WACKY,

WARPED, &

WICKED

Secrets Organizations

Don't Want You

to Know

Bruce Hadburg

ISBN-10:   0615830161

ISBN-13:   978-0615830162

WEBSITE

Visit the Wacky, Warped, & Wicked website at:

www.wackyorganizations.com.

COVER ARTWORK

Cover design provided by Sandra Kischuk; Tampa, Florida

Names have been changed to protect innocent persons. Geographies have
been changed to protect guilty organizations.

Printed in the United States of America.

DEDICATIONS

Heartfelt "thank yous" to:

- My wife Heidi for putting up with me through idea bouncing, proof-reading, printing, promotion, and subsequent processes

- Daughters Michele and Sarah for strong – make that very strong – suggestions especially regarding websites

- Friend Dave Clagett for taking time and energy to review my draft and offer valuable suggestions

- Scott and Maggie Mascitelli of Safety Harbor Computers who rescued me when my computer misbehaved at crucial times during writing and publication; and

- Wonderful editor Sandra Kischuk for asking the tough questions and not being satisfied with my first response.

CONTENTS

~*~*~*~

FEATURES

continued

FEATURES *(CONTINUED)*

~*~*~*~

CHAPTER 1

INTRODUCTION

Enron. WorldCom. Tyco International. Adelphia. Peregrine Systems. Arthur Andersen. Countrywide Financial. Madoff Investment Securities. Washington Mutual. Big firms that fell hard, took down the hopes and financial security of thousands of unsuspecting investors, and trashed the careers of thousands of employees. The names have become synonymous with corporate greed, irresponsibility, and deception.

Investigators discovered the extent of these crimes—well after the fact—through the process of forensic accounting. Too late. If only there had been trip wires or red flags available to identify the unscrupulous activity before the damage had been done.

This heinous corruption did not just happen. Activities (either good or bad) are preceded by intent. And intent can often be determined by careful observation and evaluation.

Movie producer Brian Grazer, as guest host on PBS's The Charlie Rose Show, interviewed Malcolm Gladwell, author of *The Tipping Point*, *Blink*, and *Outliers*. Gladwell noted that, in post Enron America, "'authentic' replaced 'cool.'"

In response to this value shift, newsmakers sought facial and body language coaching to learn how to control their subconscious physical expressions. The goal? Ostensibly, to present a better face to the public. Translation? To make it more difficult for the public to discern reality.

Not that the public appreciated these efforts.

Brian Grazer noted a clear trend—"heightened sensitivity to detecting the lie." In Gladwell's opinion, people responded to the more polished public faces with increased skepticism and a follow-on demand for investigation. "We will know authenticity when we see it or feel it," Gladwell said. "You cannot coach authenticity; it is bigger than your character."

I want to build on Gladwell's comment about "knowing authenticity when you see it."

Why Wacky, Warped, & Wicked?

Organizational behavior is not 100% rational. Stuff happens. Changes to competition, regulation, international laws, tax codes, employees, suppliers, availability or prices of raw materials, facilities, natural disasters, acts of war or terror, investor perception, media scrutiny, and mergers and acquisitions require a response from management.

Executive management's response reflects the internal politics, and relationships between the CEO and the Board of Directors, business, with suppliers and customers, with bankers and investors, and, yes, even between lovers and cheaters. Add to this the ever-present executive focus on bonuses and you have created the perfect environment for less-than-optimal decision-making and behavior.

Executives' decisions may benefit themselves — these actions are short-term wacky. Executives' decisions may not make sense to employees and investors — these are warped. Worst case, executives' decisions may do personal, mental, and financial harm to employees, suppliers, customers and others — these are downright wicked.

Organizations go to great lengths to present a unified, positive image to the public. They make effective use of the media. Our challenge is to guide you through the rosy images to determine the underlying truth about an organization. Let us begin with a look at how the changes to our culture influenced organizational and managerial behaviors.

Organizational Wackiness

With my coaching, you will be able to detect lack of authenticity and to identify wackiness, hypocrisy, suckiness, and dysfunction in an organization. Here are tools to uncover and realize the extent and depth of intentional or unintentional lies — whether from politicians, corporate executives, physicians, professors, customer service representatives, military leaders, business or volunteer colleagues, and even family members — people you deal with in everyday life. Even the most skilled liars betray themselves . . . if only observers are sensitive to the signals, and *see* and *listen* as much with their intuition as with their eyes and ears.

The first step in discovering inconsistencies is to be aware that something is amiss. The company or individual is not going to announce deception — at least by way of the traditional definition of announce. From a financial standpoint, the use of forensic accounting techniques . . . and 20/20 hindsight are valuable tools for ferreting out deception—after the fact. The sensory-based tools I present will heighten your awareness of your organizational surroundings and enable you to interpret what your senses tell you to avoid being deceived—before the numbers are published.

Waiting for post mortem assessments by traditional business evaluation experts can prove disastrous. It does a job seeker little good to find out too late the organization they planned to join is a management, money, mental, misogynistic, medieval, and/or moral mess. It does an investor little good to find out why WorldCom failed six months after the money is gone. Foreknowledge, awareness that something is out of place, is invaluable for protecting the less-knowledgeable potential employee or investor. Even the least financially-sophisticated observer can apply the principles I present.

Advances are never made by ignoring problems—whether physical, psychological, or fiscal. Barry Goldwater's objection to the Civil Rights Act of 1964, "You can't legislate morality," has been adopted as a truism. No matter how many laws are put in place, individuals and organizations will invent new ways to get around them. Corruption, whether corporate, organizational, governmental, or personal, is a problem which threatens financial and social stability, both today and in the future.

The scope of this book is limited to presenting the diagnostic tools and identifying and describing the link between the observed clue and the organizational dysfunction—the conclusions you can draw from what you see from outside the organization. Subsequent steps, beyond the scope of this book, would include discovering why a particular inconsistency occurred and identifying prescriptive or corrective actions to amend the organization's dysfunctions—inside tasks.

Organizational Analysis today rests on the cusp of conjecture and validation, awaiting recognition and formalization. As a study, it needs more attention to *flesh out* its body of knowledge. This book is the first toe in the water.

Real Clues

Highly reflective blue windows wrap the singular, oval-shaped 50-story building—a structure standing in stark contrast to the surrounding cluster of rectangular, shorter, clear-glass-windowed buildings. At the building's entrance, the corner of the company's square logo—highly polished chrome illuminated with bars of red, green, and blue—pierces a squat, polished black slab of granite at a 45-degree angle. The angularity and RGB (red, green, blue) colors of the company's name/logo conflict harshly with the fluidity of the building's curve and the ethereal coloration of its reflective surface.

Evaluation: The sharp angled logo, balanced precariously on its corner, juxtaposed against the smooth oval shape of the building, reveals the company as one of contrasts, inconsistency, and precarious balance. The incongruity of the primary logo colors and the non-color of a mirrored surface, which echoes more of the hues around it than having its own color, suggests a company

---

AUTHOR'S NOTE

My diverse background did little to directly prepare me to understand what I call the "Seventeen Es"—economy, environment, ethics, education, electioneering, electronics, embezzlement, emigration, end runs, enterprises, equality, espionage, evil-doers, exceptions, exchanges (in financial markets), excuses, and extravagance—the turmoil the world has experienced over the past decade.

Furthermore, I believe those with less formal training face an even greater potential for error and loss. Whether massive business failures and moral failings have increased or merely become more apparent than in the past may never be determined. The extent of the damage has never been more obvious. Today, moral deficiencies and greed threaten our society at all levels.

The old models, the ones I learned in school, do not explain what we are experiencing. I knew there had to be another *piece.* I followed my intuition and gut. Curiosity about what the *new rules* were and what drove them, led me to observe, analyze . . . and ultimately, formulate and test new theories about *what was going on.*

My goal is to promote an easy, at-a-glance understanding of diagnostic tools and techniques you will need in order to identify organizational dysfunction or organizational wackiness.

If my explanations are unclear or do not seem to work for you, please contact me via e-mail at bruce@wackyorganizations.com.

Bruce Hadburg
Safety Harbor, Florida
June 2014

~~*

which presents itself as one thing, but camouflages its true nature by *hiding behind the mirror* and reflecting the more readily identifiable forms around it.

Inside, neat 200-foot-long rows of desks and tables line the company's trading floor. Hundreds of high-powered workstations, each fitted with multiple computer screens, flash and blare the latest financial and industry information. Dark-suited men and women dash back and forth, shouting, laughing, and high-five-ing one another. A huge, domed ceiling, fractured in concentric circles of rectangular, corrugated-metal sheets, arches high above the electronic gadgetry-filled space and multi-button telephones. Two-thirds up from the floor to the dome, a thin ring of windows breaks the monotony of stark, cream-colored walls. Minimal natural light enters this cavernous space. The painted walls are bare; no artwork or photographs. Although viewed in daylight business hours, the room looks dull—but not dreary.

Evaluation: Although signifying the company's grandiose, lofty goals, the domed ceiling in the trading room is an architectural affectation more often associated with cathedrals and public buildings. Domes reflect and refract sounds in a unique way . . . such that a whisper in one location may be clearly heard in a far distant location within the dome. Thus, for a large, busy room, a domed ceiling magnifies sounds and adds auditory confusion. Designed for acoustical diffraction, the rectilinear metal plates on the ceiling shatter the structural surface, hiding its true form, in an attempt to repair a functional design defect. If hiding its true form were not enough, the insufficient natural light shows the company's dark side.

In contrast, many floors up, light spills into the executive suites of the CEO and president through twenty-five-foot-long, clear glass windows. Light over-flows through the offices' clear glass walls into the reception area. Oddly, visitors must ascend three small steps to reach the offices of the CEO and the president.

Evaluation: Metaphorically, the glass walls in the exexutive suites show transparency, but may also tempt visitors to throw stones at the windows and the offices' occupants. The long, clear walls raise the question—Do the CEO and president want or need to be on display? The additional steps to reach the CEO and president's offices suggest they feel their decisions and attitudes might be on a higher plane than those of other employees.

What organization would create so many physical examples of an environment that is counterintuitive to its stated purpose?

The company? Enron.

The important clues about the company, revealed in the architecture and interior design of the building, could have been found by any visitor to the Houston-based skyscraper before the company's fall. In the posthumous 2005 movie, *Enron; The Smartest Guys in the Room*, the filmmaker artfully and unknowingly documented key predictive features of the building's exterior, offices, trading room, and executive suite.

More Clues

Even the key players' names at Enron can provide valuable inputs. The first and last names of leading players Ken Lay and Jeff Skilling present fascinating clues. Ken Lay—two one-syllable names—sounds down-to-earth, responsible, and solid. Jeff Skilling sounds like an approachable guy, with a friendly first name, and a last name which implies or most nearly states he is talented or skilled at something—the progressive verb tense -ing transforming the brightness of the noun, skill, into an ongoing activity. In spite of this noun-verb confusion, the names are easy in that they seem to follow all the basic English language pronunciation rules and thus suggest that the organization fits the rules.

Unfortunately, there is no balance between these names, no built-in tension, no disagreement. They are *too good*. The lack of differences in the primary leaders' names provides another tangible clue to Enron's dysfunction.

In contrast, think about the names, Warren Buffett and Charlie Munger. Both have two-syllable first and last names. Warren sounds formal; Charlie (a nickname for Charles) sounds friendlier. Buffet implies a formal feast built around a fixed location, but also an aggressive, active action: to batter, pound, or beat. Sadly, Munger rhymes with hunger, often preceded by the words, victim of. Hardly the perfect, positive pairing of names. However, you can identify a built-in sense of tension or disagreement. From my standpoint, this works just fine.

These two men have presided over Berkshire Hathaway Corporation for more than 40 years. Berkshire may be the most successful publicly traded stock of all time. Its Class A share price grew from an initial valuation of approximately $500 in the late 1960s/early 1970s to its highest price of $162,000 in early May 2013. Buffet is also a strong advocate of effective corporate governance. The ideal leader's name includes *some*, albeit a minor, degree of contrast.

The reader may jump to the conclusion that this evaluation smacks of woo woo New Ageism, somewhat akin to numerology (count the letters in the name to decide whether it is good or bad). This is *not* the case. Instead, we are listening to the sound and interpretation, knowing that balance is as essential in business as it is in walking down the street. If management hiring decisions are based on too much sameness, the company will not have the necessary diversity of skills to survive and thrive. Names can provide a clue to an organization's refusal to diversify—not the only clue—just *another* clue.

Welcome

Welcome to the world of bull detection, dysfunction analysis, organizational analysis, or identification of organizational wackiness.

My original idea was to help job seekers accurately identify and assess corporate intangibles. This is not an academic exercise. Job seekers need to ensure reasonable matches, not only between their skills and the organization's expectations, but also between their values and the firm's culture and values, which may or may not be accurately communicated. As I explored organizational idiosyncrasies and their implications, I discovered my analytical tools would also benefit sales reps, bankers, suppliers, regulators, creditors, and customers or members—anyone who has any dealings with an organization of any kind. Companies do not fly flags outside their headquarters or provide handouts that list key aspects of the organization's *true* culture, More often, they pay lip service to ideals which they believe will lead to public support, or try to convince employees to adopt rah-rah mentalities that ignore reality.

I have a single purpose—to teach you to understand organizations by understanding what your intuition is trying to tell you. The last sentence intentionally included the word *trying*. Your gut will tell you what you need to know to make good decisions—but you must pay attention, not over-analyze what you observe, and not fight your conclusions.

Too often, we allow logic to override feelings. Yet, with practice, intuition can provide far deeper and more accurate knowledge than the facts, or, at least, what is presented as the facts. Malcolm Gladwell's book, *Blink,* famously attests to the power of intuition. You, too, will be able to quickly size up companies by evaluating characteristics that you think are less obvious, but which are, in actuality, more visible than the complex accounting and proprietary business practices most people attempt to decipher. In order to apply what you learn, you need do only two things—to pay attention and to trust your gut.

You want a complete solution—that is, to know both the combination of tools necessary to identify the problem and the systematic instructions to fix it. I choose to focus on the tools necessary to identify the problem. I am not a fixer. At this stage, neither should you attempt this monumental task. The problems are too complex, and the tools and techniques too much in their infancy to produce predictable results. Again, fixing is hardly something which can be done from outside the organization.

~*~*~*~

CHAPTER 2

TEN GROUND RULES

The most difficult concept of organizational analysis may be the idea of letting go. Prevailing wisdom, historical perspectives, well-placed articles about the organization and its people, and groupthink lock us into habitual patterns of thinking. Organization dysfunction analysis requires releasing these preconceptions and learning to observe, trust perceived inputs, and link these inputs to reach meaningful insights. Remember, we are dealing with degrees of dysfunction, not absolutes.

Here are ten ground rules to get you started:

Rule #1: There are no good companies or organizations; only *less bad* **companies or organizations.**

A friend lobbied strongly that I identify the characteristics of a good company. Moreover, he posited, these characteristics should permit a wide audience to agree that these characteristics are common to good companies. Keeping with my premise that the glass is half-empty, rather than half-full, I instead determined that *there are no good companies or organizations; only* ***less*** *bad companies or organizations.* Stated in a lighter vein, if it displays a logo, is connected to the government or military, includes LLC or PA in its company name, or files an IRS Form 1120-C, 1120-S, Schedule C, or Form 990 (required by the IRS for not-for-profit organizations), then it is dysfunctional. By definition, it stinks. The only question is to what degree.

How can I make this bold statement? I believe it is a reflection of the times. By 2010, employees, shoppers, suppliers, bankers, journalists, creditors—in short, nearly everyone—had become jaded. Why? I do not believe the cause was any one particular event, but a steady build-up (or erosion) of events, namely:

- The corporate excesses of the 1990s and 2000s

- Obscene CEO pay packages continuing to the present day. Median

CEO pay in 1970 was 9 times that of the median worker's salary; the 1975 ratio was 33:1; the 1980 ratio was 54:1. In 1985 the multiple was 67:1; in 1990, 130:1; in 1995, 168:1; and in 2000 the ratio was 548:1 — ten times the disparity that had existed 20 years prior. By 2005, the ratio decreased to only 465:1. (Source: Kevin Murphy, Professor of Finance and Business Economics, University of Southern California on the www.upstart.com website; formerly www.portfolio.com) In 2010 the ratio again slipped — to 343:1. The corrective trend did not continue. In 2011, median CEO compensation including exercise of stock options was 380 times that of the median worker's salary. (Source: Executive Paywatch on www.inequality.com website for 2010 and 2011 data)

- The U.S.'s declining world leadership and problem-solving capabilities

- The poor response to natural disasters by the United Nations and trusted relief agencies; accusations of favored treatment of the U.N. Secretary General's son

- The lethargic U.S. Congress's failing to take meaningful action on the environment, Social Security, the staggering budget deficit, health care, health insurance, slowly eroding standards for and results in education, and poverty

- Management problems at well-regarded national not-for-profit organizations, specifically United Way and Susan G. Komen For the Cure

- Unsolved and lingering abuse problems perpetrated by religious and some lay leaders in the Catholic Church

- Personal, moral, and/or leadership problems exhibited by Presidents Clinton and George W. Bush

- President Bush's remarks at the State of the Union address against Iraq, Iran, and North Korea — the "axis of evil," and UN Ambassador John Bolton's reference in May 2002 to "rogue states," which included Syria, Libya, and Cuba. One cannot publicly condemn nation states or leaders with whom you need to hold rational discussions.

In short, none of these situations is good. The world is steadily lowering the bar for accepted behavior by nations, nation-states, elected leaders, corporate executives, executives at not-for-profit organizations, military leaders, boards of directors of virtually every type of organization, and even industry regulators.

Rule #2. The correct foundation for your analysis is whatever you believe a certain type of business should look like.

Some may argue that they are not sure what an effective office for a tax preparer, mortgage broker, doctor, wholesale distributor, and a manufacturer of cosmetics, not-for-profit organization, or other business should look like. Whatever you believe, your own idea is correct. Do not talk yourself out of it. It is important that you leave your foundation for assessment in place and believe in it.

This may sound like an intellectual or analytical cop-out. However, based on individual experiences, as well as socioeconomic circumstances, ideas of what constitutes an effective office for a tax expert, for example, will vary considerably.

GROUND RULES FOR ORGANIZATIONAL ANALYSIS

1) There are no *good* companies or organizations; only *less bad* companies, firms, or organizations. Stated differently, *how much* an organization *sucks* or appears wacky is all that matters.

2) Start with what you believe a certain type of business or organization *should* look like.

3) Be judgmental. It is a requirement. You need to be able to say an organization is *good, neutral, or bad.*

4) Trust your intuition.

5) Learn to use and trust all your senses—see, hear, smell, taste, and feel.

6) Accept your inputs as you receive them.

7) The *cockroach theory* applies to organizations. (If you find one problem, there are probably a lot more.)

8) Any day is the right day to assess an organization.

9) Do not rationalize or second-guess adverse observations, sounds, smells, tastes, or touch sensations.

10) Although public appearances may be absolutely consistent at a company, look at the important *hidden factors* to determine the REAL situation.

~~*

A young, inexperienced worker who believes s/he needs basic assistance likely has one idea what constitutes an effective tax preparer's office. A worker nearing retirement age with specific questions about the sale of a house, planning withdrawals from an individual retirement account (IRA) without penalty, tax consequences of working while receiving Social Security payments, estate planning considerations, or tax consequences of gifts to a grandchild has a different view of what a tax expert's office would look like—s/he will seek a tax advisor to provide critical information about potential tax impacts. A small business owner has a third belief about the office appearance and demeanor of a competent tax preparer. The tax preparer for a multinational corporation will need to have extensive knowledge, access to a variety of reference materials including copies of current tax-related legislation, and a staff of experienced CPAs to assist.

In spite of the diversity, each view or belief about what a tax preparer's office should be is valid—and this is why.

An organization which serves a specific population will, if it is honest, reflect and be appropriate for the population which it serves. When an organization tries to appear as more, or, infrequently, less, than what it really is, it is not being honest. Restated, if it does not match your expectation, trust your gut. You need to feel comfortable and believe in the parameters you just established.

Rule #3. Be judgmental.

I base my entire premise on taking an open approach to various inputs while simultaneously employing a value-laden effort to judge the relative positive and negative aspects of these inputs. In plain English, you must make a decision. If you cannot bring yourself to make a judgment, then be observant, mark down the information, and compare it with your gut feeling. Once again, you do not have to agree with everything. The key is opening up to new inputs and trusting your intuitive interpretation of what you find.

Appraising the significance of inconsistencies, hypocrisy, twisting of the truth, and outright lies requires perceiving these factors, evaluating them in their environmental contexts (at what point in time, at what corporate level, in which functional area did the process become broken), adding up your evaluations, and drawing conclusions.

A person may or may not innately perceive necessary inputs. May we address the many variables used to determine personality wherein judgment is one trait? One tool is particularly useful to help you assess personality types. The Myers-Briggs Type Indicator (MBTI, registered trademark and copyright © by Consulting Psychologists Press; Palo Alto, California) identifies sixteen possible combinations of these four psychological dimensions:

1) how we interact with the world and where we direct our energy;

2) the kind of information we naturally notice;

3) how we make decisions; and

4) whether we prefer to live in a more structured way (making decisions) or in a more spontaneous way (taking in information).

Individuals are scaled along a continuum, but their profile will be based in each pair on which of the two characteristics is stronger. The characteristics are as follows:

Position 1 (Interaction):

Extraversion   ↔   Introversion

Position 2 (How information is noticed):

Sensing   ↔   INtuition

Position 3 (Decision making):

Thinking   ↔   Feeling

Position 4 (How we want to live):

Judging   ↔   Perceiving

For example, one individual's four-letter profile could be ESTJ (Extraversion, Sensing, Thinking, Judging), while another could be INFP (Introversion, INtuition, Feeling, Perceiving). Eight of the sixteen possible combinations include *Sensing*; the other eight include *INtuition*. Likewise, eight of the sixteen combinations include *Judging*; the other eight include *Perceiving*. Individuals with a J in the fourth position of the four-letter code (Judging) like to have things settled. Those with a **P** in the fourth position (Perceiving) prefer to keep their options open.

Sensing and *INtuition* refer to ways in which individuals receive information. Sensing individuals tend to trust concrete information—data and facts. Those who rely on intuition are more likely to follow *hunches*, rely on abstract, theoretical concepts, and often connect new ideas with known patterns. *Thinking* and *Feeling* refer to the way individuals process, assess, or judge, the information they have received.

Each personality type brings different strengths to organizational analysis.

The challenge is finding the right balance between judging and perceiving.

Rule #4. Trust your intuition.

REALITY CHECK: AN INCOME TAX PREPARATION BUSINESS

I vividly remember going to my first appointment at the office of a prospective consulting client in the income tax preparation business in Georgia. I parked my car and looked around before I went inside. Here is what I observed: Dying bushes; no mulch around plants, bushes or trees; scattered chunks of gravel; a large cart full of mulch occupying the gravel-covered ground next to the company's faded business sign; weeds growing everywhere; indistinct lines separating individual parking spaces, and a handicapped parking space that did not meet minimum legal painting requirements. The one-story, corrugated, tin-sheathed building was neatly painted in a pleasant, light beige color. My initial impression was, "Yuck. The freshly painted building looks fine, but the landscape is a mess." I wondered what I would find inside.

Inside, the lack of organization was immediately apparent. Scattered files littered the horizontal surfaces; partitions just inside the front door hid excess office equipment; the company had set aside no private areas to meet with clients for financial discussions; and beyond the public areas? A messy office; a messy rest room, and a messy kitchen.

The owner, Susie, said she needed consulting assistance to improve time management and set up a system to guide her firm through the income tax season. She shared that they had missed some key deadlines for clients. I cannot imagine *any* professional tax preparer missing *any* key deadlines for *any* clients! This told me the problem was far greater than one of simply missed deadlines.

My assessment of the exterior and interior confirmed what I learned in talking with Susie. I discussed the appearance issues in my follow-up email message. Susie said that, had I asked, she would have told me someone was scheduled to clean the exterior the following weekend. Speaking privately with staff members, I learned, among other things, that the exterior had been in its current condition for at least *four weeks*. The owner had tried to find middle school or high school students to complete the work for a very low price rather than pay a professional landscape company approximately $200 to clean the front of the building.

Although many people will not admit it, most of us tend to get in trouble when we *do not* listen to our intuitions or pay attention to that sinking feeling in the pits of our stomachs. No two intuitions are alike, of course. You and I may observe the same set of inputs and come away with very different impressions and analyses. Nevertheless, you need to trust your intuition or gut. Malcolm Gladwell's book, *Blink*, documents solid instances where gut feelings

One incident was most revealing. Susie and I talked in her office with the door open. In the middle of our discussion, a customer entered the outer office and went directly to the reception desk to ask a question. One of the staff members sitting near the front door started to answer the man's questions. Upon hearing conversation, Susie jumped up and went out front. She joined the conversation, answered the client's questions, and returned to her office. Her three staff members stood dumbfounded.

Assessment: I quickly identified the real problem. It was not only time management and organization; it was Susie's inability to let go, manage, delegate, and trust her staff. She had set up a hub-and-spoke management structure, rather than the more traditional pyramid-style management structure. With the hub-and-spoke structure, all information and decision-making had to pass from one of the five full- and part-time employees (the spokes) to her (the hub) for action or dissemination to the other employee spokes.

In my email to her, I described what I believed was the core issue. She did not want to hear what I had to say—or consider discussing my remedy. She also tried to argue that my hourly rate was higher than that of a large accounting/management consulting firm. Given the levels of corporate overhead and compensation at such a firm, a lower hourly rate was not mathematically possible. If her statement about their hourly rate was true, the firm would have sent a junior-level employee on this assignment. I later learned from an assistant that Susie did not select any outside consultant for help.

Bottom line: Susie had a cheap attitude toward everything inside and outside of the building, including the treatment of her staff and her willingness to get help. The building exterior and office interior were immediate and important visual clues to the dysfunctional nature of the organization. The mulch outside was the perfect initial clue to the dysfunction. If the outside had been neat, the sloppy interior space, especially just inside the front door, exposed the true situation.

~~*

or hunches proved more timely and, in many cases, far more accurate and reliable than empirical data. I intend to build on Gladwell's anecdotal concepts.

Rule #5. Trust your senses.

Forty percent of the population learns best in response to visual stimuli (what they see), another 30 to 40 percent through kinesthetic inputs (what they touch), and the remainder through auditory signals (what they hear) and, to a much lesser extent, olfactory signals (what they smell).

Organizational analysis has its foundation in our five senses—sight, sound, touch, smell, and taste. People's ability to use these skills depends on their health, their strengths, and the degree of natural skill development. A person whose strength is in what they see may find it more difficult to discern things that don't sound right.

The complexity and consistency of sensory inputs also make a difference. If the input is complicated, the mind may have a hard time discerning a pattern and identifying it. If the input is only fleeting, the mind may tend to dismiss it.

The result?

Perceptions may be flawed. Even if they provide accurate data, the information may logically conflict; that is, what you see does not match what you hear. What you see may be incomplete, partially hidden by something else, or painted in something other than its true color. Someone may put together a sophisticated PowerPoint presentation designed to elicit a certain response or create certain imagery. Fancy artwork, and, especially, a computer-generated image, can help present a product at its unimagined best.

Perceptions may be technologically altered. Communication technicians have devised a number of techniques to deliver messages to observers without triggering conscious awareness. Embedded in movies, television programming, print advertisements, and sound recordings, these subliminal visual and auditory messages bypass the conscious gatekeeper that evaluates and rejects faulty inputs. Without even being aware of the influence, individuals judge, behave, and form attitudes based on information they do not know they have absorbed.

A stimulus may be immediately obvious, but its meaning not understood. For instance, smell, because of its link to the limbic system, a primitive part of the brain, is one of the fastest, most direct routes to memory. You may recognize the smell, but not understand its link to past associations. This is why people use the smell of baking bread to sell houses. Baking smells like home. On the other hand, if something doesn't smell right, the warning may not make logical sense, but you remember—not the lesson learned long ago, but the feeling associated with that lesson.

The accuracy of your observation can also by clouded by artificial environments. Conference or convention centers, casinos, country clubs, exquisite landscaping, over-the-top décor, and elegant offices may transmit an unearned legitimacy by presenting the trappings of a healthy organization, even though what is seen is merely a façade.

Rule #6. Accept your inputs as they are.

Whatever you see, hear, feel, smell, or taste on the day you are conducting your analysis is valid and fully represents the organization. Your host/hostess may defend the appearance or smell as not the way things usually are. It does not matter. If not that specific input, it would be another that would add to your intuitive sensing.

TRANSFER AN EMPLOYEE OR FLY OVERSEAS?

My close friend Jerry worked in the reservation center for a resort. He applied for and was selected to interview for a job transfer that required different skills than the ones he now used on a daily basis. I believe Jerry was very well qualified. He had used the required skills in an executive position he held ten to fifteen years before in the same industry. A week after the hiring company's management said they would notify the applicants, management offered no information about the position nor had they made a decision. The hiring manager had jetted to overseas meetings. The hiring priority for the position slid to a distant second, third, or fourth place.

I had not told Jerry, but I believed this department was poorly run and disorganized. *When people make promises and do not follow through and when the position itself is poorly defined, the successful job applicant can expect to be subjected to constant changes in position requirements, better known as other duties as required.*

I would have bet Jerry the proverbial *doughnut to a dollar* that more than one aspect of the department was amiss. A while later, Jerry told me that the company contacted him two weeks after the deadline passed. Jerry knew the person selected, who confirmed the department faced many challenges.

Luckily for Jerry, he was not selected for this no-win position.

~~*

Rule #7. The cockroach theory applies to organizations.

The cockroach theory holds true in identification of wacky organizations—you never find only one cockroach. You seldom find a single piece of evidence of organizational dysfunction—multiple examples of dysfunction are the norm.

Rule #8. Any day is the right day to assess an organization.

Some would argue that you might have picked the wrong day to conduct your evaluation. I differ. The messages you get are precisely the messages the organization intends to send and ones you need to receive. The messages may differ slightly from day to day; however, the nature and degree of organizational dysfunction remain remarkably stable.

Whatever day you visit an organization or check its website is the perfect day to conduct your evaluation. It is what it is. If something is out of place, missing, or in disrepair, the company may offer a number of excuses. These excuses may range from claiming the company is waiting for a planned upgrade to blaming an individual employee who shirked her/his responsibility for the building's exterior maintenance. In reality, the important clues are there for you. All you need to do is pay attention.

Rule #9. Do not rationalize adverse observations, comments, smells, sounds, or touch.

Do not talk yourself out of making a note of something that does not seem to fit. Do not ignore something that appears to disagree in some small way with what you thought of the organization based on your initial observations and basic expectations. It is what it is. Observe and make notes.

Rule #10. Although public appearances may be consistent at a company, look at the important *hidden factors* to determine the REAL situation.

A company may present a consistent image to the public. However, the hidden factors provide useful information so you may assess the degree of wackiness. Hidden factors are actually the most tangibly obvious . . . although they tend to be overlooked. Some of these factors include the website, backgrounds of senior executives, landscape and grounds, front lobby, rest rooms, hallways, employee kitchen or cafeteria, promotional materials, and the employee bulletin board.

Summary

Welcome to bull detection or organizational analysis, the process of identifying dysfunctional or wacky or sickly or sucky organizations. Organizational analysis is based on one simple, timeless philosophy: There are no good organizations, only less bad. This is analogous to the pessimist's outlook on life: The glass is always half-empty, never half-full. Just remember . . . it is not the good in an organization that will hurt you.

By taking this contrary approach, we do not have to be concerned at any time with determining which factors to use to identify the so-called best organizations. Companies identified in popular business books as good to great or excellent had, within five to ten years, dropped to average or far below. Just as is the case with products, industries, countries, economies, and organizations go through life cycles. The pattern is the same: start-up/immature, mature, decline, and ultimately, reinvention or go out of business. Bull detection tools will help you identify organizational dysfunction no matter where the organization is in its life cycle.

~*~*~*~

CHAPTER 3

WEBSITE

You cannot walk in the front door of the company and, merely, by doing so, claim you are ready to meet your client, prospective manager, or customer. Before the scheduled meeting or job interview, you have plenty of work to do. In decades past, this research required diligent investigation of newspaper archives and financial reports. Even then, information was limited and flat.

Today, companies of all sizes maintain websites, primarily as marketing tools. They invest in search engine optimization to get their names as close to the top of the page as possible when someone searches for terms the companies consider critical to their businesses. They post information about what their companies do, what they claim as values, significant historical events, who their clients are, jobs within their organizations, and how to contact them.

Companies consider websites indispensible for their success. However, the website also is an invaluable pre-meeting tool for anyone who is considering a relationship with an organization—not only for the information it supplies, but for how well it is presented and what is left out.

Why is this pre-meeting work so important?

It enables you to develop a thesis about that organization.

When you eventually meet with an organization's executives, a thesis provides a framework to ensure your questions are effective and complete. The answers the executives provide will help validate or contradict your thesis. Pay close attention to their answers and especially to:

1) *Diversionary tactics:* where they seem to answer the question but take the response in a totally different direction from that which you clearly intended;

2) *Distraction:* where they start to answer the question, but then something else *comes up* (the phone rings, someone comes into the office, your question reminds them of a joke/story);

3) *Information omission:* either through diversionary tactics, distraction, or *sliding over* critical details; and

4) *Incomplete answers:* where you may *think* you got an answer, but the respondents stopped talking about it just before the answer was actually provided.

The *lines* between these four are indistinct, but the result is the same. You do not get answers to the questions you have asked. Your response should include changes to your line of questions so that you may learn what you need to know in order to fully evaluate your thesis.

Website Purpose and Design

The organization's website is often your first introduction to an organization. I am not a web designer. I do not know the technical, type font, white space, layout or graphical requirements and limitations involved in creating a website, nor do I know the tricks experts use to overcome any limitations. However, I have looked at hundreds, if not thousands, of websites while conducting business and personal research. I can sense when a company or an organization presents essential information clearly and logically and the site just makes sense. So can you.

I become concerned when websites attempt to impress more with complex artistic design or technological gimmickry (specifically, use of *Flash* software and associated moving images) than with conveying important information and providing logical site navigation. Any page that tells you that the site is loading is not a good way to start just as bloat in any part of an organization is a sign of inefficiency. Blinking icons; irritating sliding banners; advertisements; unasked-for sound messages/music; or slick technological tricks which are not related to the company's activities do not belong on professional websites. The rule?

Some image, preferably the company's home page, should load immediately to the browser so you know you have reached your desired destination. Anything less suggests the company might be evasive or delinquent in answering legitimate queries. Clicking or typing in a web address is equivalent to asking a question.

How quickly and well is that question answered?

Poorly designed navigational schemes which require seven or eight clicks to find even basic information may indicate poor internal corporate organization. When an organization creates its website for an internal audience, instead of the real world we know, the organization is inwardly, not outwardly, focused.

Inwardly focused organizations are marked by a strong culture where everyone fits in, often to the detriment of quality. The organization's founders, its history, cultural norms, and ethics strongly influence the products and services offered as well as the content of its website. The website navigation is difficult, links are not clear or logical, and the site is likely to contain jargon unique to the organization. An internally focused website may be characterized as one created for approval by the organization's leadership, not for easy navigation and understanding by a website visitor.

In contrast, an externally focused website is designed for easy understanding by the first-time visitor. Navigation is easy, page layouts are clear and easy to read, color is used appropriately, and the use of jargon is minimal. Obviously, a web site designed with an external focus is far preferred to one aimed at an internal audience.

Here is the short list of what to look for on a business-related website:

Website—Organization and Speed of Loading

People go to a company's or organization's website to get information. How well does the website present that information? The website's organizational structure is a combination of individual page layout, the flow between pages, and the logical mapping that facilitates navigation to the desired information.

- *URL.* Has the company chosen a URL (Uniform Resource Locater or web address—the string of letters that appears in the browser address bar) that relates to the company's name or business? A logical web address makes it easy to find and correct typed-in errors. If the company is large, has it taken the added measure of buying up similar addresses and redirecting them to the correct address?

- *Home page content and organization.* A good home page should combine the best features of a table of contents and an index. This is a tall order. The table of contents contains the six to ten main categories of information a person might research; the index refers to the subcategories under each of the main categories.

- *Fast loading home page.* Some websites immediately open to a picture that shows progress of the home page loading onto the browser. The viewer wants to see the home page quickly and efficiently. I interpret the "loading home page" message as a sign of IT or marketing functions gone badly. This approach is not customer-focused; it shows either that an organization's focus is inward, or the techno-geeks have been allowed too much play time.

A few sites, thankfully very few, play obnoxious music while you are waiting for the home page to load. A *noisy* site is presumptuous—it assumes the viewer is never busy with other professional communications when accessing the page, and needs the website to dictate *listening content*. Most Web interactions are visual, not auditory. Just because it can be done does not mean it should be done.

Website—The Look and Feel

- *Initial look and feel.* The home page should feel welcoming; hence, the name *home page.* A professional website has a clean layout, an effective combination of colors and logos, and well-designed and appropriately sized buttons which function as a built-in index. I have seen websites where the buttons were so large they took up more than one-half the width of the page. As a result, the screen cut off the last four words on each line of the text message on the right edge of the page. This is a coding error; nevertheless, someone approved the final version without checking it on a variety of browsers.

- *How well written is the website?* A company's writing abilities relate not only to its communication abilities and professionalism but also to overall competency. Typos, misspellings, poor grammar and syntax, and unprofessional tone hurt the organization's chance to present a positive image. We have a higher level of trust for those who can write well, especially for a website.

- *White space.* White space may or may not be white—what the term refers to is the blank, undecorated parts of a page . . . and the spaces between the words and graphics. White space is part of the organization of the page, and functions by grouping and separating various categories of information.

The effective use of white space lets the words *breathe* and helps give meaning to what is written. Liken it to pictures on your wall. If you jam a whole bunch of pictures corner to corner, ceiling to floor, no one will know what is important or which pictures are related. Setting the pictures off with space around them communicates the *group* they belong with, as well as their individual importance. I cannot give you an ideal percentage guideline,

---

Clean Sheets of Paper?

I shared some of the key aspects of pre-meeting and on-site research with students in my Business Communication classes. Students' universal reaction was, "Bruce, why don't you get a clean sheet of paper and a pen, open your mind, write what executives tell you, and then analyze their information?"

My response was consistent. Moreover, it is what I sincerely believe. I responded, "I need to have formulated some opinion about the company—good, neutral, or bad—before I meet with executives. Otherwise, the executives will fill my head with BS and the information and images they want me to take away. I need to arrive with some understanding of the truth or a sense of the situation as it really is in hopes of leaving with an accurate assessment."

For this reason, I always created a thesis about a company before I actually met with their executive team. My theses were simple, such as:

- This is basically a good company.

- This company has made tremendous headway in its efforts to turn itself around and show a profit or enter a new market.

- The pointy-haired boss from the cartoon strip Dilbert © is alive and well. These guys and gals are clueless.

- The CEO is a megalomaniac; this is reflected in the company's operations.

- The organization is schizophrenic; the company is manic depressive; the firm is obsessive compulsive.

- It's only about profit. Everything else takes a backseat.

- Executive management has done a great job balancing the conflicting demands of customers, shareholders, employees, suppliers, regulators, and competitors.

~~*

such as 15% or 25%, for white space. However, the right combination of page layout and white space sends and reinforces a positive message.

- *An appropriate, descriptive logo.* A major challenge is the design of an appropriate logo for an organization, a company, its product, or its service. A good logo reinforces the name of the organization and links that name with the types of products or services offered.

- *Professional or amateurish look.* Most webpage design programs encourage professional design. Despite the availability of good tools, some webpage designers want to push creativity to the bleeding edge. Bleeding edge technology is that which is so new it is relatively unsupported and tends to fail. It is usually promoted by techno-geeks who revel in showing off. Bleeding edge creativity is creativity which may appeal to the avant-garde, but which your average viewer won't get. In this case, it is the creative genius showing off. Amateurish web pages are offensive because they assume the viewer is too stupid to notice the errors. Bleeding edge design is offensive by its attempted claim to superiority when it works and clumsy and amateurish when it fails.

A common error is to use a wide variety of font styles, colors, and weights. Font characteristics should be controlled so that changes convey meaning—the size and style consistent for the level of information (e.g.; HEADINGS, Text, *photo captions)* throughout the website. Again: Just because something *can* be done doesn't mean it *should.*

Professional-looking web pages combine these structural elements:

Appearance

- Consistent contrasting or analogous (also called monochromatic) colors. Once the color scheme has been established, it needs to be continued throughout the website.

- Effective amount and use of white space

- A type font that reinforces the company or product message and/or logo. Avoid all caps, since this is the electronic equivalent of *shouting.* Also avoid extensive italics and script style fonts since these are more difficult to read. Creative fonts draw attention to themselves, compromise credibility, and distract from the company's message.

- Attractive graphic elements that highlight important information and facilitate following the page

- Industry-relevant and company-specific drawings and photographs

Navigation

- Clearly-defined navigational tools, with navigational links consistently located in a sidebar or at the top of each page

- Easy, organized menu access and navigation between screens (hitting the back button six times to get back to the home page is not good navigation)

- A minimal number of clicks to retrieve desired information

- A site *search* feature or site map

- An easy to locate *log in* and *log out* (if required)

- Links to other sites or pages that work!

Website—Content

Within the website, the business (company history, founders, current management, products, services, support, careers, benefit package, corporate culture) should be described in commonly-used terms, not industry-specific or company-appropriated jargon. The twelve web-based aspects of a company you can research in advance of your visit to the organization are divided into three main areas:

Institutional factors, which include:

- Institutional Description

- Business Partnerships and Synergies

- Finance-related Information

- Products

- Distribution Channels

- Customer Service / Customer Support

People factors, which include:

- Executive Management

- Organization Charts

Other indicators, which include:

- Organizational Culture and Work Environment

- Patents Received (for a technology-based company)

- Lawsuits Filed

- Community Involvement

Institutional Factors

TWO WEBSITES—INTERNAL VS. EXTERNAL FOCUS

Years ago, I helped my daughter, Michele, search for colleges. She knew she wanted to attend an undergraduate business school. We looked at websites for the Anderson School of Business at the University of California Los Angeles (UCLA), the Marshall School of Business at the University of Southern California (USC), the Haas School of Business at the University of California Berkeley (UCB), the Olin School of Business at Washington University in St. Louis, and The Wharton School at the University of Pennsylvania (Penn).

To simplify the analysis, I will discuss the extremes—the best and the worst websites. Wharton created the easiest-to-navigate site, by far. Two mouse clicks and the correct and complete detailed information we needed magically appeared. At the opposite end, the website for Washington University required seven to nine clicks to access any substantive information. Moreover, no answers were complete on only one screen. Every basic question required viewing at least two screens after going through the seven to nine previous screens to arrive at the basic topic.

I am not certain what we can accurately discern from these disparate experiences. Is Washington University an administrative nightmare or second-rate school? Is Wharton the "business-school-heaven-on-earth"?

I have never visited Washington University's business school. It is well-regarded and ranked # 22 in the top 50 graduate business schools in the *U.S. News & World Report* 2012 rankings. Nevertheless, something does not fit. I view the Web site as one that reflected an institution focused on good internal communication and coordination, but lacking a sense of logical organization in its outreach efforts.

Institutional Description

- *In which city are the company's corporate headquarters located?* A head-quarters location must closely match the nature of the business.

For example, Wal-Mart's headquarters is in rural Bentonville, Arkansas. Its initial placement of stores in small towns throughout the South and Midwest spurred its early revenue growth. Rural America is the foundation of Wal-Mart's *corporate DNA* or origin. Accordingly, the company understands well the fashion, house wares, home entertainment, home décor, sporting, toy and game, automotive, jewelry, office supply, and related needs of small town America.

As the company grew, it expanded into larger cities and suburban shopping centers. In 2005-2006, in order to continue its revenue growth, the company announced a foray into more upscale merchandise. The company faced many challenges in its efforts to offer higher profit margin merchandise. Its struggles with the new model were not solely about price. Because of the company's very strong rural roots and corporate DNA, I hypothesize that it simply did not fully understand the psychographic, demographic, and quality requirements of relatively upscale urban and suburban shoppers. Plus, it had its rural image to overcome.

If the Washington University site also showed an inward-looking focus, its convoluted navigation also demonstrated a near disdain for its prospective students, a semi-elitist attitude, and a confused leadership style. Not investing the time, money, or thought into how the site would be used clearly indicates a proclivity for shortcuts. This could be a warning of short-staffing of counselors available to students and prospective students . . . a shortage further exacerbated by the website's tortuous data trail.

By comparison, Wharton ranked #3, behind Harvard and Stanford, in the Top 50 graduate business schools in the same *U.S. News* survey. In February 2004, I attended a one-day conference at The Wharton School. There was a sense of high energy in the air unlike any school I had ever visited. Although I worked in Silicon Valley for a company that had access to Stanford's main library, the business school, and its business school library, I never felt a similar energy in any Stanford building. To me, Wharton is a special place. The sense of high energy amplified the impact of the one-day program, the presentation of its leader, Paul Schoemaker, and fellow attendees' experiences.

~~*

- *How complete is the company's description?* You can expect sections on
  history, executive management, products, customer service and support, key partnerships, financial/investor information (required if the
  company is publicly-owned; if it is, the company's stock is traded on
  a stock exchange), ordering information, company address and telephone and fax numbers, and how to contact the company via email.
  (You would be amazed at how many businesses or organizations ignore providing information about the company and its basic history).

It is interesting to identify which sections the company or organization
omits or makes difficult to find. What is the company or organization trying
to hide by not disclosing specific information or burying it deeply in some
obscure location? Sensitive areas may include: executive compensation;
director additions, resignations, and compensation; press releases for any
less-than-positive news; current and pending litigation; adverse accountants'
opinions; order backlog; and revenue recognition. Why can they not make
any public statement about the organization's challenges or capabilities in
meeting these challenges?

- *What is the organization's history?* What does the company choose to
  say about itself? A complete discussion includes names of founders,
  when and where and who founded the company, product history,
  key corporate milestones, significant changes to physical plant or location and the reasons, patents held, and directions for new product
  or service development.

To get a good idea of the present situation and possibly the future
direction, one has to have some knowledge of the organization's past. Just as
an individual's past influences his/her future, an organization's past leaves
an imprint. Not being *aware* of history can be risky. But, *forgetting* what you
once knew can be just as dangerous. "Those who cannot remember the past
are condemned to repeat it," the oft-quoted saying made famous by George
Santayana warns.

Not-for-profit organizations have histories. So do law firms, management consulting, accounting, medical, and other professional firms. Military
organizations, government agencies and all levels of schools, whether public
or private . . . *any* organization has, since its inception, from the founder's
first conceptual spark, had a reason for being and an interrelationship with
its physical, cultural, social, and fiscal environments. The responsive inter-
play of the organization and its environment builds its history.

Business Partnerships and Synergies

Technology-based companies need to be located in the same geographic areas as other technology companies. For example, Gateway Computer could not long remain in North Sioux City, South Dakota; it moved to a suburb of San Diego in 1997. Synergies are important, specifically:

- The availability of an appropriately educated labor force

- The ability to easily share technical information face-to-face

- The opportunity to find business and technology partners with whom your company can work and grow

- Access to capital through venture capitalists

- The ability to have the financial needs of growing companies met by bankers who understand them and who are willing to assume the associated risks

- Access to accountants who understand specific requirements of the business model: the revenue recognition, tax credits, stock options, customer service revenue and expenses, and leasing versus buying real estate considerations

- Access to attorneys who understand intellectual property, stock options, technology-based partnerships, and joint ventures

Finance-related Information

Has the company included summary balance sheets and income statements from past years and current quarters? Does the website show graphs illustrating the year-to-year growth of sales and profits? If the stock is publicly traded, is it easy to find the company's ticker symbol?

Products or Services

- *What are the firm's products and/or services?* The organization's website should list the products and services offered. The site should contain a relatively complete description of each product, a model number to use in the ordering process, and the required hazardous or safety warnings for the product. Photos, line drawings, or blueprints would also be helpful.

Distribution Channels

- *Is there a full or partial list of key clients?* If publication of a company as a client is not restricted by Non-Disclosure Agreements (NDA), this list helps a potential customer compare the relative size and type of customers and ensures a good potential match up of prospect and client. A list of the kinds and duration of projects worked on adds considerably to this information category.

- *Can you easily find the names and locations of local retailers for the product/ service?* If a company sells its products through retailers, you need to be told. The company's website should list the names and cities of its major retailers. Ideally, a separate search engine enables you to find a retailer located in or near your postal ZIP code. You may choose to visit that retailer to do a *hands-on* inspection and evaluation of the company's products.

Customer Service/Support

- *How easily can you contact the company via telephone, fax, e-mail?* How easily can you find the company's street address? How easy is it to send an email with questions to appropriate departments (HR, finance, operations, marketing, purchasing, or any executives)? How quick is the response and are the answers relevant and complete? How easy is it to contact individuals you might need to contact by telephone? If you leave a message, are your calls returned promptly?

- *What does the website tell you about product support and service?* What customer service and support does the manufacturer offer? How long is the warranty period for key product classes? Can you get technical assistance via the company's website? Do you see a toll-free phone number to call for technical or sales assistance? Does the organization offer *chat* capabilities between you and a customer service representative or technician?

People Factors

Executive Management

- What does the website tell you about executive management? A reasonable expectation is for the website to provide the names, education, and business backgrounds of each member of the executive management team. Additional information might include memberships in professional, honorary, or strictly social organizations, such as the Elks, Moose, and veterans organizations (not country clubs—yes, one executive of a Florida-based company listed his country club membership!). Community or college alumni involvement is fine. However, watch for excessive involvement in activities that have nothing to do with that person's business. You will know excessive when you see it.

For a service business (management consulting, accounting or auditing, contract scientific research or laboratory services, repair services for technical products), I want a separate list of staff member names and bios. At minimum, the site should show the educational background and work experience for each key employee. If this information is not disclosed in some manner, however abbreviated, then I wonder about that firm's work environment and corporate culture. When you hire a service business, you hire all the employees. You want to learn something about people with whom you will be working.

Organization Charts

Organization charts can provide information, not only about those areas of responsibility the organization considers most important, but about its management philosophy. An organization with thirteen vice presidents reporting directly to the CEO (a flat organizational structure) will be far different than one where the CEO has two vice presidents each overseeing a half dozen department heads, who in turn manage the numerous section heads (a vertical organizational structure).

Although the vertical organization structure is older, competition for the few positions at the top can create a hostile working environment. A more horizontal structure can improve productivity and collaboration because of improved communication, less high-level administrative oversight, and less political jockeying for the few top-level positions.

Other Indicators

Organizational Culture and Work Environment

- *What specific traits define the corporate culture?* In 1982, Deal and Kennedy defined corporate culture as *the way things get done around here,* and identified four cultures:

- o *Work hard, play hard:* rapid feedback/reward, low risk

- o *Tough guy macho:* rapid feedback/reward, high risk

- o *Process oriented:* slow feedback/reward, low risk

- o *Bet the company:* slow feedback/reward, high risk

To these four, the author adds:

- o *Tradition bound:* rigid management, methods closely follow what has been done in the past. Enables quick decision making . . . but not always the best decisions.

- o *Family-owned/family managed:* financial control flows from the family, decision making may be quick or slow based on family dynamics and interests . . . decisions may or may not be in the best interests of the company depending on which family members are in control.

- o *Family-owned/professionally managed:* financial control flows from the family, decision making is less constrained by family dynamics and interests. Decisions are more likely to be in the best interests of the company as opposed to the interests of family individuals. However, professionals who make decisions not in alignment with controlling family members risk dismissal . . . and changing family dynamics can result in professional management churn.

In 1992, Edgar Henry Schein, a former professor at MIT Sloan School of Management, defined a number of what he referred to as corporate culture artifacts—which included virtually everything physical: facilities, offices, furnishings, visible awards and recognitions . . . as well as the dress and the interactions of the staff with each others and with outsiders. These artifacts, tangible, overt, or verbally identifiable elements included company slogans, mission statements, and other operational creeds.

At a less visible level, Schein defined espoused values as how the organization's members formally describe themselves to each other and to outsiders. At a third, deeper level, shared basic assumptions, the commonly held, but often taken for granted or even unrecognized behaviors, are the essence of the organization's culture.

Schein's levels of corporate culture provide a construct to understand paradoxical organizational behaviors. Yet, these levels are interrelated in that the most visible level—the physical—can effectively *flag* anomalies in less visible layers. This is critical. Only when an organization's leadership recognizes the *signs* and understands the origin and implications of now-exposed beliefs and habits can these managers develop and implement effective change strategies.

To Schein's more formal elements of corporate culture, the author adds some which may seem of less consequence—motivational posters, the condition of the refrigerator, and the condition of the restroom. Why? These are things companies are less likely to connect with corporate health. Through my research, I have found these less obvious indicators often provide far more accurate reads on what is going on within an organization.

- *What are the cultural forms of the company?* In 1988, Harrison Trice defined cultural forms as the linking mechanism to communicate ideologies, values, and norms to the organization's employees. These include:

  o *Rite:* elaborate, formalized activity, usually performed for an audience

  o *Ceremony:* linked rites combined in a single occasion or event

  o *Ritual:* Standardized, detailed activities with emotional benefit but of little, if any, technical importance

  o *Myth:* An imaginary story developed to explain something

  o *Saga:* A historical narrative, often of heroic proportions

  o *Legend:* A historical narrative, with added fictional elements

  o *Story:* Often a combination of truth and fiction

  o *Symbol:* Something which conveys meaning by representing something else

  o *Language:* Unique written and verbal communication styles

  o *Gesture:* Body movement used to communicate meaning

  o *Physical:* The physical setting

  o *Artifact:* Manufactured materials to facilitate cultural communication

- *Can you describe the character of the organization?* How is the organization involved in the community? What social and environmental issues, multicultural/diversity concerns, work/play/family balance philosophies, or religious values does the organization promote?

Does it offer unusual benefits? Has it received community service awards? What is the work style?

Some of the styles suggested by The Institute for Business, Technology, and Ethics (and modified by the author) include:

o   Open vs. closed

o   Accountability and personal responsibility vs. lack of accountability and blame

o   Reasonable risk-taking vs. same actions, different day

o   Do it right vs. clearing the item off one's 'to do list'

o   Tolerate and learn from mistakes vs. only perfection and repeating the same mistakes

o   Unquestioned integrity and consistency vs. arbitrary actions and lack of standards and procedures

o   Collaboration, integration, and holistic thinking vs. *collection of cowboys* mentality, silo-based actions, and inside-the-box, cover-one's-butt thinking

o   Courage and persistence in the face of difficulty vs. cowardice and diversionary actions in the face of difficulty

Management consulting firm Booz & Company created the www. orgdna.com website to help evaluate corporate culture or, as they call it, *organizational DNA*. If you are already employed at a particular company, or if you are lucky enough to have a friend willing to answer a brief questionnaire about the organization, this website evaluates and prepares a report of the organization's management style and the strengths and weaknesses of that model. The questions cover:

o   Decisions and Norms

o   Motivators & Commitments .

o   Information & Mindsets

o   Structure & Networks

o   Organization Demographics

The organizational styles provide, by their names, a pretty clear idea of how the company operates and include: Passive-Aggressive, Fits-and-Starts, Outgrown,

Over-Managed, Just-in-Time, Military Precision, or Resilient. The www.orgdna. com website is an excellent tool to help you determine organizational DNA.

An organization's beliefs can affect more than the organization and its internal functioning. For instance, some organizations repeatedly emphasize their support of religious values on their websites; others may mention religious values only once. The Atlanta-based *quick-food* drive-in restaurant chain, Chick-Fil-A, is a good example.

A REMOTE WORKFORCE MEANS REMOTE RELATIONSHIPS

Imagine a small company with a unique software product that integrates the ability to analyze attitudinal, behavioral, demographic, and geospatial data. The product permits a company's management to evaluate customer data in more detail, gain insight into customers' needs and market trends, identify extensions and improvements to current products and services, and recognize opportunities for new service implementations. The CEO has a PhD from a well-respected university in eastern U.S. and extensive relevant business experience.

Imagine this small company with Jeff, the CEO, and four staff—the VP of Operations, a marketing specialist, a database specialist, and an administrator—in an office in Miami, Florida. The VP of Technology lives and works from his home in suburban Pittsburgh, Pennsylvania. The VP of Data Management works at home in Boulder, Colorado. Last, the Director of Business Development lives and works from his home in Tampa, Florida.

This situation is not imaginary; it is real—surreal in fact. How well does this geographically-scattered organization function? I attended a strategic planning session where all employees of this company were temporarily united. This planning meeting was the first to assemble this group of executives and staff. Here is what I observed and learned:

- The out-of-towners did not have enough time during breaks and mealtimes to get to know one another. The lack of a water cooler or coffee room meant there was no casual gathering place to exchange small talk. Building personal relationships during the meeting became equal in importance to planning for the organization.

- Jeff tried to preside over the meeting, but the non-local VPs took over and directed focus to their own areas of priority. **These two situations revealed outward signs of a lack of organizational cohesion and project focus.**   ▷

The company's outdoor signs tastefully state, "Closed on Sunday," at the bottom. In interviews, the founder, S. Truett Cathy, says he operates the chain based on biblical principles. The website proclaims this in an understated, almost hidden way. "Closed on Sunday" gives employees time to worship, be with family, or engage in fellowship. "Closed on Sunday" also means Mr. Cathy does not handle money on the Sabbath.

On a syndicated talk show on June 16, 2012, Chick-Fil-A's president and chief operating officer Dan Cathy decried the audacity people had in thinking they could redefine God's definition of marriage. In an interview published on July 2, Cathy stated, "We are very much supportive of the family—the biblical definition of the family unit."

- I learned this was a family-owned business; the CEO's brother served as venture capitalist and Chairman of the Board of Directors. I discovered Jeff paid each VP $50/hour as an independent contractor. An independent contractor is subject to the full 15.3% Social Security and Medicare taxes on net profits. While $50 sounds like a high hourly rate, the extensive backgrounds of these experienced professionals merited far more compensation. One man had a PhD in electrical and computer engineering from top-rated Carnegie-Mellon University— and three technology-related patents. Another had a degree in geography and geospatial systems and solid industry experience. The third had an MBA in management information systems, served as a U.S. Air Force officer and had extensive senior-level experience in industry. **The CEO hired the best but avoided paying what each key employee was worth—cheap, cheap, cheap. What is more surprising is that these individuals were willing to work for him at a less-than-market price.**

- The CEO dumped projects on whichever VP was available, notwithstanding that person's lack of necessary skills and expertise for the assigned task. For example, another consultant/contractor, the VP of Technology researched and wrote the presentation for the planning meeting on the company's future direction. **Although this may be an interesting exercise in rapid learning and coordination with other executives, the CEO's actions showed disrespect for this consultant's time and took advantage of the consultant's broad expertise—and Jeff paid him peanuts.**

Cathy's publicly anti-gay marriage comments sparked divisive debates and nationwide retaliatory boycotts. A couple months later, Chick-Fil-A shifted position and publicly announced that it would no longer fund anti-GLBT organizations. In spite of what could have been a public relations disaster, an effective change strategy stabilized, and actually improved, Chick-Fil-A's business.

The issue in such a case as this was not the owner's beliefs; it was the extent to which those beliefs became part of the owner's organizational culture or DNA, his public proclamations, the degree of dysfunction that resulted, and the negative impact which reverberated beyond the organization.

As with religious beliefs, an individual's philosophical beliefs shape or

---

- Research on the Internet validated the situation just described. The www.glassdoor.com website showed this company made a job offer with a salary of $40,000 to an experienced data management professional who was earning 30% more at another company. Here is the significant contrast. Jeff claimed that he liked to be intellectually challenged by his VPs. In contrast, through his hiring practices, he surrounded himself with relatively passive, willing-to-be-underpaid, non-threatening, lower-level employees.

- The CEO decided to introduce his software product and service to a new market. He selected this market because he and his wife had a friend who has worked in this market for 25 years. In order to validate the demand for the product, I conducted a telephone survey of five potential customers. These diverse companies varied by geography, current brands sold, number of stores (if part of a chain), and number of employees. I learned that, no matter how good the proposed new product, participants in this relatively static market had heard far too many sales pitches that promised a solid measurable return on investment—that did not deliver.

Despite all five potential buyers' admitted to me their great skepticism, this CEO went ahead—and lost a lot of money in a short time. What is scary is that the CEO had another option. He could have licensed his company's technology to a larger business partner with established distribution channels and a receptive customer base in exchange for a share of revenue. Jeff would not do it; he wanted to control and manage it all.

One hundred percent of nothing equals nothing.

~~*

---

are shaped by the individual's organization. During the 2012 presidential race, Mitt Romney, in what he thought was a private Republican fundraiser, commented that 47 percent of the U.S. population believed they were "victims," and that these same people were "dependent on government."

Whether Romney truly believed this, whether he was repeating the party line, or whether he crafted a statement which he felt would appeal to the pocketbooks of his well-heeled audience, the comment was not well received by those outside the room. Yale Law School named it the number one quote of the year.

A major political candidate, and, by association, the party to which s/he is affiliated, can hardly expect to win an election by disenfranchising 47 percent of the potential electorate—particularly during economic hard times where many who would prefer to be working—and *not* dependent on gov-

---

POOR WEBSITES

We contrasted two University's websites—one poorly- and one well-designed. We outlined the desired content and format of effective websites. Further research found most existing websites at least adequate—some were even good. The bad ones were notable, and, as in the case of any highly-visible faux pas, invited ridicule—which the website, www.webpagesthatsuck.com, provides each year. This site identifies poorly designed or ineffective Web sites. From its list of "nominees" for the first six months of 2013 and calendar years 2011 and 2012, I selected five:

- Pulcinella Restaurant (www.pulcinella.ca). The home page opens to a constantly moving picture album of black and white photos with superimposed transparent (insipid) orange bands and words flipping across the surface. Navigation? Two buttons, "Explore" and "Reservations," and a single arrow on each edge, each of which only reveals its target on mouseover (menu, philosophy, reservations, certification). Clicking on the "Reservations" button reveals an online reservation form. The "Explore" button provides a transparent strip with a menu for home, reservations, menu, philosophy, certification, news, and location. The only way to return to the home page is to click on the correct edge arrow. This is not explained nor is it intuitive. The map does not show the city in which the restaurant is located; I found it by reading the text in the Philosophy page. And response time? All the coding bloat from the constant site activity makes this site unresponsive. Click a selection. Maybe you'll get there.

ernment—remain jobless. This was merely one egregious example of many which highlighted the disconnect between a dysfunctional government (public *servants*?) and the population governed.

What other beliefs can negatively impact an organization? Many. Whether a belief relates to the organization's ethical, environmental, social, employee, customer service, or quality responsibilities and whether its origin comes from the organization's history, its industry's history, management attitudes, or indigenous government and culture does not matter.

- Most Holy Family Monastery (www.mostholyfamilymonastery.com). The home page is a hodge-podge of seemingly unrelated information. A row of small religion-oriented photos stretches across the top of the page, followed by the organization's name, its slogan, "Defending the Catholic faith . . .", and the monastery's address and phone number. So far, so good. Then the visual nightmare—a collage of changing "news story type" photos fills the left half of an informational strip and offers videos such as "how to peel a head of garlic in 10 seconds" and "Dog Rescued After Being Frozen to Ground." Huh? On the right side of this strip, the site presents a 4 x 5 matrix of available topics beneath a black top border with five additional topics. Clicking on any topic populates the area below the band (and initially offscreen) with a scrollable list of links to related articles and videos. These lists vary in style—with inconsistent formats, and font colors, sizes, and styles. A reader must scroll down to see the complete listing of links to articles and videos.

- Art Institute of Pittsburgh Online (www.aionline.edu) requires a user to sign in (and provide a name, ZIP Code, email address, and telephone number) before learning anything about the school's online course offerings.

- School of Architecture, Rice University (architecture.rice.edu) – This site is best characterized by its distracting "hot pink" colored background. Small white lettering on a black background is very difficult to read.

- Sixties Press (www.sixtiespress.co.uk) A strange, faded background wallpaper, blocked color behind the words, and "psychedelic," discordant letter colors makes the site difficult to look at and the text especially difficult to read.

~~*

Dysfunction is dysfunction.

Other things to look for?

- *Do some or all employees work remotely?* A new work style—working remotely—evolved as a result of rapid changes in technology. To work remotely means to work from home, from a hotel, in a car or van, or yes, even in a coffee shop—no need to go to an office. Meetings can be held via multi-participant video conference, telephone conference call, or Skype, an Internet-based video service that connects two or more parties.

  Look closely at the organization's website. On the website, do you see references to work-at-home, working remotely, road warrior, or very flexible schedules? If so, this organization is likely to use remote connectivity as the foundation for its day-to-day operations. If you're a prospective employee, you need to verify this during your job interview. There are considerable limitations in an organization where key executives, managers, or nearly everyone works from different physical locations.

The limitations of working remotely include:

  - o Not being able to build personal relationships with your teammates
  - o Logistical difficulties with strategic planning and problem resolution
  - o Limited key inputs due to scheduling/time zone conflicts
  - o The likelihood of being underpaid in salary, benefits, or both
  - o Requirements that employees be available unquestioningly via computer, cellphone, or chat capability for extended periods of the day

- A project-driven—not strategy-driven—work methodology
- A struggle for the employee to work effectively with a recently promoted manager who is learning the ropes in this new capacity
- Likely under appreciation of one's accomplishments, since the manager cannot actively see the effort the employee puts into a particular project
- *Is this a family-owned business?* Family-owned and managed business can be deadly for the job seeker. It's *all* about owners' control; money

for the owners; a "don't confuse me with the facts, my mind's made up" attitude; and the sad, glaring fact that a family-owned business will almost never oust a family member, however ineffective that person may be. "It's the family, stupid."

Patents Received

A company which is actively pursuing patents is one with a focus on the future. Note in particular the trend in the number of patents. If the company registered a number of patents ten years ago, but has not registered any since . . . it will be in trouble in ten years. U.S. patents are only good for 20 years . . . and they are not renewable.

Lawsuits Filed

A company may or may not include information about lawsuits filed against it on its website. However, a quick Google search may turn up some interesting information. You will have to evaluate the information to determine the legitimacy of the legal suits.

Community Involvement

- Does the organization have a program where it matches employees' donations to not-for-profit charitable organizations or colleges and universities? Does the organization provide funds as an endowment for a professor or scholarship fund at a college or university?

- Does the organization participate in discussions at local colleges and universities on business issues, politics, government regulations, the environment, taxation, and research and development initiatives?

Summary

Your first stop for research is the organization's website. At minimum, the website should provide information on the history of the organization, the mission or goals, the leadership, its people, the products and/or services, its location, and the means to contact the organization whether by telephone, email, or live chat capability. Nice-to-have information includes examples of social and/or environmental responsibility, a full or partial list of clients, and list of retailers where one may purchase the product.

~*~*~*~

CHAPTER 4

MARKETING

Marketing is not merely the type, quantity, and scheduling of advertisements and messages a company sends. It includes product design, description, and categorical placement—both within the organization's product line (is it a Ford or a Lincoln?) as well as in relation to competitors' products (is it comparable to a Chevrolet or a Cadillac?).

Marketing also includes distribution channels (the environment in which the product is sold—online, in a retail store, in a brand specific dealership, through a partnership, in the customer's home), and after-market product support. At the advertising level, considerations include: advertisements/slogans/logos/songs, advertising choices, whether the company focuses excessively on the future vs. the present, use of coupons, and warranty promises.

Products

Evaluate new products using seven factors—the product's design, product's description, category placement, customer testimonials, independent assessment of the product, early adoption by the U.S. military, and the use of photos rather than drawings.

Product Design

Does the design appear to be functional for its intended purpose? Or does it appear to be overloaded with *extras* that provide little added value but increase the likelihood of product failure? Products with all the bells and whistles you don't need are not a bargain, even if those extras are thrown in for free. You are probably paying for them in decreased quality in the essentials. Don't get so sold on the extras that you miss the fact that the product does not do what you need to have done.

Product Description

Brochures and/or the website should provide a clear explanation of the

product's features and benefits. Do not settle for a list of technical specifications—that is *not* enough information to evaluate the product. Additionally, technical specifications may be inaccurate or outdated. If appropriate,
the marketing information should provide a list of uses for a multi-function
product. The full range of uses may not be obvious to a first-time user.

Category Placement

Companies often offer a variety of products at various price points to
address the products' capacities for fulfilling different functions and levels
of functions. Commercial grade will usually be more heavy duty than consumer grade . . . and the economy model may have a far shorter product
lifespan than the premium version in the same product line. Additionally, a
company will often carry a product which it wants the customer to identify
as equivalent in function to a competitor's product . . . but which it wants
potential customers to perceive as better—in style, durability, quality, function, features, etc.

Customer Testimonials

A couple of solid testimonials add credibility. However, too many testimonials make you wonder about the product's *real* capabilities. Moreover, overly
laudatory testimonials may indicate something is amiss. Not every testimonial
can be a superlative; one or two good ratings would be acceptable—and add
considerable credibility. If all the testimonials are superlative, it may indicate
that the company cut some sort of deal with the persons or companies providing the testimonials. If all the testimonials sound like the same person wrote
them, the testimonials are more likely written by the marketing or public relations department than by actual customers.

Evaluations by Independent Market Research or Product Testing Firms

Is the market research or testing firm truly independent or is there a
required/implied business relationship? Is the product review a balanced
one—one containing positives and negatives? Did the third-party reviewer
raise any valid, significant negative points or does the gushingly positive
review appear to have been written by the company's PR department?

Early Adoption by U.S. Military

If the company documents a military use of its product, it's a good sign.
The military is a demanding customer and sets high standards for its contractors, technologies, products, or applications. The military may be involved

with the product from an early stage, thereby ensuring the product meets its stated requirements.

Use of Photos or Drawings

I prefer to see color photos of the product on the Web. A drawing may be of a *planned* product and the final version may not look the same. The photo does not have to reveal the inner workings or unique technologies contained in the product. From a different standpoint, why *not* show the product exterior to prospective customers? If the company fails to show at least the exterior of the product, then that company has something to hide; it is not straightforward in its business dealings; and the company or its key employees may indicate a dark past.

Product Support

Evaluate product support by examining three factors—the description of customer service/support options, in-house or third-party support for consumer products, and length of product warranty compared to that offered by the competition.

- *Description of customer support or service options is critical.* Poor support tells you all you need to know about the company's *real* attitude and beliefs. The day is long past when a company can make and sell a product, and then walk away.

- *In-house or third-party support.* Support from the manufacturer is generally better. A well-known third-party organization offering nationwide support and post-sale service, such as the programs offered by Best Buy, Target, K Mart, Radio Shack, and Sears, is acceptable. Interestingly, some of these larger retailers actually subcontract their repair service to a third party—often the same one the manufacturers use. Regional or local appliance or electronics store or chains are fine if you do not plan to move away. Ultimately, the quality of the product from the manufacturer is what counts. Do your homework *before* you purchase an appliance or home electronic item. Obviously, no listed support is the worst possible situation; do not buy that product.

- *Length of warranty vs. that of the competition.* The longer the warranty the company offers, the more faith the company has that the product it produced is not going to require warranty service. A significantly shorter warranty is a warning sign. For example, most new personal computers include a 90-day warranty. A company offering a one-year warranty (not an extended warranty) is making a strong positive statement; one offering a 30-day warranty is making a weak statement.

South Korea's Hyundai Motors' initial entry into the U.S. auto market was less than successful. Its vehicles were unreliable. After considerable effort, Hyundai greatly improved the quality of its vehicles. To reinforce the notion of improved quality with U.S. consumers, Hyundai became the first auto manufacturer to offer a 10-year, 100,000 mile warranty on the engine and select transmission/transaxle components. For 2011, U.S. sales of Hyundai and Kia brands (Kia vehicles are manufactured by Hyundai) were sixth, eclipsed by long established brands GM, Ford, Toyota, Chrysler, and Honda. Hyundai-Kia came from nowhere to set sales records and sell more than 1.2 million cars in the U.S. (ranking seventh) in 2012.

Distribution Channels

It is easy to overlook distribution channels. Most consumers are not aware of all the various channels a manufacturer can use to distribute and support its products. Some distribution channels are relatively simple. Take cars, for example. New car dealers sell new cars off the lot and through the Internet.

A NOTE FROM THE EDITOR

Friends recently bought a Vizio television. Vizio support (US-based!) appears to come directly from the company. If you call with set-up problems, you will complete product registration at the time you call in . . . and their customer support will either immediately answer your questions or put you on hold while they check other, more complex or obscure questions. (such as "Which screws do you use to mount the brackets to the back of the TV?") They will also *reset* your TV remotely if the software requires updates.

Does Vizio seem to understand its customer's concerns? Absolutely! The quality of their customer service was the primary reason I recommended Vizio to these friends. However, I don't have experience with Vizio's *on-site* service . . . if someone has to physically come out and repair the TV. Hopefully, the television's one-year warranty is indicative of sufficient quality that it will never need on-site service.

~~*

New car dealers sell one or two brands, mega-dealer Carmax sells a variety of used cars, and publicly-traded company AutoNation sells a variety of brands of new and used cars. Other sales outlets for used cars include corner used car lots, individuals, independent auto repair shops, rental car companies, auto brokers, and large companies selling vehicles from their fleets.

Exhaustive research on every company's distribution channels is not necessary. However, when purchasing a sophisticated product (especially a technology-based product such as a personal computer, notebook/ultrabook/tablet computer, plasma television, flat-panel computer display, combination printer-fax-scanner-copier, video game player, etc.), identifying obvious and sometimes conflicting changes in the manufacturer's distribution channels can give you a clue as to the underlying health of the manufacturer.

Stated simply, a company that is adding distribution channels is preferable to a company that is dropping distribution channels. Dell is famous for its single distribution channel—order a customized product in advance via the Internet or telephone and pay in advance. In May 2006, Dell announced it would open two retail stores. Other technology-based companies sell through retail chain stores, individual retail stores, computer distributors such as Ingram Micro or Tech Data, computer resellers, and companies specializing in serving a particular industry (such as a specialized system designed exclusively for use by small- to medium-sized credit unions).

Dell's decision to expand into retail store distribution channels succeeded because of its strong market presence (albeit web marketing- and mail order-based) and brand name recognition. Adding physical stores provided the advantages of hands-on product display and a physical location for customers to take their computers should technical problems arise.

Here is what to look for:

- *New or dropped product resellers.* Focus on the large chain store retailers. Suppose Best Buy, H.H. Gregg, Sears, J.C. Penney, and Rex Appliance Stores distribute the products of a particular consumer electronic manufacturer. If you read that any of these resellers stops carrying the product, try to find out why. Just as the manufacturer needs sales outlets, sales outlets need quality products that are in demand by the public and supported by manufacturers after the sale. By asking "Why?" you will learn a great deal about the manufacturer and retailer.

- *Look for basic changes to the distribution model.* A significant change in the fundamental distribution model is a warning sign. If a company is selling through wholesale distributors to retailers (called *two-tier* distribution), then decides to sell directly to retailers (called *one-tier* or direct distribution), one must question this change to the company's basic business model. This major change may indicate looming financial problems. When a company changes distribution channels, it is usually done to save money (the financial payoff). In return, the customer generally receives poorer service, especially if the first level of support is through the product's distributors.

- *Search for international distribution and support.* Although you are not likely to move overseas, international distribution and product support separates the big dogs from the lap dogs of consumer retailing. International distribution also shows the company's adaptability to different consumer, safety, electrical, ergonomic, and regulatory requirements.

- *Look for cross-channel conflicts.* What is cross-channel conflict? Perhaps a manufacturer is successfully selling its products through retailers, resellers, and distributors. Cross-channel conflict occurs when the manufacturer competes with its established distribution channels by selling directly to a large dollar customer. Why would a manufacturer jeopardize its established distribution channels? Greater profit margin, closer contact with a key customer, greater profit margin, and greater profit margin. It's really *all* about money.

What specific problems can result from cross channel conflicts?

- The local, regional, or national retailer will feel betrayed. The retailer now has good reason to question the company's loyalty to its resellers. It may sign distribution agreements with other manufacturers to regain those lost profits by being able to offer competing products. The retailer may even decide to drop that manufacturer as a supplier, leaving the manufacturer with the job of finding a new distributor for its smaller purchasers.

- If end users of the product require significant telephone or on-site support, the manufacturer now will have to provide that service and support. Where the distributors and retailers previously offered this important post-sale service, the manufacturer will now be forced to establish an expensive in-house support organization.

This is not easy for the manufacturer since it:

- Will not fully know or understand this customer's support requirements

- Cannot ask its distributors for assistance on how to set up such a support function, since it went around them in the first place. Moreover, distributors in one geographic location share information with competitors in other regions. You can be sure that this manufacturer's distributor will share its tale of the company's shabby treatment.

- Put itself in competition with its distributors and retailers for future large or very large orders

Advertising and Promotion

Advertising is a communication tool used to gain a marketing advantage by building customer awareness of the company and its products. Done properly, advertising works; done badly, advertising creates confusion or false expectations on the part of the buyer. Ad slogans and promotional statements verbalize how the company wants to be seen.

For whatever reason, some companies create or approve *clever* slogans or characters which do not relate directly to the company's products or services. If you dissociate the company name from the slogans, it is hard to guess the name of the company advertised, let alone its industry.

Unrelated Slogans or Characters

We don't need an in-depth discussion of slogans or characters that don't work. The vague slogans below could be applied to *any* product or service. None says anything distinct about the company, its product or service, or its commitment to customers.

- "The common sense choice," Scott Corporation, paper products

- "Engineering the flow of communications," Pitney Bowes, manufacturer of integrated e-mail and document products

- "Make progress every day," Verizon, voice/data communication carrier

- "You expect more from a leader," Amoco, oil exploration, refining, and distribution

- "Make something great," Stanley Corporation, hand tools

- "Simplify," Honda, automobiles

- "Be like Mike," Gatorade, sports beverage

- "Turn promise into practice," Aetna, health/life insurance company

- "Truth, Courage, Judgement (sic—spelling counts!)," Guardsmark, security services

- "Whatever it takes," Digital Equipment Corporation (DEC), computer systems

- "Ideas for life," Panasonic Corporation, consumer electronic products

- "Five star service guaranteed," U.S. Bank, commercial bank

- "Imagination at work," General Electric, industrial products manufacturer and financial lending institution

DON'T MESS WITH YOUR PRODUCT DISTRIBUTORS

Here is a good example of the effective use of distribution channels. I worked at Wyse Technology in San Jose. A Top 5 U.S. bank wanted to order 10,000 terminals for use in its nationwide branch banking system. Internal discussions revealed Wyse was tempted to bypass its existing distributors and work directly with the bank. Why? By eliminating one or more intermediaries, the bank customer would save money and Wyse would make more money.

What did Wyse do? It made the *wise* decision for all parties—the bank, its distributors, and itself. Wyse provided the large bank with the names of all of the company's U.S. distributors and let the bank negotiate with multiple distributors. In turn, all the distributors worked with the Wyse sales force to get the best pricing, invoicing, sales support, product support, and delivery terms possible.

What were the benefits of this approach? The distributors made money, the bank's geographically scattered offices received the necessary support from a distributor with nationwide offices or from local distributors, Wyse did not compete with its product distributors, and Wyse further cemented its good distribution channel relationships.

This thoughtful, collaborative approach was a clear win-win for everyone.

~~*

Here are examples, some iconic, of good ad characters, songs, slogans, and logos:

Memorable Characters

- Mr. Clean: Procter & Gamble recently revived its use of Mr. Clean, a cartoon-like, muscled strongman dressed in white, to promote its cleaning products of the same name. This choice of character is not dependent on the availability or public behavior of any actors.

- Miss Chiquita: Miss Chiquita Banana, a colorfully-dressed, recognizable character, has represented U.S. banana distributor Chiquita Company for many years, far beyond what one would have expected.

- GEICO gecko: This lifelike *spokes creature* for an auto insurance carrier has been so pervasive in GEICO's advertising, that the voice, figure, and personality are virtually *real*. Although the gecko is unrelated to the product, the name sounds like GEICO, the name of the company. With its proper-sounding, British/Australian accent, the gecko injects humor and personality into what is perceived as, the faceless, stodgy insurance business.

In mid-2006, GEICO ran a commercial with composer Burt Bacharach singing a tune about GEICO's customer service. The newest slogan was, "Great service. Great price," designed to differentiate GEICO from its competitors. Why hire great music composer Burt Bacharach? Where did *that* idea come from? Why drop the affectionately-recognized gecko which had become part of the company's brand?

For a while, GEICO experimented with formerly-famous actors alongside unknown people to explain how GEICO was helpful during auto-related crises. A third advertising approach used a cave man to reinforce the notion that GEICO's website was so easy to use that even a cave man could do it.

GEICO wisely extended the gecko's presence beyond television ads to include print ads and billboards. Alas, no gecko appeared in the company's Yellow Pages ad. The iconic GEICO gecko joins the Budweiser lizards in a mythical animal-based advertising hall of fame, and, along with Mr. Clean and Ms. Chiquita, demonstrates that some companies *can* get it right.

Effective Songs

Popular songs play a role in consumer advertising. Two in particular stick in my mind. Bob Seger's *Like a Rock* became the theme song for Chevrolet trucks, communicating a theme of rock solid reliability. For one Christmas shopping season, Roy Orbison's *Anything You Want (You Got It)* served as a perfect linkage with mass marketer Target, the discount department store. Each song listed above reinforced the product or service offered.

More examples of catchy tunes used in effective advertisements:

- Carly Simon's *Anticipation*, Heinz, ketchup

- Rolling Stones, *Start Me Up*, Introduction of Microsoft Windows 95

- The Cars, *Just What I Needed*, Circuit City Stores, Inc., consumer electronics

- Collective Soul, *Better Now*, Kellogg Co., breakfast cereals

- T-Bones (instrumental), *No Matter What Shape (Your Stomach's In)*, Alka-Seltzer, antacid tablets

How does the selection of a song or slogan translate into an assessment of the company's culture and values? As in other aspects of an organization, if it fits and makes sense in the promotion of the product or service, then that is a good sign. If it does not fit, then something is amiss. Remember, **someone or a committee had to approve the song or slogan.** Although a company's song or slogan is one of many factors—it is not a primary factor for assessing an organization or its culture.

Appropriate Slogans

Like a well-selected song, an appropriate slogan reflects positively on a company. Examples of effective, memorable slogans include:

- "Like a good neighbor, State Farm is there," State Farm, auto/homeowners insurance

- "All the news that's fit to print," New York Times, newspaper

- "The few. The proud. The Marines," U.S. Marines, military

- "No surprises," Holiday Inn, lodging

- "We'll leave the light on for you," Motel 6, lodging

- "We try harder," Avis, car rental company

- "The milk chocolate melts in your mouth, not in your hands," Mars Corporation, M&M candies

- "Built for looks. Buy it for life," Moen, decorative plumbing fixtures

- "Computers from Iowa," Gateway, personal computers (Gateway added cow spots to its shipping boxes in the early 1990s, a clever extension and reinforcement of its slogan.)

- "You deserve a break today," McDonald's Corporation, fast food restaurants

- "Saturn. A different kind of company. A different kind of car," Saturn Corporation, automobile manufacturer

- "Can you hear me now?" Sprint Corporation, cellular phone service provider

- "Never Stop Improving," Lowe's, home improvement

- "More saving. More doing," Home Depot, home improvement

- "You never actually own a Patek Philippe. You merely look after it for the next generation," Patek Philippe, manufacturer of luxury watches

- "The Ultimate Driving Machine," BMW, automobiles

- "The Pursuit of Perfection," Lexus, automobiles

Here is a notable exception to the rule—the tag line "SC Johnson—A Family Company." In an impersonal world, the company differentiates itself by linking itself with unnamed *family* values. Without knowing anything else about the company, a reasonable assumption is one of a close-knit, supportive, positive organization that produces good quality products your family could use. However, the contrary position must be brought up. Most family companies are run for the benefit of family members and are dysfunctional at a number of levels—unqualified family members holding key positions, heavy internal politics, lack of follow through on projects, not keeping one's word to do something, possible safety issues, and making unnecessary changes to distribution channels or product support capabilities.

Bottom line: It is fair to say that, based on product history and product ratings, the SC Johnson Company is far from dysfunctional.

Good Logos

A good logo provides a visual anchor for its company. Even when products change, the positive image of the company remains, established through association of the logo with quality products in the past. Here are examples of effective corporate logos:

- The red script letters in Kellogg's, manufacturer of breakfast cereals

- The letters in *CAT* printed close together in bold black sans serif letters, representing Caterpillar Corporation, heavy equipment

- The 3M logo where no space appears between the number 3 and the letter M, Minnesota Mining and Manufacturing Company, product conglomerate

- IBM's distinctive logo with alternating bands of thin light blue lines and white space reinforce a high-tech, yet friendly and approachable company

- Mercedes Benz's three-pointed star inside a circle is instantly recognized

Fabio, Lizards, and Frogs

We can only imagine how much money Unilever paid many years ago for romance novel cover model Fabio to recite, "I can't believe it's not butter." What is the linkage between a long-haired, 20-something male model and low saturated fat, low calorie, zero trans-fat margarine? Fake butter is sexy? Who approved *that* concept? On the other hand, the clever, but long-defunct Budweiser lizards and frogs did not relate in any logical way to beer, the company's product. However, it is difficult to forget some of the lizard's and frog's famous lines: "Let it go, Louie." "You are one sick lizard." "Your mother's half iguana." And, "Frankie, eventually every frog's gotta croak."

Bottom line: Appropriate slogans and logos which are memorable and product-linked are strong indicators of organizational strength. True, slogans and logos are small in comparison to total organizational operations. However, the extensive work required to identify a product's or company's strength and create a good slogan and logo demand a unified management team, and an organization that knows itself and knows its target purchaser.

New Logos for Unilever and Microsoft

In May 2004, Unilever released a new logo. The logo combined 24 dis-

ent? Are employees at client companies no better than or their thinking no different from dinosaurs?

This advertising solution may instead reflect the company's stagnant creativity, its inability to come up with something memorable, and its failure to generate an idea that was relevant, original, and fresh.

Recap: Marketing Promotions and Organizational Dysfunction

Vague marketing statements, motherhood statements, inappropriate mascots or spokespersons, and poorly crafted songs or slogans which could be applicable to any business highlight five symptoms of dysfunction:

- First, and most important, the company does not know itself. A company must know, believe, and live what it represents. A company must understand its capabilities and limitations. **Poor ads reveal a company's major plans are often unrealistic; the firm believes it has exaggerated personnel and financial capabilities.**

- Second, the company does not know its customers. The company does not fully comprehend its customer's demographics and psychographics. The company's aim may be off—its target is generally too broad. **A company may believe it can be everything to everyone. In the end, it winds up as nothing to anyone. Inward focus, a narrow planning horizon, possible infighting between finance and marketing, substandard customer service and support, and confused messages characterize the organization.**

- Third, since the company approved these poor slogans or characters, **the company's decision-making processes are unclear or overly political.** Who thought it through? Who acted as the voice of reason? Who overrode that voice? Why? Or Why not?

- Fourth, the company under-funded its promotions and advertising. For a consumer products company, this is a serious miscalculation. For a company that sells to other businesses, the impact may be less severe if the company correctly employs other aspects of its marketing budget. For example, in business-to-business (coolly abbreviated as *B2B*) marketing, the company may increase its trade show budget, and may introduce a new product at the leading industry trade show instead of advertising it in traditional print media. In consumer marketing, a company must employ an ever-changing mix of newspaper and magazine ads, coupons, social media contacts, website features, television and radio promotions, in-store product demonstrations/ samples, point-of-purchase (POP) displays, or billboards, mailers to homes, flyers, and direct mail to keep its message and products in the minds of consumers. **Underfunded promotions may represent another clue of an organization's *finance vs. marketing* battle.**

- **Fifth, at a higher level, poor promotion represents an inefficient or incorrect allocation of resources, which in turn, reflects a poor overall strategy.** For a consumer goods business, mass promotion is critical. For product sales to other businesses, effective use of third-party distribution channels can overcome poor or lacking promotional efforts.

Bottom line: It is difficult to create good slogans, ads, jingles, or characters. It is more difficult to create a great slogan, ad, song, or fictional character. **Clever slogans, ads, or characters reflect an active, customer-oriented company. Inappropriate or vague slogans, ads, or characters reflect a passive, inwardly-focused company. A song or slogan is a consistent indicator to help you evaluate an organization and/or its culture.**

Advertising Channels

Advertising channels are the mix of promotional methods used to reach potential customers. The promotional methods will vary based on the product, target, and budget. A high-tech B2B firm may find it more beneficial to invest its advertising dollars in laptop presentations for its technical sales team, advertisements in industry-related technical journals, and participation in trade shows. A local high-end boutique will spend its advertising dollars targeting the local population that values fine clothing and has the money to pay for it.

With the growth of the Internet, even local businesses can gain a worldwide presence with the proper advertising. For example: Internet auctions now allow people from all over the world to bid for one-of-a-kind jewelry and fine art pieces. Reaching a large enough audience to ensure a successful event requires a completely different type of advertising than when the jewelry store was operating at the local 9 to 5 brick-and-mortar level.

Take note of the channels a company uses to place its advertising. Does it use high-gloss, full-color, die-cut, heavy paper for its brochures and annual reports? Are its television advertisements loaded with high-cost special effects and high-profile stars? Is this high-cost, extra-effort consistent with the product type, grade, and targeted customers? Or is the company over-reaching . . . attempting to impress customers with *quality* that is not characteristic of the products it produces?

Always Writing/Talking about Future Products and Plans

Sadly, some companies choose to emphasize future products or services more than current ones. ***Selling futures* takes away the pain of talking about a company's current reality.** Future products or other opportunities seldom materialize as described—unforeseen supply chain, manufacturing, staffing, and technical problems sabotage the vision. The promised products are generally very late to market and face tough competition from competitors who delivered earlier. Other opportunities—partnerships, joint ventures, overseas expansion, outsourcing, mergers, acquisitions, divestitures, restructuring—don't measure up to the hype. **The corporate culture in this case is clearly one of lethargy, inertia, and bureaucratic decision-making rather than risk-taking, forward-thinking, and decisive action.**

A dated example is Microsoft Corporation. In 2000-2005, the company failed in its attempt to develop and sell digital music players and television set-top boxes, which are required to receive digital cable television broadcasts. An August 3, 2006, article in the *Financial Times* put Microsoft's situation in perspective. Craig Mundie, at that time the company's newest technology strategist, defended the company's false start on television set-top boxes and its complete miss on the digital music business—two fast-growing and now very large businesses.

Mundie claimed Microsoft was "the only company to have a potential leadership product in every category." He then added, "You can think of Microsoft as the 'Magical Morphing Microsoft.' Every person who has said to us, 'Here's the new thing and it's going to be the thing that unseats you,' has always neglected the fact that the company is willing to change and has this deep technological investment pool."

In these comments, Mundie indirectly admitted Microsoft's product weakness. The company had the willingness to change and the required funding, but lacked focus and follow through. Mundie emphasized *potential efforts*—not *actual results*.

My view differs substantially from that of Mr. Mundie. Between 1995 and 2006, Microsoft spent $42.7 *billion* on research and development. For this incredible sum, Microsoft developed operating systems for personal computers and small to mid-range servers—Windows for PCs, Windows for

Servers, Windows NT—and upgrades to its Office software suite, plus Xbox, a single consumer product that played video games.

To put this in perspective, companies such as IBM, Hewlett-Packard, Tandem Computers, and Digital Equipment designed and created operating systems for sophisticated large computer systems that supported up to 3,000 users, were virtually hacker-proof, and ran mission-critical software applications. The cost to create these operating systems hovered between $100 and $300 million, not *billions* of dollars.

Basically, Microsoft may have, in Mundie's words, a deep technological investment pool, yet it has proven itself incapable of leading the development of new, exciting business and consumer products beyond a relatively unsophisticated personal computer operating system and office suite software. Sorry, Mr. Mundie, Microsoft can't have it both ways. The company is either a player in new technology market spaces or it is not. Potential doesn't count; only successful new products count.

Microsoft not only sells futures, it brags about its past marketing and technological prowess. While Microsoft talks, others develop and sell real products and do the tough groundwork to open new markets and reach new customers, some of whom were formerly Microsoft customers. From 2010 on, Microsoft has been a late entrant to the fast-growing markets for tablet computers and electronic book readers.

For the company in 2012, little had changed. Microsoft introduced a few niche products, but nothing technically advanced or market-changing. Specifically? The company created a version of Windows operating system for cell phones, added enhancements to its Xbox 360 video game console, and introduced the Slate ultra-portable tablet computer concept which included built-in capabilities for Bluetooth, webcam, touch screen, and HDMI connectivity.

However, products built around the Slate concept are marketed by Samsung, Fujitsu, ExpoPC, Motion Computing, ASUS, and Acer. Microsoft also started marketing a tablet computer product called Surface in Q4 2012. By December, industry pundits were predicting that Surface sales would be fewer than one million for its debut quarter, due, in part to its slow release, restricted sales channels (at that time Microsoft had only 31 retail stores and 34 holiday specialty stores), and poor independent product reviews.

Microsoft bought the popular Skype video conferencing company and created Bing, a search engine with capabilities to effectively rival Google. Its Zune product enables cell phone, personal computer, or Xbox video console to play music, movies, and television programming. In a nutshell, these products are largely extensions of its existing products, purchased technologies, or copies of competitors' products.

Microsoft recently fine-tuned its retail distribution channel (AKA, copied Apple) by establishing proprietary retail stores. By May 2013, Microsoft had opened 67 retail stores throughout the U.S./Canada/Puerto Rico to sell Windows 7 PCs, Windows phones, Kinect for Xbox 360, the Office 2012 software suite, and other Microsoft products. However, ten companies (Acer, ASUS, Dell, Gateway, HP, Lenovo, Samsung, Sony, Toshiba, and VIZIO) already sold PCs based on Microsoft's Windows 8 operating system. Two companies (Nokia and HTC) sold and supported Windows Phones.

Fast forward to June 2013. The company announced it will transform its Xbox product beyond gaming and become an entertainment hub for users' television. Voice commands will allow users to seamlessly switch between movies, games, television, and music instead of the current practice to close one application before opening another. The company believes it can leverage both the 76 million Xbox model 360s sold and its Xbox Live service with 48 million subscribers. With this pending new product, Microsoft will challenge the companies that make hardware and the television networks that provide programs.

What more did Microsoft feel it had to offer when it already had major established players promoting its products? Perhaps Microsoft was seeking to emulate Apple's mystique, enhance its prestige, and build a dedicated following around its products. Instead, this is a great example of confused distribution channels or copycat marketing—a window-dressing alternative to "Show us the innovation."

Excessive or Unfocused Customer Coupon Publication

Certain local restaurants consistently place ads in the approximately 350,000 daily circulation *Tampa Bay Times* (formerly *St. Petersburg Times*) and place smaller ads in coupon books mailed to residents in select ZIP codes. These restaurants advertise $5 off a $25 check and $10 off a $50 check. Some local restaurants advertise as much as 50% off meals using the on-line coupon site, www.groupon.com. The few times I stopped by, these restaurants were not busy.

Heavy use of print or on-line coupons characterizes the promotional efforts of new restaurants. Such promotion may also indicate a business which has lost focus and is making a last desperate attempt to survive. While a new restaurant can be expected to cast a *broad net* as it searches for the right combination of publications in which to advertise, an established restaurant's lack of focus indicates it is unsure of its target audience. Possibly, the quality of the food, service, or ambience changed for the worse and the restaurant is trying to regain lost business.

Consistent use of coupons in targeted publications is appropriate and effective. It is a matter of degree. Too many or too frequent coupon use can change a restaurant's image from one of high quality food and service to one which discounts its price—suggesting the fair value of the food is less than the menu prices. Coupons then become habit; customers will not eat at the restaurant *unless they have a coupon*.

Effective restaurant ads combine the use of coupons with image ads, whether in print or on the Internet, television, or radio. For personal services, such as relaxation massages, hair styling, or manicures and pedicures, the use of coupons tends to bring out only the cheapskates who will gladly try the bargain service, but will *never* return to pay the full, too expensive price!

Requesting Detailed Personal Information for Completion of a Warranty Registration Card

If you must mail a newly purchased product's registration card to a post office box in Denver, Colorado, then your personal information feeds a huge database. This database information is analyzed and the results are resold to companies. Your hobbies, reading habits, likes/dislikes of spectator sports, preferred participant sports, automobile ownership, and toothpaste and shampoo usage are nobody's business but your own. **Companies that participate in this information-gathering program are trying to take a rational, data-driven approach to understanding their customers.** Kudos to them. However, you are under no obligation to help.

The only required warranty information is your name, address, date of purchase, place of purchase, and serial number or other identifying information from the product. If you expect to keep your current Internet Service Provider (ISP), then you may want to list your email address to receive product and promotion information. However, before doing so, check the company's policy on sharing your email address.

If the site permits unrestricted sharing or sharing among selected business partners, do not provide your email address. Your definition of selected business partners may widely differ from those selected by the company. In other words, you never know who will gain access to your email address and for what purpose. You never know how long the database company maintains its information or how many times it will sell your information to so-called related companies . . . and where those companies eventually will sell it again.

Summary

Marketing is the first operation-related topic for discussion. Why? Marketing is important. Marketing, then sales—not finance—drives the growth of an organization. We subdivided the broad topic of marketing into products, support, and promotion.

For products, the evaluation referenced an appropriate number of testimonials, independent evaluation, and an often-overlooked criterion, early adoption by the U.S. military. While not every product or service has a military-related application, early adoption by the U.S. military is a strong indicator that advanced applications exist for the product.

Two aspects of product or service support are relatively straightforward. In-house support beats that offered by third parties. And the longer the warranty, the better. Two other aspects require additional fact- or impression-gathering. Distribution channel dysfunction is when the company sells its products through too many or conflicting outlets. In the most obvious cases, the manufacturer tries to bypass its established outlets, generally for a very large sale to a single customer. Additional research needs to be done to identify lopsided partnerships. The lopsided nature may be due to incompatible organizational cultures or significant differences in the size and negotiating strength of the partners.

Dysfunction in promoting the company, its people, or the products/services offered quickly becomes apparent. You can identify the differences between good and bad slogans, effective and ineffective promotional characters, memorable and unmemorable songs or jingles, and well-thought-out and hurriedly created logos. Marketing, as an outreach to customers, is critical to the success of an organization.

Finance and Accounting, our next topic, provides a measure of an organization's internal health.

~*~*~*~

CHAPTER 5

FINANCE & ACCOUNTING

You do not need to pore over every single number or calculate every known financial ratio to find an organization's finance- or accounting-based warning signs. Critical finance-related factors include:

- How complete is the financial information?

- Is it easy to view key financial data?

- Who generally speaks for the company?

- What are the reasons given for an earnings shortfall?

- What does the *segment information* tell you about the company?

- What is the ownership structure for publicly traded stock?

- How aggressive are the company's accounting policies and practices?

Completeness of Financial Information

Does the company provide a summary of key data *and* all supporting financial information? Key data without supporting documents leaves a lot of room to hide what is really going on. Too much detail with no meaningful summary makes it difficult to sort out the impacts of the various contributions to gain or loss.

Is the material presented in a way that promotes understanding? Is the information easy to find? Does the report use an easy-to-read type font? Does the format include sufficient white space? Does the information include an income statement, balance sheet, and cash flow statement?

The answers to these questions should be an unequivocal "yes." Obfuscation, omission, illogical ordering, overly couched wording, and use of jargon or unfamiliar terminology or unexplained abbreviations tell of an organization trying to hide a bigger, likely more damaging, story.

Each quarter, a few companies publish press releases which contain only a summary of the key data that includes revenue, net profit, and earnings per share. The company has filed the required public disclosures with the Securities and Exchange Commission (SEC). However, the details are not made readily available to the general public . . . which *should* raise the question—why? I cannot think of an acceptable answer. Be wary of less-than-full-disclosure in any quarter or year.

Companies sometimes submit *pro forma* financial statements. *Pro forma* means provided in advance—in advance of the full situation or in advance of full knowledge of a situation. Jokingly, *pro forma* is an accounting term for, "This is a guess and most likely the best case estimate," or, "This is what we want the investing public to know at this time, although it could change for the worse." Seriously, why would any investor, employee or future employee, supplier, lender, or customer want to read fiction? If, in its written discussions, the company emphasizes *only* *pro forma* statements, then run—do not walk—away from this company.

Too-brief summaries and *pro forma* statements are more about marketing than financial accuracy. They suggest untrustworthiness, set unrealistic expectations, and create an environment of hype rather than one of problem prevention, problem solving, and truth. Moreover, the company's emphasis on the future is designed to de-emphasize its likely deteriorating present situation. If this hardheaded indictment forces just one company to drop its *pro forma* fantasies and publish real numbers, then it will have been worth exposing the man behind the curtain.

Are Key Numbers Readily Available?

Is the information complete? Is it easy to read? Key numbers include:

- Revenue/percentage change in revenue year-over-year

- Gross profit/percentage change in gross profit year-over-year

- Operating profit/percentage change in operating profit year-over-year

- Net profit/percentage in net profit change year-over-year

- Earnings per share/fully diluted earnings per share (which take into account all grants of stock options)/change in earnings per share year-over-year

Year-over-year compares data from the same quarter for the current fiscal year against the same quarter the previous fiscal year. This eliminates the substantial effects of seasonality (e.g., higher retail sales during the end-of-year holiday season).

You would be surprised at how many companies do not readily disclose basic financial information. If all key financial data is not readily available in a single location, then I believe the firm is hiding something. To ferret out the missing information, check these additional sources: Form 10-K (annual financial report with emphasis on the Exhibits), Forms 10-Q (quarterly financial reports), Form 14-A (annual proxy statement), and the company's website for financial information. Be sure to read the footnotes placed throughout the Form 10-K. Focus especially on the balance sheet section in the Form 10-K to learn about off-balance-sheet financing, a big potential source of financial problems.

I can almost guarantee that you will find something of significance buried in the footnotes or in the company's Statement of Changes in Cash Flows. Why do I say this? The Statement of Changes in Cash Flows links the numbers on the Balance Sheet with those on the Income Statement and discloses increases or decreases in discretionary accounts such as reserves, write downs or impairments, provisions for loan losses, or provisions for bad debts.

Bottom line: Financial alchemists end up hiding most of their manipulations in these last four accounts—which are good places for an investigator to start.

Who Generally Speaks for the Company?

Does one executive speak consistently on behalf of the company? Does the CEO speak if the company has a good quarter? Does the Chief Financial Officer (CFO) speak when the financial results for the quarter are bad or do not live up to consensus Wall Street expectations? Who presents the information at the quarterly earnings conference call with Wall Street analysts and mutual/hedge fund managers? Who answers questions from analysts and portfolio managers? One warning sign—if the CEO speaks for the company on the conference call with analysts and investors *only* when the firm announces good results. In the same organizations, the Chief Financial Officer (CFO) will speak for the company on the same quarterly conference call when the firm announces less-than-expected or less-than-forecasted financial results.

Does the company schedule an annual tour/meeting with financial analysts? It should. The CEO and all operating division heads, and vice presidents should attend. This is a big deal. At least once a year, the company needs to keep the financial community aware of what is going on in the organization. Remember, in the financial community, no news over an extended time frame is the same as bad news.

What are the Reasons for an Earnings Shortfall?

Do the explanations given sound believable? For example: The management of Krispy Kreme doughnuts reported the company fell short of its quarterly earnings due to the sudden popularity of the Atkins Diet. Utter nonsense. Why did the financial impact of a diet trend/fad suddenly hit in a single quarter and create such significant financial damage? The Board and shareholders pay senior managers to realistically manage the business and thereby prevent an earnings shortfall. If earnings are expected to be below Street expectations, management should provide an early, realistic warning of and likely reasons for the expected shortfall. Executives are paid big bucks and/or many stock options or both to create plans to prevent catastrophes, manage risk, and/or address critical events.

Bottom line: The effects of the Atkins diet did not magically manifest themselves in a single quarter. Management at Krispy Kreme was either not straight with investors or it was clueless—neither case is indicative of good management. One has to wonder what else was amiss at Krispy Kreme.

What does the Segment Information Tell You about the Company?

The SEC requires that companies disclose specific information about their business segments. Using segment data, you can unlock the specifics of a company's operations by ascertaining each segment's contribution to revenue, operating profit, and its use of assets. Footnotes in the segment information section will tell you which operating divisions have higher sales, greater profits, and require higher capital investment as well as those with lower results and requirements.

Bottom line: Compare the difference between each operating segment's business and the company's stated plans or vision. This data shows the harsh realities. Be very leery of any diversified company that claims to conduct 100% of its business in a single business segment. Some companies will show 100% of their business derived in a single broadly defined segment to prevent competitors and investors from learning factual details. You need to see the complete data set so you can accurately assess how each operating division is doing.

Does the Company Always Meet or Exceed its Forecasts for Revenue and, especially, Profit?

A *normal* company cannot consistently meet or exceed its revenue or profit forecasts. Stuff happens. The stuff that happens is not necessarily big or bad. However, be wary of any company that consistently meets or beats its forecasts, despite some analysts' defense of the management of such a business.

An egregious example is American International Group (AIG), the property and casualty insurance company formerly headed by Maurice "Hank" Greenberg. The company reported strong profits and earnings per share for at least 10 years without a financial hiccup. In reality, the company engaged in aggressive accounting practices in order to meet or exceed its earnings targets.

On the other hand, Walgreen's, the retail pharmacy chain, shows steady, but unspectacular growth. Although the demand for prescription drugs continues to increase steadily, the company has occasionally missed analysts' quarterly earnings estimates by a penny or two. Walgreen's results are closer to real-world performance—what we expect to see.

If a Company Buys Back its Shares of Stock, How Often does this Happen?

At the direction of the Board of Directors, a publicly traded company may purchase outstanding shares of stock. This act reduces the number of shares outstanding and lowers the divisor when calculating earnings per share.

Some investors consider share buy-backs as effective use of company funds. From a purely corporate finance standpoint, the use of excess funds to lower the divisor when calculating earnings per share is considered good. For example, a company has 25 million shares of stock outstanding. When the company announces its profit, then that amount is divided by 25 million to arrive at earnings per share. If this company bought back 5 million shares and reduced the number of shares outstanding to 20 million, then the resulting next earnings per share would be higher since the profit is divided by a smaller number.

Here is a different take on share buy-backs. Share buy-backs are an admission that the company can no longer effectively use its capital to increase revenues, profits, and earnings per share. Of course, in order to buy back shares, companies must have large cash balances and continue to generate additional cash each quarter.

Share buybacks are a sign of marketing weakness and financial deterioration or, stated differently, a transition from a marketing-driven to a financially-driven organization. Whether a firm is marketing-driven or financially-driven, the company's practice of using excess cash to purchase shares of stock sends a confusing message to current and potential investors. On one hand, the company is reducing the number of shares outstanding so reported earnings per share will increase. On the other hand, the company is saying it cannot effectively use its capital to increase profits or company valuation.

Share buybacks are usually done infrequently. If the company buys back shares more than once every five to eight years, then the firm is screaming, "We have no real strategy to grow our business. Whatever we tried in an attempt to grow our business did not work and we did not have any backup plans. Executives are quite happy in our little world and our CEO has managed to persuade the Board that all is well."

Announcements of Large War Chests for Acquisitions

On July 21, 2006, Pfizer, the world's largest drug maker, announced a $17 billion war chest that it planned to use to acquire companies within the following 30 months. Its stated reason was that a number of its drug patents had expired. This announcement may be viewed as, "We need to use some of our banked money so we can buy a company already generating revenue in order to make up for potentially lost revenue from drugs with expiring patents."

Executive management and the Board *knew* the life cycle of these patents; the expiration date is always twenty years after a company applies and receives the patent—with the option to extend that patent up to fourteen more years if the drug is eligible. Twenty years of not noticing a ticking clock?

When Pfizer stated its intentions to purchase other companies, the company signaled it had few potential drugs in the pipeline to replace the expected lost revenues from the drugs with expiring patent protection. By announcing its war chest and its need to acquire a smaller company, Pfizer increased the likelihood that it would overpay for the company it wished to acquire.

To say nothing would have been the better approach. On January 26, 2009, Pfizer agreed to buy pharmaceutical rival Wyeth for a combined $68 billion in cash, shares, and loans, including some $22.5 billion lent by five major Wall Street banks, making this the largest acquisition in the history of the pharmaceutical industry.

Why make the announcement? The company or its board of directors must have felt pressure from a few large institutional investors (mutual funds, hedge funds, pension funds, foreign investors, non-U.S. based hedge funds, foreign governments) to improve earnings per share for the current quarter, even though the announcement, in the long term, would compromise its financial strength. Shame, shame, shame.

A Significant Change in Capital Expenditures

Divide the amount spent each year for purchases of new equipment or new facilities, known as capital expenditures (often called "CapEx") by total revenue. Compare the change year-to-year for this percentage. If the company shows a three-year trend of decreased CapEx spending, then that is a warning sign. When a company does not replace depreciated or worn out equipment, it decreases its capability to remain competitive. If a company uses heavy machinery in its manufacturing process, then this is an early warning sign of an expected decrease in productivity, followed by a drop in sales and an increase in work-related accidents. Older equipment, unless extremely well maintained, becomes dangerous with wear.

Ownership Structure for Publicly-Traded Stock

Stock can be issued in different *classes*. Some firms use two classes of stock where each class of stock has different voting rights. Beware of a company where the stock owned by company founders has retained nearly all the voting power. Lopsided voting power says, in a nutshell, "We can do whatever we want and you can't stop us."

Newer publicly-traded technology companies are famous for the dual share structure. Google began the practice in 2004, followed by (in alphabetical order) Facebook, Groupon, LinkedIn, Yelp, and Zynga. Berkshire Hathaway has a dual class structure to its shares; however, voting power is not concentrated with Warren Buffet, Charlie Munger, or their families.

The dual class of stock has spread to the sports world. The UK-based Manchester United (Man United) soccer team, which went public in August 2012, will use such a lopsided system. The US-based Malcolm Glazer family will retain voting control of Man United through the use of shares that have 10 times more voting power than publicly traded shares.

Accounting

How aggressive are the company's accounting policies and practices?

A company discloses its basic accounting guidelines in the publicly-filed SEC Form 10-K. The section called *Management's Discussion & Analysis* shows the details of a company's policies as they apply to arcane items such as revenue recognition, cash flow, assumptions for valuation of assets, or expensing versus capitalizing certain expenditures.

Over long periods, company reporting policies should be consistent—which may require researching previous years' Form 10-Ks. Perhaps a tedious job—but companies which change their policies count on people not noticing when and how they've made these changes. More aggressive accounting tactics serve only one purpose—to show an increase in the company's profits and reported earnings per share and ultimately boost the financial value of the company. Changing *how things are done* often becomes a tool to deliberately hide what is really going on.

Accounting is part science, part art. From the scientific side, accountants must follow broadly written rules called GAAP (Generally Accepted Accounting Principles). From the art perspective, accountants have a great deal of latitude in the application of GAAP rules. Abraham J. Briloff, a retired accounting professor, passed away in 2013 at the age of 96. A famous critic of GAAP, Briloff created the acronym CRAP, which stood for *Cleverly Rigged Accounting Ploys*. Simply stated, Briloff believed one had to look beyond the stated numbers to get the full picture of an organization's financial health.

American essayist and poet Ralph Waldo Emerson famously stated, "A foolish consistency is the hobgoblin of little minds." I do not know if Mr. Emerson was also a successful investor. I know investors prefer consistent and repeated executive management practices and actions. When the policies change, the bottom line numbers no longer mean the same thing as they did previously.

Unfortunately, it can be difficult to determine if a company's financial consistency is foolish or brilliant. In financial theory, it is better for companies to borrow money to help fund growth than use reinvested profits that would go to investor shareholders. Many companies in technology businesses maintain huge piles of cash so they do not have to borrow money for expansion, for acquisitions, or to implement major strategy changes. When a technology company that uses conservative accounting and financing practices suddenly borrows a billion dollars the investor needs to know why this was done.

When the SEC cites a company using unapproved, aggressive accounting practices and forces it to recalculate and restate its financial statements, investors punish the company. They sell their shares of stock. They are reactive. They no longer trust management to the same degree they once did. Why should they?

In March 2006, General Motors (GM) delayed the release of its 2005 annual report and said it would restate its annual financial reports (SEC Form 10-K) from 2000 through 2004. Following the announcement, the stock price fell from $22.22 to $21.13 per share, a one-day decline of 5.2%. It's not nice to fool Mother Nature—or disclose results of operations using inconsistent financial reporting practices.

Bottom line: Watch for changes in a company's accounting policies. This is important because investors, suppliers, future and current employees, creditors, and bankers prefer conservative accounting policies. If a company becomes more aggressive in its accounting and subsequent financial reporting, then this is a sign of deteriorating reported earnings quality. A responsible and honest management meets the challenge of growing earnings without resorting to accounting or other financial tomfoolery.

Corporate Finance

Corporate finance represents the playground for the corporate big dogs and leading investment banks (called *bulge bracket* banks). Investment banks must complete transactions or, more commonly, simply *do deals.* Only upon completion of a deal, do companies pay these banks the negotiable fees of 3% to 7% of the amount of money raised.

Unfortunately, investment banks' actions are not always in the best interests of client companies, investors, employees, and creditors. Here are four examples that demonstrate the pervasive influence of corporate finance on corporate cultures.

Pay Far above Market Price for Acquisitions

The financial community (read: investors) expects a company to produce a certain net profit growth rate over a three- to five-year period. Companies can grow profits through internal expansion or acquisition.

Acquisition may look easier . . . so it is often the first strategy companies resort to when they want to grow. It has been proven repeatedly to be the less successful approach—impediments to success include integration of management styles, corporate structures, physical plant, operating procedures, and diverse technologies (in particular, merging databases)—all of these tend to present more problems than originally predicted. An investment banker or financial analyst can compare similar companies. Specifically, bankers or analysts use established metrics such as price/earnings, price/book, price/sales to readily determine the financial value of a company. They do not often prepare an assessment of the company culture.

No matter how good a match between two companies appears, the acquiring company should not pay too much to add new assets and capabilities. Companies with billions of dollars in the bank may be tempted to pay a premium for a much-desired acquisition target in order to sustain the growth of earnings per share (EPS). Paying too much for an acquisition now may overshadow the long-term goal of continued EPS growth.

Here are a few examples of how a company might end up overpaying for an acquisition.

- Getting into bidding wars for target companies rather than refusing to raise the bid.

Some companies do not know when to stop. A bidding war may cause the price to exceed the calculated value of the company by a premium of, say, 10%. A smart company knows when to stop playing bidding leapfrog.

Unfortunately, management egos at many companies get in the way of sound financial judgment on acquisitions. They may feel they can absorb the premium. Or, the acquiring companies may already have invested so much time and energy in trying to close the deal, they may be willing to overpay because they hate to see all that effort go to waste. Often, in their minds, they have already begun to integrate the new company with theirs.

Some companies refuse to overpay for acquisitions. In early 2006, consumer health products powerhouse Johnson & Johnson walked away from an ever-increasing price for Guidant Corporation, a maker of implantable cardiac devices. J&J stopped bidding at $71 per share. Boston Scientific beat J&J, paying $80 per share for Guidant Corporation.

Netherlands-based consumer research giant VNU wisely dropped out of the bid for pharmaceutical market research vendor IMS. After dropping out, VNU's CEO resigned, since the Board had lost faith in his ability to lead the company.

Other examples of the perception of overpaying for an acquisition target include:

o Office Depot paid a 42% premium to acquire Viking Office Products in 1998.

o Berkshire Hathaway paid $21.7 billion in 1998 to purchase

General Re, the reinsurance company. Although the price may have been right, the share price for Berkshire Hathaway fell 25% within the following six months.

o   Clear Channel Communications paid a 41% premium to acquire television station owner AMFM, Inc. in 1999.

o   Office supply company Buhrmann paid a 24% premium to acquire Corporate Express in October 1999.

o   The AOL/Time Warner merger was significantly overvalued. In April 2002, AOL/Time-Warner took a $54 billion charge as a write-down for the excess AOL paid Time Warner so the merger would go through.

o   In June 2006, data storage manufacturer EMC offered a 44.6% premium to acquire RSA Security, a vendor of security software.

o   In late July 2006, Advanced Micro Devices offered a 24% premium to acquire ATI, a Toronto-based manufacturer of graphics processors.

o   In August 2012, the chairman of Best Buy Corporation made an offer to buy the 80% of shares he did not already own at up to a 47% premium to the stock's closing price.

• Technology-based acquisitions seldom work out as planned.

Mergers and acquisitions are easy to strategize and difficult, if not impossible, to complete. Failed mergers and acquisitions litter the technology landscape. General Motors (GM) acquired Electronic Data Systems (EDS) in 1984. In 2008, as part of its corporate restructure, General Motors sold EDS to Hewlett-Packard (HP) for $13.9 billion. HP acquired UK-based software firm Autonomy in August 2011 for $10.3 billion, considered at the time an expensive purchase in light of the company's strategy-related issues. In early August 2012, HP took an $8.0 billion charge against earnings to more accurately reflect the greatly reduced value of EDS and Autonomy.

Other less-than-great tech mergers or acquisitions include ATT/NCR, Compaq/Digital Equipment Corporation, and Compaq/Tandem Computers. AOL/Time-Warner is in a class by itself. Since the merger in January 2000, the combined company lost approximately 81% of the value of the investment. Specifically, the $350 billion combined value at the time of acquisition decreased to $67.6 billion as of July 25, 2006. By August 8, 2012, the market value of company shares had plummeted to $3.2 billion, a staggering decrease to less than 1% of the combined peak value of the companies. In March 2013, Time Warner spun off AOL, Time Warner Cable, and Warner Music Group. On January 31, 2013, the combined market capitalization of only AOL and

---

THE VERY NEAT AND WELL ORGANIZED RECEPTION AREA

I visited a friend at his office; he worked for a hedge fund. Naturally I arrived a few minutes early; doing so gave me a chance to observe the work environment.

- First, the wood furniture—coffee table, the two upholstered chairs, and the étagère—was dark in color.

- Second, the arrangement of the items on the étagère was perfect. Not one item was out of place; the arrangement showed visual, near artistic, balance.

- Next, a clock, set to the correct time; small nautical mementos; about 20 hardcover books; and a silk plant sat in a precise, neat grouping.

In fact, the reception area looked too neat. Everything had a definite place; all designed to convey an image of a solid, controlled, and efficient operation—one that could be trusted. As I looked more closely, I noticed the books pertained to topics of interest ONLY to the founder/CEO. He clearly liked history and sailing. In the general population, these topics have limited appeal. Moreover, there were no magazines or newspapers related to people, weekly news and world events, or finance. Specifically, I found no issues of *Institutional Investor, Forbes, Barron's, Investor Business Daily, Business Week, Business 2.0, Time,* or *Newsweek, The Wall Street Journal,* the *Financial Times,* or *The Economist.* This combination of factors told me *it's all about him*—the CEO/founder is a control freak; *all* decisions must pass through him.

I saved my best observation for last. The fund was located on the second floor of a two-story building where the office space on the second floor was equal to the space occupied by five or six retail businesses on the first floor. A long covered walkway linked the entire row of offices. The overhang from this covered walkway impeded the amount of natural light that entered the office spaces. Surprisingly, just after the noon hour on a sunny day, the reception area was actually dark. There was not a single incandescent or fluorescent light available to counter the lack of sunshine and brighten the reception area. Could the founder intentionally want visitors to enter—and remain—in the dark?

Time Warner rebounded to $60.7 billion.

Does anyone pay attention to historical (hysterical) lessons in mergers and acquisitions? Although history suggests extra caution is required to successfully merge technology-based companies, firms continue to attempt this

---

In the past, I heard joking references to the owner as a *psychopath*. Re-checking the dictionary definition, a psychopath is *one who operates without a conscience*. Is it possible that this fund's success is due in some part to borderline behavior by the founder/portfolio manager? My mind immediately linked the dark interior space with dark behavior.

Obviously, I do not have access to the investment and trading records for this firm. I cannot validate the thesis I raised in the previous paragraph. However, I believe it is worth mentioning. Based on the strongly incongruous lighting and lack of appropriate reading materials in the entry area, this hedge fund did not initially fit my image of a solid financial services firm.

Is this firm reputable? I did not find any negative references to this firm. However, by definition, hedge funds operate on the margin of the financial services industry. They are largely unregulated, despite selective efforts by the federal government through the Securities and Exchange Commission (SEC) to regulate them. In fact, the U.S. Supreme Court declared some of these efforts illegal in July 2006, dampening some of the regulatory efforts.

Hedge funds are not suitable investments for everyone. To invest in a hedge fund, investors must have a personal net worth of at least $1 million, agree to the fund's fee structure (1-2% annual management fee), agree to pay 20% of the fund's profits to the manager, and agree not to redeem their funds for at least five years. These sophisticated investment vehicles, suitable for institutional investors—union pension funds and university endowments—and wealthy individuals take a greater-than-average risk to earn a greater-than-average return. Hedge funds may buy stocks, short sell stocks, trade commodities, trade currencies, trade metals or agricultural products' futures, or any combination of these and other investment vehicles.

The firm *does what it does* and *is what it is*. It is a hedge fund. The founder/CEO of this particular fund may not operate on the dark side. My observation-based thoughts may not be as Machiavellian as I initially thought. However, I must point out this gut-level observation.

~~*

near-impossible challenge. If one technology-based company with annual revenue greater than $10 billion plans to purchase another similarly-sized technology company—run, do not walk, from the stock of the surviving company. In greater than 90% of the cases, it is a strong warning sign. Years of negative experience have shouted, *mergers of similarly-sized technology companies do not work.* Nevertheless, corporate strategists and members of the board of directors continue to believe their planned merger or acquisition is different from the many previous attempts—and that this time, it will work out. If a prominent analyst, investment banker, or market commentator says, "This time, things are different," I suggest you pay more attention to other analysts, bankers, or market commentators and run from this investment opportunity.

- Spin-offs

The implications of spinning-off internal business divisions as independent companies are not as potentially risky as acquiring external companies. A company will spin off one or more subsidiaries so the stock market will recognize the inherent value in the spin-off company. What is the thinking behind this?

Before the spin-off, one or more operating divisions produce solid financial results. However, the overall company's finances, usually fair to average, obscure the superior financial results from the subsidiary organizations. As part of the spin-off, the parent company typically retains a 40-60% ownership in the new company. Sale of the spin-off company to private investors is also an option.

Examples of technology-based spin-offs include:

o   AT&T/Lucent Technologies (1995)

o   HP/Agilent Technologies (1999)

o   Agilent Technologies/Avago Technologies (2005). Kohlberg Kravis Roberts (KKR) and Silver Lake Partners led a group of private investors which bought the business from Agilent in August 2005 for $2.66 billion.

A major goal of spin-offs is the separation of businesses so that the stock market better recognizes the value of each component. If a spin-off is successful, then the combined stock market value of the two distinct firms will be greater than that of the single blended firm.

A company must know its financial limits. No matter how good the strategic match, a company must not overpay for an acquisition. If a company pays too much now for an acquisition, then its interest payments will be higher and shareholder equity will be diluted. These are the two most common results of overpayment. In addition, the challenge of integrating any two companies is difficult and often plagued with hidden costs. The actual integration may not yield the expected results.

Summary

Finance and accounting deserve our focused attention. These seemingly arcane disciplines can provide excellent clues to an organization's dysfunction. Obscure or incomplete business segment information in required financial reporting documents; incomplete, illogical, or obscure financial information presentation; poor earnings shortfall reasons; a dependency between the chosen spokesperson and the financial results reported; CEO monopolization of any and all external organization communication and interviews; multiple classes of publicly traded stock with the founder retaining absolute voting power; and conservative to aggressive accounting policy changes provide solid clues of corporate dysfunction.

_*~*~*~

CHAPTER **6**

ADMINISTRATION & TECHNOLOGY

Five administrative topics provide accurate clues to a company's degree of dysfunction. You are likely to see at least one example before you visit the company and none of them requires any extra effort to obtain. They include:

- Travel arrangements
- Quality of stationery paper
- Quality of printing on stationery
- A focus on the past
- A refusal to answer direct questions

Travel Arrangements

If your prospective job requires relocation, the company may make travel and lodging arrangements for your interview. Here is a great early opportunity to observe the company in action. Are the travel arrangements convenient for you? Must you travel overnight on a *redeye* flight? Are connecting flights so closely scheduled it is virtually impossible to get from one to the next? Do you have long layovers, with a good possibility of flight delays for connecting flights, at busy airports such as Chicago's O'Hare, Dallas, New York's LaGuardia, or Atlanta's Hartsfield? At what hotel will you stay? Is it a business class, suite, executive, four- or- five star, resort, or economy hotel? Do you need a rental car? Does the hotel offer free pickup and drop-off service between the airport and the hotel? Are restaurants and other conveniences located within walking distance, a short drive, or in the hotel? The way a company treats you before they want to hire you is a good indicator of their future treatment of you as an employee.

Does the company want you to charge the room and, if applicable, food and beverage expenses, to their business account with the hotel? Do they prefer you pay your expenses, and then fill out an expense report for later reimbursement? Make sure you fully understand in advance of your travel. Evaluate how quickly the company reimburses your out-of-pocket expenses.

The key things to note about your travel arrangement documents are appearance and completeness.

- Are the documents neat and easy to read?

- Do your documents show confirmation numbers?

- Do your documents show telephone numbers to contact in case of changes as well as an after-hours contact number?

- Did the company make *all* travel arrangements—home to airport transportation, air travel, rental car or shuttle bus, lodging, food, and airport to home return?

- Did the company make only certain arrangements? Did they book only the nearby hotel and leave the airfare and ground transportation to you? Best case, the company made all necessary arrangements for you at a hotel that is near restaurants and the company's offices.

- If you drive your auto from home to your local airport, at what rate does the company reimburse your mileage expense? It should be the same as IRS guidelines. If the company does not reimburse for mileage for at least the statutory rate, then this is a warning sign—the company is cheap and does not value its employees.

- Did the company give you a complete set of instructions, reservation information, and confirmations the first time? Or have you had to chase the missing pieces?

- Did the company make last minute changes?

- Did the company do anything in a manner that did not meet your expectations?

Stationery Paper

What quality paper does the company use for its business stationery? The best specification: 24-pound, cotton rag content, and white or off-white color. Reality dictates use of anything except standard white copy paper. A company's or organization's stationery, often viewed as part of one's first formal encounter, should be congruent with the public perception of the organization's quality. We expect IBM to use high quality paper; Wal-Mart's use of a similar high grade of stationery paper would contradict the company's image as a tight-fisted, hard bargainer with its suppliers.

Let us now assume the organization uses appropriate quality paper for its letterhead stationery. What is the quality of the printing and clarity of the logo? The highest-quality letterhead printing is engraved. Run your fingers over the name and address of the company; you will feel raised letters. On the reverse side, the reverse of the letters will be slightly indented. Thermography, which is baked-on raised ink, is less expensive than engraving yet produces a high-quality image—the backside behind the lettering will be flat. Is the logo easy to read and interpret? Do colors run together? High quality printing reflects sound attention to detail.

Bottom line: Incomplete or unprofessional-looking travel documents, and poor quality stationery paper and printing reveal a company's callous attitude toward its employees and the public. The organization's focus is inward, not outward.

Lawsuits Filed

The New York Stock Exchange, the American Stock Exchange, NASDAQ, or one of the few remaining regional stock markets lists the stocks of publicly traded companies. Public companies are required to file a report once a year with the Securities and Exchange Commission (SEC). One section of the required report addresses lawsuits. Be sure to thoroughly read this section and look for:

- *Types of lawsuits the company has filed:* Is the company actively protecting its patents and proprietary information? Has its defense been successful?

- *Types of lawsuits filed against the company:* Lawsuits against the company pose a serious threat to the firm's financial and operational well-being. Additionally, lawsuits can threaten a company's reputation, regardless of outcome. Lawsuits of any type require executives to devote attention, emotion, time, travel, and meetings to nonproductive purposes. Lawsuits are hugely expensive; the only clear winners in any lawsuit are the lawyers.

- *Reason for the lawsuit:* Anyone can sue anyone else. In business, companies sue others to prevent them from copying or disseminating technical information, to deter ex-executives now working at a competing company from raiding talent, and to attempt to prevent a competitor from expanding into the company's established distribution channels.

Although often perceived as a nuisance legal tactic, securities-related lawsuits can have a material effect on a publicly traded company's finances. If the company's Form 10-K or Form 10-Q disclose any securities-related litigation, regardless of the outcome, this is a strong negative. The government has nearly unlimited resources. Fighting this type of legal action is costly and time consuming for the company and distracts executives from their usual day-to-day tasks.

Consumer/class action lawsuits are filed by individuals or groups of individuals based on alleged harm caused by a company's products, fraudulent activities, or business-activity behaviors endangering its employees, employee families, and community neighbors. These lawsuits can have a significant effect on both the company's financial bottom line . . . and its long-term survival. Clean-up funds can hardly begin to repair the damage done by air pollution, dangerous working conditions, and irresponsible toxic dumping on property and into rivers.

- *Without merit statements:* Ignore any statements that imply that the suit is without merit. The company cannot make any definitive public acknowledgement on the relative merits of any case filed against it.

- *The number and severity of lawsuits:* Most companies state, in effect, that the firm is a party in some number of normal lawsuits in the normal conduct of its business. If the company believes that a lawsuit may have a material effect on the company's finances (usually equal to an expenditure in excess of five percent of annual revenue), then it must disclose that information.

A Focus on the Past

If the organization's spokespersons wax poetic about excellent products, people, flexibility, responses to ads or effective distribution channels from more than two or three years before, it's ancient news. What is the company doing today for its investors, employees, customers, bankers, etc., and what is its vision for tomorrow?

Bottom line: **This culture looks backward, not forward. Decision-making, employee motivation, market share, financial results, organization** structure, and executive management are stuck and unable to move for-ward due, most likely, to poor leadership.

A Refusal to Answer Direct Questions

Unless the question clearly involves the disclosure of confidential infor-mation, senior managers should provide well-thought-out, straight-forward answers to direct questions. **Anything less than a complete straightforward answer to a question indicates the representative of the company lacks focus, is overly concerned with *turf* issues, or is reflecting a culturally-ingrained (and accepted) evasive attitude.** Executives/key employees may hoard critical information to build empires or maintain job security in an en-vironment characterized by threatened/looming layoffs—a human response. However, a spokesperson's job is to be aware of issues, company news, cor-porate response to internal changes, and legal, economic, competitive, staff-ing, and business environment impacts—then communicate the company's information and position to the community.

Bottom line: **Poor external communication—to customers, suppliers, lenders, and regulators—mirrors poor internal communication.**

Technology

Patents

Patents represent one more piece of the puzzle. Although not a critical item, they are nevertheless worth exploring.

- *Number:* Patents show a company's interest in growing and main-taining a competitive edge. Although some patents may appear friv-olous, the U.S. Patent & Trademark Office nevertheless did approve them. There is a reason why companies such as IBM, Hewlett-Pack-ard, Sun Microsystems, Oracle, Canon, Apple Computer, Nokia, Advanced Micro Devices, Microsoft, Samsung, and Intel are lead-ers in their respective industries. They invest significant amounts in new technologies. They hold many patents and vigorously protect this intellectual property (IP).

- *Technologies patented:* Just because a company has many patents does not automatically confer winner status. Do the patents link directly to their core business or do they represent new directions? Do the patents link to new products or new processes?

- *Broad versus narrow application:* Do the patents link to areas with broad or a narrow application? Broader applications result in a higher value.

- *Use of patent protection:* Does the company really use its patents to make products or does the company use them to create legal infringement problems for competitors? In June 2006, the U.S. Supreme Court determined, appropriately in my opinion, that patents must be used in a company's products or services to be defensible. No longer may companies create an inventory of patents mainly so they can litigate. In August 2012, Apple Computer prevailed in its lawsuit against Samsung for patent infringement on full-featured cell phones.

- *Trend:* What is the trend in the number of patents awarded to the company? Increasing? Decreasing? Staying flat? Comparing year-over-year changes is not as meaningful as tracking a three-year or five-year trend in the number of patents.

Technology Adoption

Although not directly related to technology-based patents, a company's adoption of newer technologies to increase productivity or efficiency is worth noting. For example, a chain of fast food restaurants that adopts a new technology for cooking and warming its entrees is noteworthy. A few observations may help us see and better understand the complete picture:

When a company announces continued investments in new products or processes, everyone rejoices. Investors love it. Employees face new learning challenges. The community likes improvements. If financed with the issuance of bonds or other debt instruments, commercial bankers love new business. However, investments per se are not the problem. Problems arise when a company continually invests in the latest gimcrack or unproven technology.

Some companies invest in the latest unproven technology and love to play beta site for these new technology-based products. In return for thoroughly testing and documenting product errors and needed improvements, the company gets a head start against its competitors and, often, receives a large discount off the purchase price for its participation. The computer product or software manufacturer may require the company to act as a reference site for the product when (and if) all the bugs are successfully fixed.

Investments in computer technology have paid off, but financial and productivity returns are often woefully inadequate compared to vendors' promises. The computer and communications companies have consistently over-promised and under-delivered. In few instances does the use of technology deliver the productivity with the expected cost savings.

Computer manufacturers, software companies, data communication carriers, and tele-communication carriers have not delivered on the promise to improve productivity through extensive use of the use of advanced computers and communications. The returns are positive, but are nowhere as great as originally forecast.

Right now, companies face a huge challenge in the integration of existing software applications. The expense and time needed to effectively integrate software applications is compounded by the additional expense and time needed to train personnel and address the security challenges posed by spyware, malware, computer trojans, and computer viruses. Computer and communication technology plus the Internet equals hacking, potential employee theft of data, and potential employee theft of proprietary software applications.

Since the introduction of the Microsoft Office integrated software product, vendors have not introduced any unique, significant, broadly integrated business application software. Programs with slightly varying functionalities and interfaces, yes—but something which revolutionizes how things are done? Hardly. Improved flat-panel displays, high-capacity disk drives, portable high-capacity disk drives, and backup storage farms have contributed in only a peripheral way (pun intended) to increased productivity or lower computer operation costs.

Partnerships

Partnerships occur when two or more companies combine efforts in order to produce synergistic results. This desired outcome does not always happen . . . and depends on:

- The nature of the partnership

- Partner affiliations, when based on products using a certain technology

- Whether the partnership is one of equals

- Whether the corporate cultures are compatible

Nature of the Partnership

Partnerships may be used to expand distribution, to enhance technology or intellectual expertise, to improve service and support, or to promote co-marketing opportunities. At the retail level, technology partnerships are not particularly important—the companies have already fought the technical battles behind the scenes.

Partnerships among manufacturers can be hazardous to the health of each of the partners. The product jointly produced and marketed will most likely be a match for each of the partner's target markets—consumers' demographics, psychographics, and socio-graphics—suggesting that the strength of the partnership might lie in the companies together being able to garner a greater total market share.

However, for technology-based products, it is possible for a company to pick the wrong partner. Unfortunately this incorrect choice cannot be determined in advance. Sales of the new product will tell you if this partnership did or did not work.

Successful partnerships are rare. Success becomes more elusive when the new product involves pioneering technological approaches. If one partner selects and implements the wrong technology, the failure of the product will injure both companies' reputations with customers—especially damaging the closer these customers are to each company's core customer base.

USAA—A SMART USER OF TECHNOLOGY

An excellent example of the effective implementation and use of technology is United Services Automobile Association (USAA), a San Antonio, Texas-based member-owned property and casualty insurance company. USAA's 9.1 million customers comprise current and honorably discharged U.S. military members, their dependents, and some higher-level employees of the federal government and their dependents.

The company built its customer service and business processes around mainframe computers starting in the early 1970s. USAA served as a *beta site* (test site) for IBM's first document imaging system in the 1990s, and was one of the first companies to implement a true company-wide client/ server computing architecture. Customers call one 800-number and the call is automatically routed to one of six U.S. regional customer service centers. Service reps field customers' phone calls; the computer updates transaction records every night. The key is selectivity—USAA does not implement every new technology offered by every vendor. Because of good technology choices, USAA is able to provide consistently better customer service at lower cost.

~~*

Success in any leadership role is a challenge. It is axiomatic that in technology the *pioneers are the ones with the arrows in their backs*. Partnering to achieve leadership may increase the likelihood of failure—every interface between the organizations is one more link that can potentially fail, leaving behind a mess far more difficult to untangle than if the errors were completely internal to a single organization. Was failure due to technical inferiorities or mismatches? Poorly targeted marketing? Miscommunication or misallocated responsibilities? Cultural incongruities? Or was it the result of the inability of two organizations to respond effectively to changing consumer needs and market dynamics? Better to wait, be the second company to enter a market after evaluating the relative strengths and weaknesses of the first market entrant, and realize, *it's the second mouse that gets the cheese.*

Let us extend our technology discussion to the microprocessor market, now dominated by Intel Corporation. Intel got its start by manufacturing memory chips, not microprocessors. Although Intel invented the world's first microprocessor in 1971, the company did not achieve high volume shipments of this product until 1981 when the IBM personal computer (PC), based on an Intel microprocessor, made its debut. Microsoft provided the necessary operating system.

In the Intel/ Microsoft partnership (dubbed by the techno literati *Wintel*, for Microsoft Windows and Intel) vs. the world battle, Intel reigned supreme over many microprocessor competitors, some extremely well-established and well-financed—Advanced Micro Devices (AMD), Motorola, National Semiconductor, IBM, Fairchild Semiconductor, MIPS, Sun (its microprocessor product was SPARC), Hewlett-Packard, Zilog, MOS, and Intersil (owned at one time by General Electric).

Although over the years Intel dramatically increased sales of its microprocessors to IBM and manufacturers of IBM-compatible PCs, competitors Motorola and Advanced Micro Devices (AMD) made greater gains in microprocessor technology.

For a while, AMD out-designed Intel and sold a broad range of advanced products: 64-bit microprocessors, 32-bit low-power microprocessors, and dual-core microprocessors. Intel promoted the higher clock speeds on its chips—hardly an advantage.

Any company can theoretically outperform its competitors on one benchmark test. However, consistently outperforming competitors on a variety of benchmarks implies superior microprocessor design—good semiconductor design leads to good results in semiconductor benchmark competitions. Yet, as we have seen, a better product does not guarantee a larger market share, especially over a long period of time.

By late-2005/mid-2006, Intel's main competitor started winning an increasing share of Intel's residual market. Intel invested heavily to leapfrog its technical capabilities over those of AMD and widen its market lead in microprocessors, a trend which it has since strengthened. The new marketing campaign, built around the *Intel Inside* slogan, and reinforced by the *Intel Inside* sticker on new personal computers, bolstered Intel's technology and market leadership positions. From 2008 until 2012, Intel owned a market share in the low 70% range, AMD processors in the high 20% range.

Any discussion of computer technology must include Microsoft. Microsoft is *the* major technology partner/competitor. Microsoft's partnerships

---

SPECIAL TECHNOLOGY SITUATION—CORPORATE AIRCRAFT

One could say that the addition of corporate aircraft represents an investment in technology. If the company's headquarters is in an out-of-the-way location and the company supports global operations, a corporate jet makes a great deal of sense. The wasted person-hours traveling to the nearest major airport with limited choices of flights to many destinations, security hassles and time lags, plus the expense of higher priced airline tickets may well justify the investment. If the company's headquarters is in a major metropolitan area and a very busy airport serves that city, then the investment in a jet may be justified on the grounds of avoiding flight delays.

It is difficult to believe that *any* company requires, say, nine corporate aircraft, no matter how far-flung the operating divisions. The company jet has become a status symbol, the airborne equivalent of owning a Hummer sport utility vehicle. Rationally speaking, not many people *need* a Hummer. Likewise, not many companies need a jet to transport a large number of employees at one time to the same location.

Let's say a private business jet appears to be the appropriate practical transportation solution. Sophisticated companies do not allow more than a certain number of executives to fly together—the risk to the company should the plane crash or terrorists take it over would be too great. Since some of the executives would have to fly on a commercial airline, why not divide the executives' flights among commercial airliners and skip the expensive private jet?

~~*

generally support enhancements to past products, not the creation of new ones. Despite a plethora of partnerships—joint marketing agreements, easy-to-use and widely used application development tools, a program for the technical certification of computer support personnel, and a constant stream of new operating systems for PCs and servers—Microsoft continues to face increased competition from Linux and other open source software and from Apple Computer's Macintosh (or Mac family). New tablet computers from Apple, Samsung, Google, and Amazon present a growing challenge to Microsoft's market position.

It is not what Microsoft has done—it is what Microsoft has not done or has done poorly. Over time, users, especially corporate users, have become less willing to put up with constant operating system security attacks by hackers, substandard system management or data storage capabilities, and newly released operating system software that requires up to a year of ongoing patches or upgrades to stabilize before it will work correctly and consistently. Windows Vista required nearly a year of software bug fixes before it became stable enough for business use.

Feature-laden operating system Vista was a computer resource hog, a techno literati term for a computer that needs a lot of RAM (Random Access Memory) and hard drive storage in order to work properly. Vista needed a minimum of 512 MB RAM to start, 1 gigabyte to operate at a functional level, and up to 4 gigabytes of then-expensive RAM to run smoothly. Windows XP-based systems required a minimum of 64 megabytes RAM, with an optimum of 128 megabytes—basically an eighth to a quarter of what Vista demanded.

Vista was also notoriously *clunky*, a mock technical term for feature laden, slow in response, and difficult to use. It acquired such a bad reputation that many businesses and individual users postponed new system purchases and operating system upgrades, virtually forcing Microsoft to introduce a massively overhauled version of Vista, called Windows 7.

In 2000, Bill Gates stepped down from his position as CEO, but maintained a position as chief software architect until 2006. His partial abandonment of Microsoft to the leadership of Steve Ballmer created questions about Microsoft's future. Its relatively low stock price in Summer 2006 reflected those concerns—although it was acting like a big company in terms of designing, coordinating, and manufacturing new products, its product-based wounds (lack of innovative new products), ever-changing specifications, and date of introduction delays were self-inflicted. In other words, competitors' actions did not cause these major problems.

In mid-June 2012, Microsoft announced its Surface tablet computer, a late-to-market product to compete against Apple's iPad, which had a market share of approximately 60% and five generations of products in users' hands. Again, Microsoft was late to market with another *me-too* product. In November 2013, Steve Ballmer resigned as CEO.

- *Affiliation with one or the other technology **camp** can impact and limit subsequent marketing and business options.* In the early years of personal computers, the selected platform limited who could communicate with whom and the types of software that could be run, a real problem when most data transfer was accomplished by *sneaker net* (floppy disks distributed by walking them over to the next computer). The early combatants were:

  o   Microsoft vs. non-Microsoft (Unix, Linux, Macintosh, other proprietary operating systems)

  o   Java (Sun) vs. .Net (pronounced dot net, created and promoted by Microsoft)

Across computer hardware platforms, software which served the same function was not compatible. Data from one program could not be converted into understandable information on a different system except through extraordinary, time-consuming conversion measures far beyond the capabilities of most system users. An example? Word vs. WordPerfect.

Microsoft Word, initially released in 1983, was ported to the MacIntosh platform in 1985, where it provided the first WYSIWYG (actually pronounced wizzy-wig—what you see is what you get) word-processing experience. From 1987 on, Microsoft synchronized its MacIntosh and DOS (PC) versions. In 1989, Microsoft released its first Word for the Windows operating system, which soon became the world leader in IBM PC-compatible word processors.

WordPerfect, developed at Brigham Young University for use on the Data General Minicomputer, was redesigned to work with the IBM PC-compatible DOS platform in 1982. During the 1980s, WordPerfect, available for a wide variety of operating platforms, dominated the word-processing market.

Slow adoption of a Windows interface (1991—a year and a half behind Microsoft Word's Windows version) and operating system incompatibilities led to WordPerfect's decline in popularity for general word-processing. However, WordPerfect still is strongly preferred by the legal profession because the product (now owned by Corel) has been highly responsive to the needs of that niche market.

Selection of one CPU technology over another (IBM-compatible-based vs. Mac-based) constrained future software choices and dictated which peripheral brands and models—disk drives, printers, tape backup systems, and video display monitors—could be used. For most computer users buying a

HARD CHOICES—

TECHNOLOGY-BASED PRODUCTS AND PARTNERSHIPS

In short, it is possible for a company to join the wrong technology-based partnership. Two examples come to mind.

First: The mid-1970s battle between Sony with its Betamax technology vs. the VHS technology created by JVC and promoted by Matsushita under its Panasonic trade name. Although the Betamax format produced superior quality video, its recording time was limited to one hour per cassette compared to two hours per cassette for the VHS format. More importantly, JVC/Matsushita created a partnership among major vendors of consumer electronic products. Its partners included Hitachi, Mitsubishi, Sharp, RCA, Magnavox, Sylvania, and Sears. Even though Matsushita introduced VHS technology two years after Sony introduced its Betamax format, the overwhelming marketing force behind VHS technology helped it gain rapid acceptance and ultimate market victory over Betamax.

Second: The 2005-06 battle in high definition video recording technology between the Panasonic/Sony *Blu-ray* format and the Toshiba *HD-DVD* format. In June 2006, products based on both technologies were available. Unlike the lopsided 30-year old contest that pitted Sony against an international consortium of manufacturers, the marketing combatants on both sides in this 2005-06 jousting match were unusually well-balanced. Each team contained two or three strong, consumer marketing-oriented players with solid name recognition and well-established distribution channels.

Blu-Ray won.

However, there were no early or easy clues as to which technology would prevail. Technology-based consumer marketing battles seldom leave a nice trail of breadcrumbs for purchasers to follow in order to make the *right* decision. That is why you sometimes need to wait for a clear determination of the technology battle winner before you invest your money, particularly in a big ticket item.

~~*

single system, this was not a problem. Other users, especially those at large organizations, needed to be conscious of the long-term financial implications of their technology choices. Although purchasing a company's product did not create a partnership in the strictest sense (it was not bilateral relationship except to the extent that the seller supplied ongoing support), the decision *did* create a relationship.

A major technology purchase locks an organization into a near unhealthy dependency on the supplier—that the product will meet the organization's long-term needs, that the product will perform as advertised, that the supplier will survive in the competitive market and be able to continue its product support, and that the surviving supplier will be willing to stand behind its product and provide needed customization, upgrades, training, and guidance.

Such a purchase does not produce a partnership of equals. If the product/seller fails in any or all of the listed expectations, the seller may be forced

---

HEWLETT-PACKARD AND INTEL—
CORPORATE CULTURES THAT DIDN'T MIX

Hewlett-Packard (HP) and Intel are a favorite example of a lopsided corporate partnership. For many years, HP designed its own microprocessors in-house and used third-party foundries to manufacture the semiconductors used in its computer systems. Eventually, HP realized that it could not sell a sufficient number of low-end, mid-level, and high-end computer servers to amortize the rapidly increasing expense of its next generation microprocessor design.

Around 1994/1995, HP *partnered* with Intel with the intent of producing a new 64-bit microprocessor within three or four years. One key requirement— the new microprocessor had to run programs written for HP's existing proprietary operating system as well as the new server version of Microsoft Windows. This was a near-impossible technical task, analogous to trying to build a Chrysler automobile using Chrysler and Ford components, marketed and supported through Chrysler's dealer network.

In addition, the organizational cultures were about as far apart in Silicon Valley as corporately possible. HP typified a group of nice guys while mid-1990s-era Intel embodied a bunch of paranoid hard asses. Bill Hewlett and Dave Packard built and handed down the *HP Way*, based on models of cooperation and trust. In contrast, to this day, *constructive confrontation*, as Intel calls it, is an "Intel core value." Intel is proud of this organizational trait.

by the buyer to reverse the sale; the buyer, however, is then forced to retrench and find a new solution, having lost valuable time and the financial investment incurred in trying to make the failed technology work.

- *Is it a partnership of equals?* Conversely, does one partner benefit significantly more than the other partner does? Does the more critical partner derive less benefit? If so, the imbalance is a danger signal, since the more critical partner may be inclined to investigate and invest in other, more profitable alternatives.

- **Are the corporate cultures of the partners compatible?** Conversely, is a group of nice guys trying to create an equal partnership with a bunch of hard-charging folks? If so, the hard chargers will win. Guaranteed.

I worked with a bunch of ex-Intel engineers. In a typical meeting, Intellectuals (pun intended) would take you 'round and 'round just so they could have some fun and get much-needed mental exercise. Unfortunately, you never quite knew where the Intel folks stood or if they would honor the commitments they made.

In the end, Intel beat HP. The first two generations of Intel 64-bit microprocessors did not directly support HP's operating system as requested. Rather than facilitating an easy transition from existing computer servers to new servers using the planned microprocessor, HP was forced to sell its customers on a new operating system and application software package, and then help them transfer business or scientific processes and data.

Why did Intel win? Although each company brought something to the table, Intel held all the technology cards. It had the semiconductor design and manufacturing expertise, distribution/partnership relationships with every name-brand manufacturer of PCs and servers, compilers, rapid application development tools, and an extensive network for product support. To Intel, HP represented only one thing — it was just another customer or user of Intel's microprocessors.

Assessment: HP needed Intel; Intel did not really need HP. Intel outflanked HP by dominating — both in technical prowess and negotiation strength. In retrospect, HP did not expect this level of difficulty and failed to prepare either a Plan B or a Plan C — Worst-Case Scenario Plan as back up.

~~*

Companies must increasingly work with other firms. Companies work together so they can penetrate new markets; gain sufficient volume in order to reduce manufacturing and/or distribution costs; economize on advertising and promotional costs; build a critical mass for market acceptance; build a critical mass for third-party product applications, customer evaluations, and customer purchases; and build critical mass so they may provide better support and service. **However, the mere presence of a partnership does not ensure success for either party.** Partnerships should be of equals and corporate cultures should be compatible. Getting together for the sake of a perceived technological or marketing advantage is not sufficient justification for this major step.

Summary

Dysfunction can be found at the administrative level and in the technology decisions made. Clues about the health of an organization can be found from how travel arrangements are made down to the quality of paper and printing. Communications from a dysfunctional organization emphasize past issues or future promises, but not the present. How and who represents the company to the public is another critical clues.

Dysfunction can be found in the types and qualities of the partnerships formed. Major questions arise when companies collaborate: who leads, who follows, and when; who makes technology choices and who is dependent on those decisions, or is the partnership one of equals; and, between the partners, are the technologies and marketing strategies compatible?

~*~*~*~

CHAPTER 7

EXECUTIVE MANAGEMENT

We look next at the executive management team; then, in far more detail, the CEO.

The backgrounds of the executive management team members and CEO help explain the culture at an organization. If the current or long-established CEO is also a company founder, then that person's influence is deeply rooted. Among executives, experience, capability, and values are what matter most. Factors that will help you assess the background of the executive management team include:

- Breadth and depth of executive team experience

- Executive stock purchases or sales

- Executive's first jobs out of college, if listed

- The firm's hiring preferences

- Executives' participation in *extreme* sports

- Titles of executives

Breadth and Depth of Executive Team Experience

For better or worse, the team of executive managers leads the company. Their experience, education, behavior, and attitudes will permeate the company culture from the top down. The behaviors they accept in their subordinates will impact your life and career. As a newcomer, you cannot expect to change what is there when you arrive. To ensure a viable top management team, review their individual backgrounds. Look for:

- *Decisive leadership in other companies.* Strong situations that called for effective leadership include: business turnaround, the integration of one or more acquisitions, recall of tainted pharmaceuticals or food products, managing the outsourcing of operations overseas, problems with key operations, dealing with regulatory issues, significant downsizing, and corporate restructuring.

- *The kinds and cultures of organizations where they previously worked.* If required, did this executive successfully transform or re-energize the culture to address significant problems?

- *Diverse, career-broadening experiences.* Did a marketing executive also work in finance or operations, or vice versa? Conversely, did the executive show continued growth and development in one business function—marketing, sales, finance/accounting, operations, support and service, or legal?

- *A willingness to meet challenges and take advantage of opportunities to grow and learn.* On the other hand, the executive could have repeated the same basic tasks for 10 or 15 years.

- *A sense of work-life balance, information which can be gleaned from executive biographies.* This includes family, community activities, seats on Boards of Directors or advisory boards, fund raising involvement (local United Way campaigns, for example), leadership at a religious institution, community activities (parades, art auctions, wine tastings, etc.), sports (participatory or spectator), or coaching of or playing on sports teams.

Count the number and relative importance of each outside activity. Politics make a huge demand on one's time. If someone is active in politics, that person cannot be effective in business. More than three or four non-company activities for an executive at a multinational Fortune 500 company are unacceptable. Very few can successfully juggle that many competing demands on their time and emotional and physical energy. One cannot do everything. Some aspect—whether required or optional—of that person's job is not going to get the attention it deserves. There is also a limit to what one can effectively delegate.

Bottom line: **This is a critical item. Ask yourself: Is this executive spread too thin?**

Executive Stock Purchases or Sales

A company must file an SEC Form, 8-K, within 15 days of executive purchase or sale of company stock. A company must file Form 8-K to reflect:

- A change in company ownership (e.g., when an individual, mutual fund, or hedge fund purchases shares greater than 5% of total outstanding shares)

- A merger or acquisition

- Bankruptcy or receivership

- A change in the public accounting firm that certifies the financial results

- Resignation of one or more directors

- Detailed information about acquired real estate or other business assets, or

- Other material information

Watch the pattern of common stock purchases and sales by company executives. If an executive's sales of company stock show a pattern—the same number of shares every month or quarter—then that person is, in fact, diversifying her/his investment portfolio. Transactions that involve the unprecedented sale of a large number of shares at one time indicate possible future problems for the business. Likewise, periodic purchases of company stock are fine. Large purchases, especially those outside a grant of stock options, could indicate better financial times ahead.

Bottom line: It is not the act of buying or selling shares that is important. More importantly, note who, when, how many shares, and the percent of the executive's total shares owned or optioned which are represented by each transaction. Look, too, for any discernible trend or pattern to the buy/sell activity. If many company executives sell significant numbers of shares within a relatively short time, for whatever reasons, those actions are viewed by professional investors as discouraging.

Executive's First Jobs out of College, if Listed

Does the biographical sketch for each executive show graduation from an undergraduate college or university; vocational, specialized, or industry-specific training; military training; graduate degrees; and/or professional certifications? Does the biographical background for each executive list the complete progression of jobs since graduation? Did the executive's first job show leadership potential, acceptance of a great deal of responsibility, opportunities for personal growth, exposure through travel to other countries and peoples, and a sense of real accomplishments? Did the future executive get hired by an organization known for its first-rate training program? Or was the executive's first full-time paid exposure to the working world lacking in some key way?

Each industry has its top companies. For example, in computer technology, a first job working for (listed alphabetically) Apple Computer, Hewlett-Packard, IBM, Intel, Microsoft, or Oracle confers status on the job holder. This is not to demean or diminish the opportunities at start-ups. While the opportunities for professional and personal growth may be far greater in a smaller organization, early exposure to a sound training program pays dividends later.

Great first jobs include: U.S. military officer, employment at a prestigious law/ accounting/ actuarial firm, staff positions with Federal elected officials or not-for-profit organizations in Washington, D.C., fellowships at leading medical centers for medical researchers, and internships/residencies for doctors at well-regarded hospitals known for exceptionally good care of patients with specific medical challenges.

The Firm's Hiring Preferences

Many organizations talk freely about diversity. However, many have unwritten hiring preferences. Preferences can be linked to race (whites only), gender (no or disproportionately few women), ethnicity (no Asians or Latinos), athleticism (hires mainly jocks), religion (preferences for one religion or against other religions), geography (Americans, not Canadians or Europeans), preparatory schools or colleges attended (Ivy League preferred), regionalism (we hire *good ol' boys*), and physical characteristics (tall, muscular, and slender).

Look in the annual report or Form 10-K for the list of executives and members of the Board of Directors. Can you find hidden hiring preferences? During your visit to the company, look at the rank-and-file employees. If you don't find women, Asians, or Latinos, then this organization is dysfunctional.

Executives' Participation in *Extreme* Sports

Some organizations may prefer to hire athletes. However, these athletes' activities are confined to organized competitive team sports or individual performance sports such as golf, archery, and skeet shooting. Do its leaders or senior managers actively participate in extreme sports such as body building, weight lifting, boxing, marathons, triathlons, long distance bicycling, or long-distance swimming?

Are executive retreats built around activities such as rock climbing, auto or dune buggy competitions in the desert, swimming or sailing marathons, auto races, or the like? An organization with a high number of upper-level people engaged in extreme sports cannot be effective; these leaders and employees devote considerable time and emotional energy to being the best at something within their control. If these companies succeed, it is often the result of fortuitous timing and good fortune, not dogged determination. What happens when the luck runs out? And even if it holds, these employees' emotional energy is spent on non-company activities. Imagine what could be accomplished if this group spent this same amount of energy on the organization they were hired to lead.

Titles of Executives

Yes. Even the titles of executives can help you identify a dysfunctional organization. Appropriate titles include: Chief Executive Officer, President, Executive Vice President, Senior Vice President, Vice President, Director, Manager, and titles that briefly describe the card carrier's function. Good examples include Phillip Jennings, Senior Software Engineer or Raylan Givens, Financial Analyst.

Technology companies started the trend toward unique job titles. In the 1980s, Guy Kawasaki at Apple Computer was dubbed *Corporate Evangelist*, a non-threatening title for someone whose sole job was to recruit technology partners, usually software companies.

I found some of the most outlandish titles at ValueAmerica, a now-defunct web-based retail giant. The company, detailed in the book, *In the Company of Good and Evil*, was unique—none of the executives had titles on their business cards. As the firm expanded, titles changed. How about these doozies? Executive Vice President, Operations and Information Technology. Group EVP of Consumer and Office Products and Presentation Marketing. President and General Manager, Advertising, Sales, and Technology Products. Executive Vice President, Government and Business-to-Business Development and International.

Straightforward and simple titles reflect a simple and straightforward organization. Too long or overly descriptive titles expose out of control internal politics and lack of integrative thinking. It's all about the individual's function, not the good of the organization or the customer.

Summary

It takes more than a competent CEO to successfully run a business. Look especially at the backgrounds of other executives—higher education, the number and nature of activities outside the organization, these executives' experiences, and a sense of work-life balance. Research the purchases and sales of company stock, the timing, the number of shares, the dollar value of the transaction, and the percent of total stock holdings affected by the purchase or sale.

Look, too, at the names and appearance of executives and staff. Search for hidden hiring preferences and evidence of participation in extreme sports. The leaders may be winners other aspects of their lives. Sadly, though, this dedication to winning does not permeate the organization. Winners in extreme sports may be losers in working as a team, building and maintaining client relationships, and mentoring subordinates. Fancy titles speak only of dysfunction; straightforward and descriptive titles work best.

~*~*~*~

CHAPTER 8

CEO—QUALIFICATIONS

The company CEO, executive director, commanding officer, mayor, governor, or president rates a detailed evaluation. After all, the success or failure of the organization and your career ultimately rests with this person. The first chapter of our three-chapter evaluation will first explore topics related to the CEO's qualifications, namely:

- Education

- Past corporate affiliations

- Military service

- International experience

- Volunteer/charitable/community activities

- CEO's health

- CEO's signature

CEO's Education

Whenever possible, check out the CEO's background. *Forbes* magazine devotes one issue each year to a summary of the educational backgrounds of CEOs of the largest publicly traded companies. You could also *Google* or *Dogpile* or *Clusty* the name of the organization's leader or candidate and see what appears.

- Where did the executive grow up? Was it an urban, suburban, or rural setting?

- Did the executive attend college? Did the executive attend an Ivy League college or university? Did the executive attend a state school? Did s/he graduate?

- What was the executive's major at the undergraduate college level? Did the executive pursue graduate studies? In what?

- Was the executive affiliated with any college or professional sport, either playing or serving as an assistant manager, go-fer, cheerleader, etc.? One would hope that serious involvement in sports ingrains the discipline, teamwork, goal-setting, and competitive skills important in business.

- Did the CEO work her/his way through college? Summer jobs count. No job is too menial; one can learn from any job.

- In which other collegiate activities did the executive participate? Was the executive a leader in any of these organizations?

You may be able to discern key abilities and skills from their early years. Was the person a student body leader, a student mediator, editor/writer/photojournalist, business manager, or advertising sales rep for the newspaper or yearbook? Was that person a friend or helper to everyone, teacher's pet, star athlete, player of one or more musical instruments, drum major/majorette, cheerleader, whiz kid, or a unique combination of these characteristics?

If the CEO attended college, which school did s/he choose? Did that person attend an Ivy League school? A state school? Is a technical school education part of his/her personal DNA? What was the CEO's academic major? Was s/he involved in college sports, student body politics, committees, and social sororities/fraternities? Did s/he receive an academic or sports scholarship or perhaps one or more of each? Did s/he study her/his butt off and graduate summa cum laude, magna cum laude, or cum laude? Do any articles mention if the individual worked his/her way through college? On the other had, did that person belong to an elite clique, become involved in the less-than-savory parts of student elections, or participate in groups that shared exams and submitted one another's term papers? Although you may not easily find the answer, it is worth asking the question.

Would a CEO's/exec's membership in a fraternity or sorority have an impact on dysfunction? Possibly. Some Greek residences were poorly-managed party houses. On Saturday nights, the police knew to expect phone calls from neighbors about students disturbing the peace.

Other fraternities/sororities required members to maintain solid grade point averages, participate in a broad range of college activities, do SOME charitable work, and act as good neighbors. Also, these houses were well managed.

More research is necessary. What was the fraternity's reputation? How important was the Greek System (fraternities and sororities) in the college's social scene? One conclusion is possible. Members of a fraternity or sorority generally have good social skills, a prerequisite for executives.

Answers to these questions help give you a solid sense of the leader's DNA and help to better understand a person's motivations and behaviors, especially those created and fostered after their formative years.

CEO's Past Corporate Affiliations

An executive's past business affiliations can also reveal a great deal. In the technology business, the seal of approval has for years gone to current and former employees of IBM, Apple Computer, Hewlett-Packard, and Intel. A current or former employee's longevity with any of the gold seal companies tells you about the person is well-qualified for their stated line of work as well as the kind of corporate culture where that person worked. If s/he remained with the company for three or more years, the organization's culture definitely rubbed off on that person.

Corporate attitudes and cultures are varied. We will explore organizations distinguished by top-down decision making, mission-driven focus, their ability to thrive on paranoia, go-along-and-get-along personal interactions, and those where an outsider would view the organization's people as highly competent but not arrogant.

- IBM used to be a strictly top down organization; if you worked there and your title was below that of vice president, you had little or no real decision-making authority. You knew whose butt to kiss and whose butt to kick. Under the effective leadership of past CEOs Lou Gerstner and Sam Palmissano, IBM transformed itself and pushed decision-making to significantly lower levels throughout its worldwide operations.

- A mission to provide easy-to-use computers and, later, other devices for the world drove Apple Computer. Unfortunately, internal splits and schisms also characterized the firm. Steve Jobs handpicked employees from within all divisions of the company to work in the secretive, newly-formed Macintosh Division. How would you feel if, as a professional who was considered good enough to work at Apple, you were not selected to work in the Mac Division? In the old days (pre-iPod), there were also huge differences in status and financial resources available to different divisions and their employees. During the 1990s and into 2001, Apple re-invented itself with the introduction of its iPod device for recording and playing music files. Has this organizational re-creation led to a reincarnation of the bifurcated corporate structure and schizophrenic company culture? Do the iPod, iPhone, and iPad groups occupy a first-line status position, and other product segments follow far behind?

- Intel is at a different end of the corporate attitude spectrum. Intel's corporate attitude stems from the self-professed personal paranoia of employee number four and its CEO during the 1980s and much of the 1990s, Hungary-born Dr. Andrew Grove. In reality, Intel's so-called paranoid attitude is a wonderful front for its hand-in-glove relationship with Microsoft. Each company needs the other to continue to leapfrog raw computing horsepower with advanced software capabilities. Intel is as much of a monopoly as Microsoft.

- There is another type of corporation—*go-along-and-get-along*. Hewlett-Packard (HP) is a go-along-and-get-along type of company. I worked in the late 1970s and early 1980s with HP employees, many of whom were recent Stanford MBAs whose first post-MBA job was in product marketing.

After working together for two or three years, I noticed the aggressive, curious employees had left the firm. These MBAs' personal styles did not really fit with what was required to advance into HP's executive ranks. Are many of HP's current long-time executives the equivalent of a one trick pony? Do they successfully execute one key project and the rewards continuously flow on essentially very old news? Is the key factor for success at HP one of "Don't make waves"?

The company's strategy and performance after the EDS, Compaq, and Autonomy acquisitions has not changed for the better, despite many promises. In fact, analysts and pundits in mid-2012 have begun to question if HP even has a viable corporate strategy. The company has cut costs in order to barely make or miss its target quarterly earnings per share results. Any large company cannot continually cost cut its way to glory, respectability, and sustained profitability.

When the HP Board hired Carly Fiorina in July 1999, she was the first outsider to serve as CEO. Immediately after Ms. Fiorina was hired, one securities analyst friend of mine noted that Carly's style did not match that of HP and that she would soon be gone.

From day one, Carly focused on her overall image and jetted around, rather than paying attention to the day-to-day changes required to keep up with competitors and the rapidly changing tastes and requirements of consumer and business customers.

Her plan to acquire Compaq was her final effort to demonstrate a strategic thinking capability. Compaq had acquired Tandem Computer, which created the first computers with built-in backup hardware capabilities, as well as pioneer minicomputer manufacturer Digital Equipment Corporation. Unfortunately, the integration of the two company's diverse products and cultures was a challenge she could not accomplish. A little over five years later, the HP Board of Directors woke up, recognized its error, and, consistent with my analyst friend's early assessment and prediction, ended Ms. Fiorino's employment.

Here is an example of good corporate DNA. Silicon Valley-based market research firm Dataquest (DQ—previously owned by A.C. Nielsen, then Dun & Bradstreet, and since 1995 a subsidiary of Gartner Group) stood out in a positive way. The firm employed a disproportionate number of Stanford and Harvard MBAs with electrical engineering or computer science undergraduate degrees or technical PhD degrees. DQ also hired bright, hard working graduates of other colleges and universities as well as experienced senior managers from technology-based businesses.

Everyone worked together to ensure high-quality information and analysis. The data set built upon two key metrics—the number of high-tech products shipped and the corresponding dollar value. DQ's areas of expertise included personal computers, scientific/technical computers, CAD/CAM systems, semiconductors, printers, video display terminals/monitors, word processors, telecommunication services, data communication products, and copying and duplicating equipment.

The difficult task was to create an accurate and defensible five-year forecast of the number of products shipped and the corresponding dollar value. It was an internal axiom that, "Forecasting is a dangerous business."

Despite its well-respected position in technology markets, Dataquest was considered competent but never arrogant. Grant S. "Skip" Bushee, a former vice president in the computer group, said, "Our clients thought our capabilities were far greater than they really were." DQers continually delivered what their clients wanted. Since the late 1970s Dataquest analysts' forecasts were appropriately conservative compared to many pie-in-the-sky forecasts by competitors.

For many start-up companies and investors, overly optimistic market forecasts lead to excess venture capital and expose the lack of real customer demand, a combination that ultimately led to business failure. Regardless of projections, companies go bankrupt when they try to enter markets properly characterized by slowing, not accelerating, growth. These new companies may want only one percent of a near mathematically impossible forecast of expanded total available market.

At the request of venture capital clients, DQ analysts often reviewed business plans for startups. No matter the technology, an analyst's concern was the start-up's target to garner only one percent of the share of the market held by the market leader. In the computer group, this translated to, "We want one percent of IBM's business." The problem is IBM is not simply going to willingly give up any percent of its diverse lines of business!

Bottom line: If real market growth is not there, then new companies will fail.

Everyone has past corporate affiliations or corporate DNA. These are very valuable when assessing a person's capabilities and motivation. For companies that market consumer products, Procter & Gamble/Duracell/Gillette, Colgate-Palmolive, and Clorox represent the gold standard. In finance, the leading investment banks include Goldman Sachs, Merrill Lynch, and Morgan Stanley. Commercial banking leaders number JPMorganChase, Citicorp, Wells Fargo, BNY Mellon, and PNC. General Electric (GE) continues to maintain its strong culture of advanced training and high expectations for mid- to senior-level managers in corporate finance, leasing, and asset financing. GE remains a great organization for employees wanting to learn about corporate finance.

Military Service

A CEO's military service tells you the executive gave up some time in the service of their country, accepted discipline and training, could follow orders, and, depending on the branch of service, could make quick life-saving decisions under fire. Those who served in the Marines and the Army best exemplify this important capability. Combat situations faced by *leatherneck Marines* and *Army grunts* bring out the best in people for real teamwork and camaraderie. The relatively easy-going Air Force is far more like a business, including the buddy-buddy aspect of getting things done.

Although military service is a broadening experience, much of what the CEO may have gained depends on the functional area in which s/he worked. Someone with an administration or human resources background does not have the operational chops or exposure to lead a broad-based organization. The real military action is in operations or direct mission support—supply, maintenance, transportation, and logistics.

Strategic Thinking or Tactical Operations?

Everyone in the military cannot be a war planner. Someone must do the daily drudge or grunt work. If your organization leader was exposed to strategic planning and required to provide diplomatic or military responses to *what if* scenarios, then this person has demonstrated a significant record of high-level thinking. Chances are far better, however, that during his/her military service, the executive had only low- to mid-level planning and execution experience.

International Experience

Did this ex-GI serve at least one tour overseas (not necessarily in a combat zone)? Exposure to different cultures, languages, traditions, religions, and world viewpoints provides a broader perspective to enhance effective decision making. All good.

In today's broad business environment, an executive who has lived and worked outside the United States is perceived as more valuable than one who has not. Whether the executive came up through the ranks in operations, marketing, finance, or a support department such as human resources or IT, overseas experience highlights that employee's adaptability and continued learning.

Bottom line: Living and working overseas is good for the executive, the company, and provides a built-in broad perspective for decision making.

Military or Business Function

In what military occupational group did the leader serve? Administration? Human Resources? Information technology? Aircraft maintenance? Vehicle maintenance? Communication/electronics maintenance? Supply management? Logistics management and planning? Hospital management and operations?

Those in mission critical departments, such as operations, or in direct mission support functions, including maintenance, supply, transportation, logistics, and medical, receive better training and experience to meet the broad range of demands in today's business environment. Human resources, finance and administration, information technology, training and education, post office, commissary (supermarket), exchange (discount department store), food service (dining facility), and household goods transportation provide sound functional discipline but a more narrow exposure to the organization and its mission. This is not to say that someone who served in one of the support functions shown cannot be an effective leader and manager with good strategic vision. It comes down to the person—their motivation, drive, ability to learn quickly and from past mistakes, the availability of a mentor, and disciplined but creative thinking and problem-solving.

On the other hand, some of those who serve in the military learned different lessons than discipline, stick-to-itiveness, a *can do* attitude, and leadership. These veterans simply become adept at taking credit for work done by

---

WHAT DID LISA'S CORPORATE DNA REVEAL?

At my local YMCA branch, I played mixed doubles tennis on Saturday mornings. Lisa, a petite mid- to late-30s newcomer, joined the crowd. She played a steady, but unspectacular, game. She worked hard to improve her serve, ground strokes, position on the court, serve and volley game, and solid play at the net. Between games one day, I asked where she had moved from and where she had worked. She said she moved to the Tampa Bay area from the San Francisco Bay area. Upon further questioning, she said she had worked as a securities trader at Montgomery Securities located in San Francisco's Financial District.

From my experience in Silicon Valley, I knew of Montgomery Securities, acquired by NationsBank in 1997. Its founder, Tom Weisel, was a near-Olympic athlete with a Harvard MBA who prided himself on hiring mainly jocks and other *driven* or *Type A* personalities. Knowing this, I forecast Lisa's tennis skills would advance considerably. They did. Within two years, Lisa was winning all the local women's singles competitions at her U.S. Tennis Association-based ranking level.

What did I see in Lisa? Her initial, steady-but-unspectacular tennis game failed to provide the necessary clue. It was her *corporate DNA*. Anyone who could work in such a competitive, testosterone-fueled environment as Montgomery Securities simply *had* to be good just to survive. It was only a matter of time before it became apparent at the Y.

Petite? Yes. An initially intimidating player? No. A not-so-obvious, self-motivated, very tough, competitive, growing-in-skill-level tennis player? Definitely yes!

~~*

others, kissing up, always saying "yes"—even in those situations where a "maybe" or "no" might have been the right answer, or participating excessively in off-duty sports programs and activities rather than developing necessary skills that are applicable and necessary to help accomplish something in the business world.

Reasons for Not Serving in the Military

Many competent executives who came of age during the 1960s and 1970s successfully avoided the draft and service in the active duty military, reserves, or national guard. Try to find out what they did instead and their reason(s) for avoiding military service. A high lottery number exempted some, but not all. Aside from that, physical or mental issues, married with children, religious deferment, and alternative government service such as the Peace Corps are the most prevalent reasons. A unique occupation also provided a valid deferment. Two examples which exempted my friends from military service—one served as teacher in a religious school; the other served as a civil defense monitor in addition to his civilian day job.

Volunteer/Charitable/Community Activities

A CEO's volunteer/charitable activities can be a definite plus or a huge minus. It depends on the nature of and amount of time spent on these activities. Some CEOs are naturally philanthropic and like working with others to help organizations that can effectively use their skills and contacts. Others want to build relationships as foundations for future career opportunities.

I met the CEO of a family-run plastics fabrication business who devotes considerable time and energy to sponsor, organize, and administer local teenage and pre-teen beauty pageants. I am unable to identify any professional benefit for this activity.

Bottom line: It is the quantity, nature, and amount of time devoted to charitable causes that differentiate a healthy sense of giving back to the community from a mechanism to escape daily corporate and/or family responsibilities and facilitate building/maintaining a potential job search network. On the positive side, many executives use their volunteer work with charities to strengthen current business relationships.

CEO's Health

The CEO must be healthy—mentally, physically, spiritually, and emotionally. So must his/her family. Any health-related distractions obviously steal time and energy from the organization. Watch for evidence of poor physical health, an excessive worry about health-related issues, the inability to deal with a mid-life crisis, the inability to deal with the ups and downs of a spouse's or the executive's own menopause (*male menopause* counts, too!), children's school or health issues, aging parents' health issues, or extra-marital affairs.

A CEO making a drastic change in the automobile driven, say trading in a Mercedes or Lexus or Cadillac for a Porsche or Ferrari or Lamborghini, signals underlying issues. Buying or building a vacation home or changing the primary residence saps time and energy from the business, as does re-decorating any home or office.

Watch for signs of gambling, attention to pornography, or an excessive interest in dangerous sports or activities. An executive changing a three-day a week business trip pattern to long trips with weekends away from his/her family suggests a possible extra-marital affair. Extra-marital affairs re-direct the executive's physical and emotional energy, compromise focus and judgment, and provide grist for the ever-present employee rumor or gossip mill. I'll bet the day-to-day emotional energy level at Boeing changed for the worse as a reflection of the former CEO's affair.

If you learn that key personnel are experiencing less-than-above-average health, then watch for similar or related signs of ill health in the organization. Organization-related health warning signs include:

THE OTHER SIDE OF MILITARY EXPERIENCE

I worked with an executive coach for a CEO for whom I assisted as a management consultant. At our first meeting, the coach walked in wearing a Darth Vader-like outfit—black chinos, black leather belt, black turtleneck, black shoes and black socks. He rattled off an unmemorable background then immediately started to spout military terminologies and jargon—incorrectly.

At that point, I identified him as a wanna-be, a phony, and someone desperate to try to burnish credibility with C-level executives. The late southern essayist Lewis Grizzard had a term that aptly described such absurd situations, "You Can't Put No Boogie-Woogie on the King of Rock 'n Roll." This so-called executive coach managed to *put the boogie-woogie on the CEO*, but not on me.

~~*

- Unexpected and not discussed reorganization of executive duties or those of key mid-level managers

- Illogical reorganization of executives and duties

- Less open communication or, at the other extreme, verbal diarrhea

- Decreased executive availability as compared to the past or the requirement for a well-in-advance appointment for relatively routine matters

- Fewer meetings with financial analysts, journalists, and industry trade organization representatives

- A drop in revenue and market share in a business environment where the market is growing

- Sudden, unexplained CEO-directed changes in the organization's long-standing relationships with outside auditors, bankers, attorneys, advertising agencies, public relations firms, trade show management firms, travel agencies, logistics management firms, and key raw material suppliers—these indicate instability

CEO's Signature

This is one of my pet peeves. Have you seen CEO signatures on public documents that are absolutely unreadable? Worse, do you see flippant curves or straight lines or squiggles with dots or dashes? **Is the CEO too busy to legibly sign her/his name? The real question becomes: Is this person an egomaniac?**

If the signature is readable, what initial impression do you get? Cautious, even strokes imply a cautious, even-tempered leader. Jagged, edgy letters typify a nervous, volatile personality. A combination of curvilinear lines and edgy angles suggest a bipolar tendency. Flourishes imply a free spirit, creativity, or someone who thinks outside the box. A look at spacing (close together, far apart), style (round or pointed letters), size, slant, pressure (light or heavy), and image (careful or careless) will provide additional clues about the executive's approach to business, life, and other people.

Summary

An in-depth examination of an organization's leaders starts with the Chief Executive Officer (CEO). Key aspects of the CEO's background include education, past corporate affiliations, military service, international experience, community/charitable activities, and the CEO's health.

Look for examples of leadership and management and in-depth involvement with a charitable organization which can use the CEO's skills. Be concerned about CEOs who are involved in too many outside activities and whose health or travel patterns suddenly change. Watch for drastic, unexplained changes in suppliers or business partners with which the organization has had long-standing business relationships. Specific firms include outside accountants/auditors, lawyers, bankers, and suppliers.

Finally, keep an eye out for distractions which will take an executive's attention away from his business. Building a dream house, buying and furnishing a vacation home, extending travel plans without including one's spouse/significant other or children, gambling or pornography addictions, increasing time away from the office at spas or other places for relaxation, fast cars, and dangerous outside activities may make an executive an interesting character—but the impact on the executive's business is negative.

~*~*~*~

CHAPTER 9

CEO—THE POSITION

Next, evaluate the business aspects of the CEO's position, namely:

- What are the current corporate and organization affiliations, including memberships on Boards of Directors?

- Is the CEO the only executive who speaks to all audiences on behalf of the company?

- How easy is it to reach the executives—the CEO and VPs—by telephone?

- Does the CEO also serve as the Chair of the Board of Directors?

- Do you see evidence of *real* leadership?

- Is the CEO constantly on the road?

Current Board/Charitable/Volunteer Affiliations

While most extra-curricular activities with non-business organizations distract CEOs from their responsibilities for running their firms, some of the links between CEOs and elected officials are important for the health of the company. A strong community presence and positive external relationships help foster a good corporate image, continued growth, and chances to meet and work with other executives for the good of the community. However, your challenge is to figure out if a particular CEO is working with the community to promote the company, out trolling for his/her next job, or is in a wanna-be role to earn an appointment to a prestigious, but not particularly effective, community organization or public advisory board.

Specific outside activities might include:

- *Seats on Boards of Directors:* businesses, orchestras/theatre groups, colleges/universities, social services organizations, religious institutions

- *Business advisory boards:* at universities, whether local or distant

- *Community organizations:* theatre, dance, music

- *Social services:* United Way, women's shelters, food kitchens, health clinics, guardians ad litem, or other programs supporting poor, homeless, abuse victims, children, adopted children, immigrants, ethnic groups, or veterans

- *Religion:* congregational leadership, lay religious activities, Fellowship/ Brotherhood/Sisterhood organizations, community outreach programs, interfaith activities

An active CEO at one publicly-traded company should not sit on the Board of Directors of more than one other company, whether publicly

---

GENERAL ELECTRIC—

ONLY THE CEO SPEAKS FOR THE COMPANY

In some cases the CEO is the only high-ranking executive with whom the public is familiar. General Electric's Jack Welch is a great example. During his tenure as CEO, he was the only GE executive ever interviewed and the only one ever quoted, good or bad, whether by industry trade publications or the general business press. Before Welch retired and the Board had to select a successor, most of the business-aware public had *never heard of* senior vice presidents Jeff Immelt, Bob Nardelli, Jim McNerney, and Larry Johnston. Each ran a large, successful business segment for GE. After the Board selected Immelt to succeed Welch, the remaining three resigned from GE to assume CEO positions with other companies: Nardelli ran retailer Home Depot, McNerny headed inventive 3M Corporation, and Johnston led turnaround efforts at supermarket chain Albertsons.

The pattern at GE appears consistent; the only person you now see or hear about in the general business press or popular media is CEO Jeff Immelt. Borrowing a sports metaphor, GE claims to have a "deep bench of talent." Who now warms the bench if the only GE player the public sees is Immelt? Jeff Immelt became more scarce at GE when, in January 2011, President Obama appointed Immelt chair of his outside panel of economic advisors, giving him an important time-consuming activity to take him away from his work at GE.

~~*

traded or privately held. Since the passage of Sarbanes-Oxley legislation, the knowledge and time demands for Board members of a public company have increased. It is almost impossible for a CEO, EVP, SVP, or VP to truly balance responsibilities to their organization plus travel, family commitments, entertainment, community or religious activities, time to play golf or tennis or poker, or go to the movies or cultural events with their significant other. There simply aren't enough hours in a day to permit an effective balance. Most of us need six to nine hours' sleep on a regular basis. In their defense, some executives may require only three to five hours of sleep a night.

Bottom line: Count the number of outside activities. Then determine the degree of the CEO's involvement with each. If the CEO is actively involved in five or six activities listed above and has a contract to run a public company, a private company, or a large not-for-profit organization, it is impossible for that person to be effective for the organization that hired her/him as CEO and, by extension, for many of the other firms s/he is supposed to oversee. From the company's perspective, the overcommitted CEO becomes merely a figurehead. If the organization is engaged in many unrelated activities, a *distracted* CEO cannot become familiar with the workings, challenges, and limitations of the diversified business. Even if the CEO delegates many operational tasks, an overcommitted staff, following the CEO's pattern, will not be able to properly oversee and coordinate all the pieces. Unfortunately, the company's business may be severely compromised by the time Board members recognize the conflicting demands on the CEO's time.

Shareholders expect the CEO to pay attention to the business s/he is charged with and paid to lead. If the CEO has become a figurehead, then who is really running the company?

Company Quotes by Only the CEO

In some companies, press releases for almost any event quote only the corporate CEO or board Chair. The leader may need to convey information and show s/he is leading the organization. However, watch for leaders who speak *only* about positive events and have an underling handle the unpleasant chore of speaking with the media when the information released is less-than-good. The issue transcends one of consistent communication and borders on a *cult of personality*; the CEO is not willing to showcase key staff members or managers of operating units when things are going well—nor does s/he want his/her name associated with negative communications.

Telephone Access to CEOs & VPs

Here is a great way to determine a company's true culture: Try to contact the CEO or vice president with a question, a complaint, or an idea you feel would be beneficial to the company. I suggest you start with a letter summarizing your request. Follow the letter with a phone call. Do not try to bypass the administrator by calling during the lunch hour or after regular business hours.

When you speak with the administrator, tell her or him exactly why you wish to speak with the CEO or vice president. In fact, you want to treat that person with the same courtesy you would the CEO or VP you are trying to reach. Be genuine, be cooperative; your goal is to get the administrator on your side. You want the administrator to think of you favorably enough s/he will pass your message on to the CEO—so that the CEO will return your call or take your call if you should have to call back.

The response or lack thereof will give you a good idea of the company's culture. In a healthy, open company, I expect the administrator to pass your message to the executive and act as your primary contact until the executive agrees to speak or meet with you.

Bottom line: If the CEO or the administrator responds, that is good. If you still have not made contact after five to ten tries (be persistent!), then you may rightly make a few judgments such as:

- The company focuses inwardly, especially the case if you learn that you need to *know someone* at the company in order to make any executive contact.

- The executives are operating in their own cocoons. They do not want any *outside* help, which means they do not want the opinions of others with different experiences. Trapped in the famed technology-based dysfunction *NIH (Not Invented Here) syndrome,* many companies will not listen to outside ideas—they focus solely on ideas vetted through their own internal cultures. Sadly, reinventing something that already exists wastes time and creative and emotional energy.

- The insular attitude confirms an inbred, encouraged, and actively-practiced culture of rudeness.

If your calls are ignored, you can write a carefully crafted, courteous letter to the CEO. This may be far more effective than leaving constant messages with the executive's administrator or the now obviously ignored voice mail messages. A representative of the company is likely to call and ask you what can be done to make things right. Your measured actions may not get you what you need, but the organization is likely to change for the better as a result of your letter to the CEO.

Bottom line: Three unrelated situations yielded essentially the same rude responses. One data point a trend does not make. Two data points may show that you are on to something. Three data points are pretty conclusive. Armed with this information, I can accurately characterize the hospital's culture as:

- *All hat, no cattle.* This derisive phrase refers to a *gentleman cowboy* poseur. In a similar vein (medical-related pun intended), this hospital poses as a great institution with little objective proof of its standing. In fact, the hospital had a large sign in front of each major facility that touted itself as one of the *Top 100 Hospitals in the U.S.* What is the source of this honor? I had to identify the organization that made these determinations. Upon what objective criteria did the independent organization base its rankings? Who sat on the committee that made these determinations? Was this organization truly independent/neutral or were there some affiliations with the hospitals evaluated? As a requirement to receive this *award* or designation, did the hospital pay a fee, buy a product, hire the firm as a consultant, or advertise in one or more industry-specific or consumer- or industry-oriented periodicals?

Is the CEO also Board Chair?

One evaluation factor is considered more important than all other factors. In many publicly traded companies, the CEO wears a second hat as Chair of the Board of Directors. **I view this CEO/Chair of Board of Directors double-hatting as a major conflict of interest.** Where is the independent oversight of the person tasked with strategic decisions and concern for day-to-day operations? More importantly, who is representing the interests of stockholders?

Management texts, whether introductory, graduate-level, or post-graduate level, emphasize the absolute need for independent overview of company operations by the Board of Directors. Such separation of functional oversight from day-to-day operations deters sloppy, unethical management practices and reduces the likelihood of a cult of mismanagement, where managers make decisions based on alliances rather than for the overall good of the company. Accounting and finance texts reinforce the need for Board/management independence. Independent oversight is the foundation of Sarbanes-Oxley legislation.

However, in spite of strong theoretical bases and common sense need for independence, a few oft-quoted business pundits and select business-oriented media continue to defend the practice of sharing roles. They support the management-oversight interlock until a business implosion occurs—such as Enron, WorldCom, or Adelphia. At that point, they righteously claim, "Exceptions happen." Or "We had no way of knowing this would happen."

Yes, you did.

If the CEO is also Board chair, then this is not an exception. Someone on a truly independent Board would know what was really going on and could muster a majority of Board members' votes to demand and implement necessary changes by company management. In the worst case, when the

---

AN INBRED CULTURE OF LATENESS AND RUDENESS

Corporate culture can encourage and spread rude behavior.

Susan, a student of mine, managed the radiology department at a medium-size local hospital. Her hospital used a large space in a suburban shopping mall for public presentations covering medical topics—at a cost of $14,000 per month with no offsetting revenue. She asked me to help her repurpose the space.

On the phone, we discussed the challenge and developed a strategy to use the space to offer basic medical, limited services. Susan scheduled a meeting for us to present the concept to her vice-president-level manager—who arrived nearly an hour late. At the meeting, we learned we needed to add a few details to the proposal. Over the next few weeks, Susan tightened it, I proofread it, and when Susan presented it to the Board of Directors, the Board adopted it. Five years later, it remained in effect with services expanded to offer mammograms in an underused part of a department store in the same suburban mall. I am proud that Susan and I created a different set of services that brought the mall location to financial break-even.

Based on my demonstrated success with this project, I sent two letters to the hospital's CEO to propose working with him on a series of strategic projects. I called 12 times to follow up (I kept track!) and—you guessed it—I *never* received a response. The CEO's two administrators were terrific—pleasant, friendly, competent, and helpful. On the other hand, the CEO's behavior provided a perfect example of an inwardly-focused, insular, haughty culture.

There are a few interesting twists to the story.

current management appears incapable or unwilling to make the changes required for the health of the organization, an independent Board can select a new management team and dismiss the old one.

There are no exceptions to good corporate governance requirements. This position represents an absolute standard and is directly critical of many contemporary situations. Just as *full faith and credit* represents the foundation of the United States government's financial business, oversight in the business world boils down to a short maxim: "Trust. Verify. Continually Question Everything." The CEO cannot simultaneously act as a key hired employee focused on corporate profits and an unbiased elected representative of shareholder interests.

A couple months later I was part of a group of select educators who toured local businesses to learn about career opportunities for graduates of this college. One of the weekly tours took our group to this hospital. The scheduled speaker was the same vice president with whom I met for the strategy discussion. Again, he was late!

Five minutes after the meeting had been scheduled to start, the young lady representing human resources gave an excellent impromptu presentation on the hospital, its current and projected staffing needs, and the preferred characteristics of the graduates they would hire. Forty-five minutes into the discussion, the vice president arrived and took over. The Human Resources representative had provided excellent, relevant information, making the vice president's presence and braggadocio unnecessary. Here was the second data point on corporate lateness and rudeness.

A few months later, Susan called me to tell me she had gotten married. Her husband was out of work. I offered to evaluate and hone his résumé and cover letter. I referred him to a job search group for professionals. I never heard from him or Susan. More rudeness, this time from my former student. Eight months later, she told me he found a job.

I recently ran into Susan at the local YMCA. She mentioned that she still managed the outpatient center, but has deferred the start of an MBA degree. For students, my "standard consulting fee" is a cup of coffee. As part of our small talk, I jokingly mentioned getting together for the cup of coffee so we could discuss the project and I could collect my unpaid consulting fee. Susan changed the subject, and then turned away. Here was a third data point on organizationally inspired and practiced rudeness.

~~*

Unfortunately, although I use a double-decker soapbox and have a solid theoretical basis, I am seldom heard. In the real world, the CEO often suggests, directly or indirectly, nominees for positions on the organization's Board of Directors. Although these nominees may come from different industries, not-for-profit organizations, the political arena, the military, or academia, the CEO's key underlying assumption is, "These are my friends or allies. After all, I was directly involved in their nomination to our Board—and plan to ensure they receive lucrative directors' fees. They will be on my side."

In addition to a biased nomination slate, companies purchase directors' loyalty through payment of high directors' fees and, in some cases, grants of restricted stock options. According to the SEC website for SEC Form DEF 14-A (definitive proxy statement), a variety of publicly-traded companies (listed

A MEASURE OF SUCCESS?

Solucient® (Headquarters: Evanston, IL acquired by Thomson Reuters in 2007) provides data and analysis to healthcare managers to improve the performance of their hospitals. Solucient created the "Top 100 Hospitals" list now maintained by Thomson, a list which designates the "Top 100 Hospitals" in each of three categories:

- National benchmarks for success,
- 100 top teaching and non-teaching cardiovascular hospitals, and
- 100 Top Performance Improvement Leaders.

As of August 2012, this hospital's website indicated it had been named a Top 100 heart hospital by *Thomson Reuter's 100 Top Hospitals: Cardiovascular Benchmarks for Success* study for 11 consecutive years—the only hospital in the United States to receive this honor. This acknowledgement says only that this hospital was either the first to recognize the advantages of this alliance or the only one to persist in faithfully repurchasing Solucient/Thompson's analyses each year. The hospital's website says nothing about high ratings from the Joint Commission, the U.S. government-based health care rating agency whose approval is required for a hospital to operate.

A hospital may purchase from Solucient/Thomson a comprehensive report detailing the observations and analyses supporting its ranking. A second available report provides an overview of comparable data for other hospitals in the relevant category. Each report costs $2,500. This so-called analytical product fails to qualify as objective data. The research organization compiles and massages the data for alphabetically) paid annual outside director's fees and grants of restricted stock in 2011 as follows:

- Agilent Technologies: $90,000 + $180,000 in company stock

- Barnes Group: $51,000 + 80,993 stock award

- Citigroup: $75,000 plus $150,000 deferred stock award

- Ford Motor: $250,000 + "other compensation"

- IBM: $250,000 + $30,000 to $61,000 additional compensation for committee chair + 4,000 shares in stock options

- Johnson & Johnson: $110,000-$130,000 plus $144,913 in stock grants

- Kellogg: $88,000 plus 2,788 shares of common stock

---

the specific purpose of selling the detailed results to its customers.

This approach makes perfect economic sense. A self-serving statistics-gathering organization creates lists of the "Top 100 Hospitals" in at least three categories. In so doing, the company creates a back-door means for 300 hospitals to become or remain customers. The organization divvies out "recognitions" to its customers, and the named hospitals may then tout their "accomplishments." On its own, neither the hospital nor Solucient is fully credible; however, the self-referral and self-justification results in a win-win situation for both. However, this process does not provide arms' length, legitimate analysis nor does it offer recommendations backed by empirical data.

For comparison, the past two U.S. News & World Report rankings of America's best hospitals included every top-notch University-related medical center and a few independent hospitals or chains. The extensive listings did not include this hospital.

In November 2005 and June 2011, the national hospital accreditation agency, The Joint Commission (called the Joint Commission on the Accreditation of Hospitals until 2007), inspected the hospital. The Commission's rating system consists of three ratings: a "plus sign" indicates above average compliance, a "check mark" indicates the organization is in compliance with requirements, and a "minus sign" indicates failure in compliance. This hospital passed both inspections and received the required Accreditation. It received a "check mark," not a "plus sign." What does all of this mean? Here are my additional characterizations of the hospital chain: ▷

- Quest Diagnostics: $65,000-$69,500 plus stock award of $113,888 & stock option award of $194,991

Sometimes, the CEO/Chair actually becomes the leader of a management team that proposes a company buyout. The sole basis for CEO/Chair's actions is the belief that the stock and/or underlying assets are undervalued. If this happens, one need ask only one important question: "If the current stock

---

- *Self promote, self promote, self promote.* In front of every facility related to this hospital, a large sign visible as one drives by proudly proclaims it is one of America's "Top 100 Hospitals." If you say something often enough, with or without justification, people will believe it. Image is everything.

- *Someone does care.* Beyond the credit-taking executives, the department managers and nursing and support staff are dedicated and caring and try to do right by the patients. The physicians are likewise dedicated. However, this caring and personalized attitude underscores a significant disconnect between the leadership and front-line employees.

- *Bigger is better.* The organizational and facility growth enable a consolidation of purchasing and provider power, not necessarily better patient care. The total number of employees in an organization often helps determine executive salaries. This hospital continues to expand aggressively in two local counties. I see active empire-building.

- *Internal politics reign supreme.* I attended a housewarming party. One of the attendees worked at this hospital. We chatted and she mentioned that the CEO promoted the vice president I previously met to run a major clinic affiliated with this hospital. Based on the two executives' past actions and words, it became apparent that the VP was a great internal politician. More importantly, it reinforced my long-held belief that "like prefers like." A person who works in a certain way would rather work with a person of similar style, in this case, one who was habitually late, rude, and needlessly took control when a stand-in was nearly finished with her impromptu presentation. Yes, if there is a personality match, like selects like, no matter how dysfunctional the individuals appear to the outside, peers, or subordinates.

~~*

price is low, who looked out for shareholder interests in the past and made a solid attempt to boost the stock price?" If the CEO/Chair wants to buy the company, then who on the Board will represent shareholders' interests? Who will ensure shareholders' receive the best price upon sale? What material information does executive management know that they have not fully shared in a timely manner with the investing public and even with outside/non-corporate members of the Board of Directors?

The separation of the roles of CEO and Chairman of the Board is a critical factor in the health of an organization. Stated simply, these two positions require two different individuals. Anything else violates basic corporate governance and separation/balance of power guidelines. If the CEO is also the Board Chair, potential dysfunctions include:

- One-man band-ism. The leader runs everything, usually due to the leader's strong personality or having founded the company.

- Empire building. Jack Welch at General Electric, Maurice "Hank" Greenberg of American International Group, Steve Case or Richard Parsons at AOL Time Warner, and William Clay Ford at Ford Motor come to mind as examples of empire builders—each was the face and voice of their respective company. The late Dr. Kenneth Lay at Enron, John Rigas at Adelphia, and L. Dennis Kozlowski at Tyco International served simultaneously as Board Chairs and CEOs.

- Development of a different type of or an increase in internal politics, since ethical and other complaints to the Board actually wind up with the CEO, who is ultimately the employee's boss.

- Creation of a *cult of personality*, since the combined CEO/Chair is model spokesperson for the company on all-important issues. In the eyes of the public, that person *is* the company.

- Decreased discussion of key issues or a policy of *not rocking the boat* since the Chair oversees committee assignments for Board members. Depending on the Board structure and rules, committee assignments often affect how much the company pays a Board member. No self-respecting Board member wants to take a pay cut.

Evidence of Real CEO Leadership

I take a real-world view of leadership. Leadership means fostering an environment where employees may create, communicate, coordinate, prevent problems or keep them small, and produce the product or service. Leaders have character. They:

- Listen and coach and mentor subordinates as needed

- Are available, use time effectively, and are not always traveling on the corporate jet

- Are decisive, realistic, and encourage change

- Keep their promises, demonstrate ethical behavior, do not offer phony excuses

- Delegate appropriately and do not practice nepotism

- Effectively oversee projects and accept full responsibility for what happens during their tenure

- Grow revenue and do not continually cut expenses to the detriment of long-term growth

Bottom line: We know the good leaders. We know who effectively turned around a corporation facing dire choices while creating or maintaining a positive work environment. We also know, but are slow to admit, that a mean, nasty person with a good PR machine cannot truly be a good leader.

The CEO is Constantly on the Road

The Chief Executive is not watching the home office whenever s/he: visits international offices or manufacturing plants; meets with key customers; lectures at business schools, alma mater, or industry conferences; meets with mutual fund portfolio managers or Wall Street analysts; or takes long weekends at plush resorts. If they are occupied with such activities, it is realistic for CEOs to delegate many decisions to subordinates.

However, an unavailable CEO sends the wrong messages, appearing to shirk responsibility by doing what he wants to do, not what he needs to do. Instead, his focus is on the glamorous image of corporate aircraft travel with family or friends and the chance to go to all the right places with all the right people He is *too busy* to prevent or deal with commonplace problems.

Presence or lack of presence is a matter of degree; the CEO must spend some time at the main office. Absence does not make the heart grow fonder; it makes other executives and the employees wonder what the CEO is doing and doubt his sincerity. To be an effective leader, a CEO must be visible. A CEO whose appearance is rare does not care.

Summary

The organizational buck starts and stops with the CEO. Accordingly, the person and the position need to be in sync. The evaluation of the CEO vis-à-vis the position included current corporate and organizational affiliations, memberships on other organizations' boards of directors, ease of reaching the CEO, the CEO as chair of the board of directors of her/his company, and the CEO's travel schedule.

Warning signs of company dysfunction include:

- The CEO serves on boards of directors of too many other companies;

- The CEO is too involved with alumni or community/volunteer activities;

- The CEO also serves as Chair of the board of directors at the company where s/he works;

- The CEO is an example of *empire builder* or *cult of personality* and is the only person to speak for the company.

~*~*~*~

CHAPTER 10

CEO—COMP & BENNIES

Finally, we examine issues related to the CEO's compensation and benefits, shortened to *comp and bennies*, which includes:

- Pay and benefits

- Retirement package

- Annual pay package after the company's stock price has fallen

Pay and Benefits

Executive pay is a relatively important indicator of corporate dysfunction. Shareholders elect members of the Board of Directors to protect investors' interests. Unfortunately, since the CEO or other members of the Board nominate prospective Board members, real board independence is unlikely. Excessive pay, stock grants, or stock options paid by the company to Board members further compromise the Board's independence, objectivity, and fiduciary responsibility to shareholders.

The U.S. Government requires publicly traded companies to annually file SEC Form 14-D, Proxy Statement. The 14-D statement includes the date, time, and location of the annual meeting; the agenda items for the annual meeting; the list of directors running for election/re-election and their qualifications; remuneration for each Board member; and major transactions that impact compensation for the firm's executives.

From this filing, I learned that Dr. William McGuire, CEO and Chairman of the Board of Directors of United Healthcare from 1991 until he resigned in 2006, received stock option grants worth a total of $1.6 billion from 1989 through December 2006. The company secretary (on behalf of the Board and with the advice—however questionable and partisan! —of company lawyers) or Board Chairman signed off on these awards, which came under the scrutiny of the Securities and Exchange Commission in 2007 for the backdating of the stock options to dates where the stock hit its lowest closing price . . . creating instant profits.

In a best-case scenario, some more objective Board members have asked the right questions and protected the interests of shareholders. It didn't happen. However, this fiduciary high-road is the exception rather than the rule. Yes, boards may eventually do what is necessary. However, it most often takes years for the Board to do what is right. When the CEO of a company also serves as Board Chair, this complicates and further delays any significant actions necessary to protect investors.

The bold fact is Board members and CEOs hang out at the same country clubs, restaurants, and resorts. In some cases, they worship together. They protect one another's elitist life styles.

Huge Golden Parachute or Large Retirement Packages for Executives

One aspect of executive compensation—the golden parachute—is particularly galling. An executive at the financially worst-performing company may still collect a substantial payment if the company is sold. Other executive-favored contracts give the executive an outsized payment if the executive leaves for any reason within a stated time frame.

One business practice compounds executive excess. A Board will sell the company when revenues can no longer profitably increase. The executive, who is often a member of the Board and, less often, also serves at Chairman of the Board, benefits directly from the perfect timing of a sale transaction.

Here are three glaring examples of the corporate *shell game,* where the money ended up in places an observer would not expect:

1) After five years at the helm, the Hewlett Packard Board fired Carly Fiorina and awarded her $22 million, in accordance with her employment contract.

2) Larry Johnston, the former appliance division executive at General Electric, who served as Chairman and CEO of supermarket chain Albertson's, received a $105 million *golden parachute* payment for selling the chain one piece at a time.

3) Ex-General Electric Chairman/CEO Jack Welch negotiated his retirement package in 1996, when GE produced very strong financial results and the Board was eager to keep his services. Upon his retirement in 2002, Welch received a retirement package that included:

   o   a $9 million per year payout

o   a Central Park apartment complete with flowers and food

o   a limited edition 2003 Mercedes-Benz SLR automobile

o   tickets to tennis matches at Wimbledon, Red Sox games, the Metropolitan Opera, and access to VIP seats at sporting events broadcast by GE's NBC subsidiary (as of January 2011, 51% owned by Comcast)

o   car phones for five cars

o   satellite television in four homes

o   five computers, complete with technical support

o   paid dues for three private golf clubs, including Augusta (Georgia) National

o   personal financial planning and tax services

Although Welch turned down $300 million in stock options, the 22 million shares of GE stock he owns are worth, as of April 29, 2013, approximately $490 million, down significantly from about $750 million in June 2006. What can be said of this package as reward for 40 years' service? It is ridiculous, excessive, and insulting to shareholders, other executives, and employees.

What does this retirement package tell us? First, Welch's timing to retire could not have been better—for him. GE's stock price was high, new products had been introduced, its GE Financial subsidiary reported strong profits, and GE had a first-rate corporate image. Welch's well-timed accomplishment led to a feeling-good Board—too good in fact—his retirement package was substantially over-weighted.

Why award stock grants or options worth up to $750 million? To be fair, GE has nearly 10.5 *billion* shares of stock outstanding; the 22 million share award to Welch won't materially dilute earnings per share. However, the Board was clearly not looking out for shareholders' best interests and may have created a precedent when it granted this package.

Second, might this be *ol' boy's clubiness* at its worst? Welch managed the public's impression of his business acumen. The stock price of GE increased on the order of 450% during his tenure. He took an active interest in the company's Crotonville, NY training center for upcoming executives and managers. He ruthlessly cut costs. He invested in businesses where GE could be the market leader or occupy the number two position.

He also had an excellent attorney or team of attorneys to advise him on the unusual terms of his employment contract. Despite these public accomplishments, may we say he acted in his own very best interests, especially as retirement got closer? Welch led the GE Board, but might he have subtly hijacked it for his own best interests?

Huge Annual Pay Packages and Bonuses when the Company's Stock Price has Fallen

Boards of directors use many metrics to measure CEO success—the most visible metric is the company's stock price. Other closely-watched metrics include return on shareholder equity or return on invested capital. Depending on the industry, important measurements may include safe operations, good environmental stewardship, strong local community involvement, completion of one or more key projects, management of expenditures, and one or more successful cost-cutting initiatives.

It is difficult for a Board to justify a huge pay package for the CEO when the company's stock price is lower than when that CEO took over. On its face, this is unacceptable. However, the public is not generally privy to the CEO's contract with the Board. The CEO may, in fact, have met the specific goals outlined in her/his contract—and the company's stock price was not the key metric driving the CEO's compensation.

Home Depot's former CEO Bob Nardelli received a pay package of $28.5 million for the year ending January 30, 2005. His guaranteed bonus, the only locked-in payout at the company, rose from $4.5 million in 2003 to $5.8 million in 2004. By June 2006, the stock traded at 7 to 10% lower than when he took over in 2000. One interesting point. With the exception of Nardelli, no member of Home Depot's Board of Directors showed up at the company's annual shareholder meeting in May 2006.

Nardelli resigned in January 2007, taking with him a $210 million golden parachute, seven times the $30 million Home Depot had set aside the previous June for stores and employees that provided good customer service. Message to employees and customers? Not so good.

By late August 2012, Home Depot's stock price had recovered some—up 66% from its mid-2006 price. For comparison, the stock price of primary competitor Lowe's rose 210% through mid-2006 and as of late August 2012 increased 99% from mid-2006.

Summary

An organization with publicly traded stock reveals significant dysfunction when it overpays its CEO, awards lavish stock options, provides extensive benefits at retirement, and offers overly generous golden parachute payments when the company is sold or the executive is fired, resigns, or retires. What ever happened to cheapskate members of boards of directors who provided realistic—not excessive—rewards for a job well done?

~*~*~*~

CHAPTER 11

MEETINGS, ACCESS TO KEY PERSONNEL, & CHANGES TO PHYSICAL PLANT

To help identify additional organizational dysfunction, the analysis of day-to-day operating modes and administration includes:

- Meetings

- Restricted analyst access to company executives

- Changes to the physical plan

Meetings

In and of themselves, meetings are not bad. However, poorly planned and poorly run meetings can easily reveal a less-than-healthy corporate environment.

Meetings with Agendas that do not Address Current Issues Facing the Organization

Example: A not-for-profit organization is facing day-to-day operating problems. In the meantime, the executive director/CEO/president is *off in the ozone*, promoting a new project or a new building. Is the leader clueless or does s/he know what is going on but prefers to promote a false initiative to avoid dealing with day-to-day problems? Does the president continually repeat the same false message to the members, in spite of overwhelming evidence that this is not the right path at this time?

There are a number of people who believe that if they (as experts, authorities, or leaders) say something, or if they say it often enough, it will become true. Some even believe that if they say something, it is true. Often mislabeled *visionaries*, these individuals, out of touch with reality, are dangerous to the survival of the organizations they lead.

Bottom line: If the Executive Director/CEO/President ignores critical issues and focuses on visions, that person is a low- to mid-level manager, not a leader. S/he is trying to manage the organization's expectations, instead of leading the organization.

CHANGED STRATEGY LEADS TO CHANGED PHYSICAL PLANT

From its nineteenth century roots as a typewriter and adding machine developer, forerunners of today's Unisys Corporation built a history of technological innovation—improving its typewriters and adding machines, and adding aircraft gyroscopes and business computers. Remington Rand delivered its UNIVAC computer to the Census Bureau in 1951. Over the next 3 decades, the company merged into a mainframe powerhouse.

In 1992, the company changed its strategy from an emphasis on selling computer systems to a strong emphasis on selling computer services. Selling systems focuses on the sale of computers; selling professional services concentrates on the sale of consulting, strategic planning for technology-related purchases, systems design, troubleshooting, designing and building customized systems or software, and effective implementation of licensed software and new technologies such as cloud computing, and data analytics. The uncertainty about revenue growth and profitability as a result of this change in strategy prompted tight budgetary constraints.

In spite of the severe budget restrictions in 1994 and 1995, Unisys added a wing to its corporate headquarters to accommodate the new computer services operation. The company also hired a senior executive away from Andersen Consulting, a pioneering organization in computer services. The timing of the construction of this new building wing diverged with the company's public statements of austerity. This expensive construction, which continued during cold eastern Pennsylvania winters, sent a message that something else was not right within the company.

I later learned Unisys fell behind in one of its first major computer services contracts with the U.S. military. The construction activity—inconsistent with the stated goals of cost reduction—was indeed an accurate harbinger of other larger organizational problems.

~~*

Hallmarks of this leaderless management style include:

- Consistent repetition of the same limited message, speaking only of a vision that something be done, with no measurable steps taken to realize this vision

- Lack of willingness to present the complete situation—pros, cons, limiting factors, and realities. By restricting information, the leader may create unnecessary factions rather instead of building consensus.

- Opinions of those who disagree are ignored, minimized, dismissed, or ridiculed.

- When one disagrees and tries to contact other board members or trustees, these so-called company or organizational leaders are equally dismissive of criticisms or suggestions of other ways to see the situation.

- The managers take advantage of organizational inertia; they prefer that the rank-and-file employees not get involved.

- To advance their personal agendas, sneaky managers will hold separate meetings for different employee groups. Groups may be based on gender, department, job function, office location, and even sexual orientation. Moreover, the content of each meeting will be tailored to fit the audience. The successful conspirator uses these segmented groups to get agreement with her/his agenda, instead of drawing on the widest possible audience for feedback, criticism, and possibly downright hostility. In this situation, the "divide and conquer" strategy works for the benefit of the conspirator(s), not for the good of the organization.

Meetings Called on Short Notice without Sending Necessary Pre-Meeting Agenda and Background Information to Participants

The person who called the meeting does not want to give participants a chance to review or gather facts, formulate questions, digest what they read and hear, and then arrive at a community-supported decision. Blind-siding works best when a person with little real power needs to get something done to make him/her look good or prevent a little problem in their area of responsibility from becoming a larger problem.

Bottom line: In this case, the person who called the meeting has a hidden agenda The person's real agenda may be to distract others from issues for which that person was responsible. Alternatively, their hidden agenda may seek to transfer blame (ah, the spirits of comic strip Dilbert © are alive and well . . . .) for an error or omission for which that person was responsible. Or, the unstated agenda may be an attempt to grab power, since the person calling the meeting is the only one who knows which cards are going to be dealt.

A hastily called meeting may be necessary due to management by emergency. By creating an environment of urgency, where crisis gets piled on crisis, management is locking control on what can be done in the organization. They say, "It's a disaster. We don't have time to think about it. This is what we must do." All other voices are drowned out . . . and even seen as unreasonable. After all, immediate response is essential.

Yes, the nature of business is such that there are occasional crises—a storm wipes out power in a geographical region, a natural disaster destroys one major factory, a competitor introduces a superior product that immediately outdates the company's product. Yet, if a company is *constantly* dealing with emergencies, leadership is failing to recognize potential problems and probably also failing to see opportunities. Or leadership team members have decided that crisis management will enhance their reputations as strong, effective leaders. After all, the heroes are the ones who walk into fires and pull out survivors, not the ones who prevent fires in the first place.

It is difficult to assess meeting effectiveness. You need to know the participants. You need to know the history of the organization. How did these participants fit in the organization in the past? You need to be aware of new coalitions formed to address particular topics or projects. You need to be aware of any large financial stakeholders. You must definitely know if these financial backers are creditworthy and trustworthy, since you do not want the organization to make a major commitment without very high likelihood of the promised financial support.

You need to have an understanding of how the company uses meetings . . . problem prevention, problem solving, or to foster a culture of crisis management. Knowing most or all these factors will help you effectively assess situations and identify hidden agendas.

Meeting Attendees Must Make a Decision of Strategic or Critical Tactical Importance in Only One Meeting

The person calling the meeting is trying to advance her/his agenda over the possible objections of other, usually better informed, managers. By scheduling a one-time meeting, particularly at a time when critical oppositional stakeholders are busy elsewhere, the desired result can be more easily achieved with less potential for blockage or proposal dilution.

Bottom line: Normal due diligence and topic exploration and discussion require at least two meetings and some passage of time. Yes, the individual calling the meeting may have been considering the implications of the matter for the past six months. However, not allowing other individuals the opportunity to provide input is disrespectful. The message is that the individual is the only person with the intelligence and acumen to figure it out.

In reality, the person calling the meeting is indeed attempting to pull a fast one. If executive managers are paying attention, they should catch this and stop the practice at once. Better yet, institute a requirement that anyone calling a meeting must distribute an agenda a couple business days in advance. The distribution list should include some senior executives.

Not Inviting all Necessary Attendees to a Meeting

The person who called the meeting usually times the meeting for a date when the opposition is out of town, at another meeting, or has another scheduling conflict. Even if multiple meetings are scheduled, the timing is *always* inconvenient or impossible for those who might object to the proposed decision. Of course, the exclusion cannot be helped . . . and it certainly is not intentional. Later, if questioned, the meeting meister's response is, "Gee, too bad; we *had* to decide without that key person's input."

Bottom line: By not inviting a person with important and possibly different views, the manager or project leader attempts to minimize opposition, make it appear idea is accepted by a majority (albeit, a selected majority), and ensure the decision goes their way.

Cancelled Meetings with Sell-Side and Buy-Side Financial Analysts

Investor relations staff members must schedule financial analyst meetings months in advance, and avoid quarterly financial reporting weeks, annual investment bank-sponsored conferences, religious holidays, vacation breaks for elementary/middle/high school/college students, key industry conferences, holiday weekends, and Board meetings. A company that schedules at least one meeting per year with financial analysts builds positive analyst relationships. The company keeps its story fresh and in the minds of analysts; creates an environment where analysts can efficiently meet with senior management; and shares new information about products, buyer trends, competitive trends, and operational plans so the analysts can learn something new.

Any delay or cancellation of this important meeting sends the wrong message. From an analyst's perspective, nothing short of a death in the immediate family explains a canceled meeting without the company paying the likely penalty of a lower stock price the next few days or into the next few months. An analyst would interpret this delay as a sign of more serious problems at the company—that the company is scrambling to cover some less-than-favorable information.

No Company Tours for Financial Analysts

Analysts like to see for themselves what is going on in a company. Financial analysts understand that, to some extent, a facility tour is *a dog and pony show.* However, they appreciate the opportunity to look around, examine the facilities, check the layout of the production floor, review the information on white boards throughout the building, check out the loading docks, look for safety-related violations, meet with vice presidents/department managers/operational personnel, and get a feel for the overall level of commitment and morale at the company.

Bottom line: Analysts do not look favorably on *any* delay or cancellation of a scheduled meeting. **What does this delay indicate?** Possible explanations include the unavailability of an adequate number of—or specific—company executives, product changeover or technology introduction problems, a new corporate structure implementation delay, financial pressures to cut costs across the board, habitual poor housekeeping, or excessive time taken up with regulatory inquiries. However, for a publicly traded company, this action signals a lack of concern for investors, both institutional and individual. Analysts say, "Good news is good for the company. Bad news may cause a drop in the stock price but, upon fixing the problem, can change to good news. Bad news also keeps the company's name in the mind of the public. No news is the worst possible option. The investor's imagination is free to roam."

Restricted Access to Executive Staff Members

Analysts or institutional investors need access to all members of the executive team in order to properly assess a company. **If the CEO restricts**

access to any or all vice presidents or director-level executives, this is a relatively major warning sign. No CEO can address the operating details and strengths and weaknesses of each department. Moreover, what does the CEO have to fear or hide? Is the CEO afraid a subordinate will say something that contradicts one of his decrees? Is there major dissension in the ranks?

Changes in Physical Plant Layout or Design

Some companies continually meddle with their physical plants. It is as though nothing is ever good enough, they do not have a clear concept of where they have been, where they are going, or what they are doing. At the same time, their corporate strategies and requirements change at a pace faster than they are able to implement. A Machiavellian interpretation suggests executive management wants to ensure no one gets too comfortable—thus the constant stream of unnecessary changes.

Examples of changes include:

- Constant redecorating of executive suite offices. Redecorating executive offices is an organizational head fake. Unless dictated by changes in local or national fire codes, these redecorations reveal a management team that cares only about itself, not the employees or stockholders. Moreover, until the dysfunction is addressed, this organization tends to focus on easy, short-term decisions; it is temperamentally unsuited to make a decision with significant long-term consequences.

- Constant redecorating the conference room/reception area. The company is overly conscious of its image to guests. Changing furniture, wallpaper, lighting, or seating after only a few years also shows a disregard for its employees and stockholders and wastes money. How does the appearance of this public area compare with that in executive offices or, more importantly, employee workstations, offices, or cubicles? If the disparity is huge and favors the reception area and conference rooms, then the firm sends "We-don't care-about-employees-or-stockholders" or "It's-all-about-image" messages. And the image is not likely to be backed by solid growth, profit, respect in the industry, and shareholder loyalty.

- Significant additions to buildings when business is bad. Such changes indicate a lack of peace within the organization. Like a someone shopping for a new outfit after losing his/her job, changing the physical environment is a *feel-good patch*, indicating a restlessness with the status quo or a need to hide a major flaw behind a new façade.

Summary

After three chapters evaluating the CEO, we explored the organization's administrative environment. When companies restrict financial analysts' access to company vice presidents or department heads or change a company's physical plant at inappropriate times, bad news will likely follow.

Meeting dynamics—how meetings are planned, scheduled, and run; who is invited to attend; whether decisions are made without input from all affected stakeholders; whether detailed information about the negative impacts of proposed action plans is obscured; and the frequency of meeting delays and cancellations involving bankers, accountants, attorneys, key suppliers, or financial analysts—provide a reliable gauge of an organization's health.

~*~*~*~

CHAPTER 12

HUMAN RESOURCES & ORG CHARTS

Most organizations say employees are their most important asset. Yet, these same companies will often blame poor results on employees, ignoring the fact that these people were the ones the organization selected and trained. In addition, senior managers are far from blameless; employees follow senior managers' instructions. Poor employee selection and training may be part of the problem, but often, it is the attitudes of corporate management, ingrained counter-productive policies, and outdated, patriarchal management styles that stifle employee creativity, ingenuity, passion . . . and ultimately, productivity and success. Look for inconsistencies.

Backgrounds of People Hired

For a technology firm, a reasonable expectation is that the company will hire technically savvy employees. For almost any firm in today's computer-driven work environment, employees must have basic computer skills.

Note when a company hires generalists with few or no demonstrated skills appropriate to the position—whether it is technology, retailing, customer service, logistics, precision machining, consumer finance, corporate finance, consumer marketing, or business-to-business marketing. **A mismatch between specific skills needed and general skills hired is a semi-critical consideration.**

Does the firm hire the physically handicapped? Do they offer the same opportunities for advancement to the handicapped? Or do they pay lip service to diversity, and dump the alternatively-abled as soon as they can cobble up a reason? If the company is not handicapped-friendly, will someone who loses their physical abilities lose their job, even if they are still able to fulfill their job functions? It happens. Famous theoretical physicist

Stephen Hawking is not a *jock*.

Wages of People Hired

If a company consistently pays below market wages, then the company sends a strong message to employees, customers, creditors, and suppliers. Even if it may seem good business to *hire the mostest for the leastest*, people talk. If you hire an outstanding employee at substandard wages, that employee is not going to perform optimally . . . at least for long. If people are not paid what they know they are worth, they will leave, and let others know how poorly they were treated. The company will find their selection of top talent dwindling . . . until what they are able to hire will be worth exactly what they are willing to pay.

Salary surveys in industry publications and those on-line reveal the range, median, and sometimes mean of wage levels for specific job functions. In times of high unemployment, a company may take advantage of the market inequality. However, taking advantage of employees by paying low salaries and benefits catches up.

When wages stay low after the economy has recovered, highly talented workers will look elsewhere. When those who are hired later receive higher wages than those with equivalent skills who were hired during more difficult times, loyalty of those left behind evaporates. And why wouldn't it? Paying low wages during harder times may be necessary for survival. But, consistently paying low wages and ignoring the loyalty of workers who have been willing to stick by the company at low wages while, at the same time, inflating the wages of new workers, is disrespectful. Ultimately, the experienced, disgruntled employees will leave, no matter the job market.

Low wages mean people are a low priority and the company does not play fairly. Consistently paying low wages is another critical item.

Use of Executive Recruiters

Some companies use recruiters to find candidates for senior- or executive-level positions. These organizations want a third-party to independently identify and assess candidates before moving forward with the hiring process. In some industries, notably Wall Street, contact through a recruiter is required for many positions. Wall Streeters are busy and feel their time is better spent doing tasks other than searching through hundreds of résumés to find a candidate for a single job opening.

There is a downside to the use of recruiters. Watch for well-known companies which use recruiters to lure employees to their headquarters because local employees acutely know the company's poor hiring and firing reputation. **Use of recruiters to hire executives to join a company with a poor HR reputation is another critical item.**

Use the Internet to conduct research on the company; look at what employees, ex-employees, clients, suppliers, independent analysts, and the media have to say about the organization and its people.

Use of Web-Based Job Posting Sites

It is easy for applicants to check on-line to see which organizations post job openings on virtually every job search website. HR departments know the strengths and weaknesses of each job site, whether international, national, regional, or local in scope. Effective use of the right job site(s) requires that someone in the HR department make a decision. **If a company's HR department takes a scattered approach to find qualified candidates, then the firm's mission, organization, internal communication, and promotional activities are likewise scattered.**

Job Posting Warning Signs

Be aware of questionable job postings. Monster Worldwide Inc. identified seven warning signs to identify questionable job postings. They are:

1) The job posting is months old or has been reposted numerous times. The position may not exist, the company has a terrible reputation as an employer, or the company is collecting information about the current employment market.

2) The post does not identify the name of the organization. Why would a reputable firm not identify itself? Are they recruiting for a position of someone who they plan to let go?

3) The job post instructs you to fax your resume to a phone number. Fax? The organization is stuck in the past.

4) The post includes phrases such as "must be very hardworking" or "must be able to work in highly successful environments." The organization will own you—no work-life balance.

5) The post lists a salary range up to $200K, $400K, or $500K per year. This is a commissioned sales job, no matter what someone tells you.

6) The job listing asks you to send sensitive information—social security number, bank account number, credit score, family information, government-issued license numbers, military information, or political or religious information. Requesting this level of personal information is inappropriate at this early stage of the employment application process.

7) The job post asks you to divulge names of contacts at companies with whom you have done business. This firm is not hiring; it is fishing for information. Again, this is not appropriate at an early stage of the employment process.

What is the Rate of Employee Turnover?

To learn this important metric, you must do extensive research. Find articles or statistics from charts or tables that compare turnover at this company/organization/firm with the turnover at key competitors. For example, in the fast food industry, turnover of 80% to 150% a year is common. Try to learn what steps the organization takes to reduce employee turnover, cut training time and cost, minimize the expense of bringing new employees on board and, most importantly, create an environment where the employees want to stay.

If the rate is significantly higher at the prospective employer, then beware. High turnover happens for many reasons:

Employee issues

- Poor quality applicant pool

- Less than optimal hiring choices

- Poor training and working conditions

- Vague definition of expectations and objectives

Organizational issues

- Unclear policies and procedures

- Blatant favoritism toward *old timer* employees

- Outright sexism

- Hidden discrimination

- Undefined promotional paths

- Questionable or illegal corporate behavior

Management issues

- Poorly-structured management (lines of reporting, responsibility, and accountability)

- Constant changes to scheduled work shifts

- Unfair work expectations (e.g., extensive overtime with less-than-full remuneration in time off or pay)

All issues listed are signs of corporate dysfunction—the organization does not care about its employees. **An organization's rate of employee turnover far greater than the industry average is another important item.**

Can You Detect Evidence of High Employee Turnover?

Businessweek magazine published an article that stated, over the past few years, Wal-Mart's employee turnover fell from approximately 150% a year to 80% a year. At that time, company ads said it was a great place to work and you could reach your potential working there. I view 80% turnover as a sign that, unless this company can contribute directly to an increase in the birth rate, Wal-Mart will run out of potential employees in less than 20 years.

One warning sign is the use of technology in response to a fundamental flaw in the company's business model. Wal-Mart prides itself on its ability to offer items at low cost due to its logistical and distribution capabilities, not on its ability to select and price items most desired by its customers. Maintaining satisfied employees and customers has been an on-going challenge for Wal-Mart in what it perceives as a logistics-oriented business. A focus on logistics negates the need to focus on staff for recognition, growth, and personal development. It also fails to recognize today's customer need for a certain amount of hand-holding, information, and acknowledgement.

Wal-Mart's claimed logistics expertise is in direct conflict with what is required to have motivated employees and satisfied customers in a retail environment. Wal-Mart's organizational strategy helps to firmly establish an institutionalized attitude of our-people-don't-really-count; fully-stocked-shelves-count.

Inappropriate Role of HR in the Hiring Process

For non-managerial jobs, it is appropriate that HR screen the applicants and pass a list of qualified candidates to the hiring manager. If the company tests applicants, HR should administer the tests. If the company uses an industrial psychologist to interview candidates (I know of one!), the HR department should coordinate the results and analysis of all interviews.

For managerial and senior-level individual contributor jobs, applicants usually contact the hiring director, vice president, COO, or CEO directly or through a common contact. In this case, HR's involvement would be minimal. The hiring executives know the kind of person and the qualifications they seek. At this level, despite solid job descriptions, HR professionals' do not excel at matching job requirements with applicants' résumés. This relatively poor record reflects equally on:

- The hiring manager's inability to understand in depth the nature of the work

- The hiring manager's inability to delineate qualifications and translate the job description into a job posting

- The hiring manager's inability to interpret resume contents and reconcile job requirements with applicants' abilities

- HR professionals' inability to ask hiring managers the right questions

- Recruiters' inability to learn the unstated requirements or characteristics, and to interpret corporate cultures

After the hiring manager receives a list of qualified candidates, which HR will have culled by verifying résumé information, contacting references, and conducting thorough background checks, the manager should schedule sufficient time to thoroughly interview each candidate. Departmental coworkers and managers with whom the candidate will interact need to be included in the interview process.

No matter how experienced the interviewer, a good interview requires about one hour. It is not possible to compress a 60-minute necessary exchange of information into 30 minutes. Plus, the additional time permits the candidate to get past the first impression phase, either slipping into areas of incompetency or exhibiting professional depth.

The finalist candidates should also have the opportunity to ask questions and to meet with their potential peers, whether in the same department or in departments with which they will work closely. The manager may get along fine with the candidate; however, co-workers need a simpatico person as well.

The dysfunction occurs when HR is involved at every step of the *new employee selection process*, **no matter how trivial the step.** Remember, HR will not work with the new employee; the managers and the co-workers in the hiring department will. Each department has its own tone and tenor—HR cannot possibly determine the best candidate for every department. Those in the department, not human resources, should determine the applicant's fit with the job, peers, and managers.

Watch for the HR department's over-involvement in the *hiring* **process, another critical item.** An overly involved HR department signals a lack of confidence in hiring managers, a politically-driven motivation by the head of HR to gain equal footing with executives with operating responsibilities, or a meddlesome person whose invasive activity has been institutionalized.

The next three items may not become apparent until the employee has accepted the offer and reported for work, which makes these particularly dangerous. If an employee can avoid getting into a bad situation where survival may require leaving almost as soon as getting the job, s/he has a better chance of building a smooth career path. People who earn reputations as job-hoppers are quite often individuals who have not learned to recognize the early danger signals and end up employed at companies with the following career-busting policies:

Poor or Non-Existent Employee Orientation or Job-Specific Training

Each company approaches its workload, specific tasks, and administrative requirements in a different way. A new employee, aware of the requirements of the job, must nevertheless receive specific training in the tasks, workflow, and key restrictions and requirements for her/his position. Corporate policies, hierarchy-based constraints, communication styles, and performance expectations should be available, in either print or online documentation. The level of detail will depend on company size and position scope.

Effective companies will hire the candidates they believe best fit the positions they are attempting to fill. In order to ensure employee success, these companies need to train and indoctrinate new employees in:

- Company culture
- Organizational values
- Key rules and regulations
- Specific actions prohibited by regulatory requirements

- Warnings about forms of sexual harassment

- Procedures to sign up for benefits

- Past celebrated events and milestones (significant corporate history)

- Short- and long-term corporate goals.

Training and New Employee Indoctrination is a Critical Item

The employee had to make a good impression before s/he was hired. Now it is the company's turn. Presenting the above information to a group of incoming employees is an efficient investment of a large company's time and human/training resources. Most importantly, this step starts the employee's assimilation process.

Excessive or Unrealistic Performance Measurements

In the finance industry, one would expect commissions generated to be the key performance measure. After all, it *is* all about money. However, one Wall Street firm set 10 quarterly performance measurement criteria for equity research analysts, specifically:

- Number of pages of investment research published per quarter

- Number of phone calls to **A** level client accounts

- Number of phone calls to **B** level client accounts

- Number of phone calls to **C** level client accounts

- Number of visits to **A** level client accounts

- Number of visits to **B** level client accounts

- Number of visits to **C** level client accounts

- Commission dollars generated

- Performance of individual stocks the analyst followed against a pre-selected peer group of stocks

- Research *votes* from key customers

SMART goal-setting requires goals to be specific, measurable, attainable, realistic, and timely. With no quantifiable numbers attached to the performance criteria, the stated goals were useless. As guidelines for activity, they only told the analysts *what* needed to be done, but not *how much*. At quarterly staff meetings, the department manager berated all 24 analysts for the few goals they invariably failed to complete to satisfaction—despite most meeting nearly every other (to them invisible) goal. After a few meetings, one analyst crafted a parody of what the manager would say at the next quarterly review. Predictably, the analyst's script mirrored the manager's tirade.

Instead of feeling chastised, the analysts listening to the admonishment were silently ticking off the points their co-worker had predicted. The manager used the measurement system to abuse his staff, who now *knew* his game. **Realistic and attainable performance measurement is a critical item. Unfortunately, you have no way of knowing about this until you start work.**

To avoid these problems, ask before you accept the job offer about new employee orientation, employee training, and job performance measurement.

Forced Ranking, then Automatically Firing the Bottom 10% of Performers Every Year

Applying a minimal amount of strategic HR-sounding spin, the concept of firing the lowest-performing 10% of your employees makes sense. This action is sensible if the organization is one making a largely similar staple product sold by others, offers minimal investment in employees through training or skills upgrades, may be family-owned where it is highly likely extended family members hold all supervisory and management positions, and has a low wage structure compared to the prevailing industry and local averages.

Microsoft provides another good example of dysfunctional HR practices. Andrew Hill's column in the July 17, 2012, issue of the *Financial Times* noted that, during its lost decade (2000-2010), Microsoft used a similar system— teams were divided into a 70-20-10 ratio for six-month performance reviews. The bottom 10% received smaller pay increases and fewer opportunities for promotion. According to Hill's interviews with ex-employees, this system was considered the most destructive process inside of Microsoft. It would be fair and reasonable to say employees planned their work days around the review process, not on creating new and maintaining existing products.

Friendly advice: Question everything. *Do not accept any corporate policies as positive unless you can see direct benefits.*

Forced Ranking—Up or Out

Organizations in management consulting, investment and commercial banking, and law practice what is known as *up or out*. Under this HR system, new employees are expected to be promoted within two to three years or they will be asked to leave the firm. The practice has been adopted in the U.S. military, where officers passed over two times for promotion are asked to leave the branch of service.

The firms which practice this are generally leading firms in highly competitive, intellectually demanding businesses where long hours are the norm, not the exception. New hires are typically summa or magna cum laude graduates of good schools and many have been inducted into Phi Beta Kappa, the liberal arts honorary society, or Beta Gamma Sigma, the business honorary society. I describe this HR model so a qualified job seeker enters such environments with no illusions. Many of these highly competitive environments expect a high percentage of undergraduate hires to leave after two to three years to return to graduate school. By establishing such a policy, the firm also retains its prestige and minimizes financial losses to the firm.

Quibbling with Employees over Relocation Expense Money

Many companies promise to pay employee relocation costs. Most companies are aware of the ballpark cost of relocating an employee and the family. If an organization, for whatever reason, refuses to pay all reasonable moving expenses, the company is not concerned about its employees. Management's focus is on money and their end-of-year bonuses, not on the people who generate the revenue. Unfortunately, you learn of this after you are hired, when the company decides that some, or all, of your moving costs are unreasonable or excessive.

If you expect to be reimbursed for relocation costs, make sure you get the agreement in writing as part of the offer letter.

Identify Technological Improvements that make the Workplace Safer

Did the company or certain locations of the company report a relatively high number of accidents or safety violations? Dangerous-to-operate equipment in a fast food restaurant's seemingly benign work environment can contribute to higher insurance rates. Installation of safety guards on equipment, built-in brakes, or dead man switches can reduce the risks of serious injuries. Most manufacturing environments have installed some type of operational override; the more obvious sign of dysfunction is if the organization did not install safety-related devices.

Does the Company Invest in its Staff to Improve Employee Productivity?

Companies generally do not invest in new equipment, methods, or training unless they expect a measurable improvement in return. The most important payback, possibly more important than safety, is employee productivity—more output per person-hour for the same level of effort. Do productivity improvements help employees *work smarter, not harder*?

Today most organizations want new employees to have already received some training in their targeted business function. By setting a higher bar, organizations need make no investment in entry-level skills, thereby saving money. Does the organization offer remedial or focused training classes to employees so they may gain needed skills? The company's offer to pay tuition for classes at a local or on-line school is admirable; however, the organization that offers tailored classes shows a real commitment to its employees and business.

Can You Uncover Safety Violations?

Safety violations can be difficult to uncover due to the scarcity of publicly available information. You could request records from the appropriate government agency/agencies under the Freedom of Information Act. However, by the time the written response from the government or organization arrived, you would probably be working for a different employer or the hiring organization's need for your skill set might have long disappeared. Alternatively, you could research stories about a company's accident rate in local newspapers, on blogs, or on government websites. If you find enough of these articles, then obviously something at the organization is amiss.

If safety violations and accident rates are high, management does not truly care about its employees. Their attitude is, "So what? We can always find someone new." That is . . . until they get sued or their insurance rates become insufferably high.

Is increased productivity the dominant metric? The mantra of *more, faster* needs to be examined in terms of tradeoffs. Indicators of productivity improvement tradeoffs include:

- An increasing accident rate

- Increased employee turnover

- A dramatic increase in unexcused absenteeism

- Office supply cabinets empty of relatively expensive office-related items, since employees feel empowered to supplement their meager wages

- Incredible nit-picking by the accounting department for employees (not executives) on every expense item shown for company travel

- Negligence in restroom and facility repair and maintenance
- Weed-filled landscape, debris, untrimmed shrubs, dead trees, bare patches in the lawn

GENERAL ELECTRIC—A SPECIAL CASE

Jack Welch instituted the practice of firing the lowest performing 10% of employees when he was Chairman/CEO at General Electric (GE). If a company such as GE truly recruits excellent employees, why would it want to fire *any* percentage of so-called low performers? The lowest performing 10% at a company with GE's reputation for hiring the best is statistically way above the performance of most employees at other firms. Why whack 10%? Why does the company not terminate the lowest-performing 15%, 20%, or only 5%? GE's board of directors is singular for buying into and espousing ex-CEO Jack Welch's nonsensical approach to HR for as long as it did. Here's why this is a unique situation. GE:

- manufactures a number of complex technology-based products (indeed, CFL and LED light bulbs and locomotives are high-tech)
- recruits top students from top colleges and universities
- invests extensively through a highly-regarded in-house education program for new and experienced employees, especially college grads selected for its highly-rated finance training program
- broadens managers' knowledge and career growth by rotating them through challenging assignments

The key is GE hires top candidates. Why would *any* organization summarily dismiss the supposed lowest-performing 10%, especially one with a reputation for hiring the best talent—and nurturing their careers? What is the likely result? A few options for employees come to mind:

- constant behind-the-scenes politicking so one is not perceived as a member of the bottom 10%
- creation of cabals that work together to *nominate* hapless souls as members of the infamous 10%
- the likely possibility that, as in the so-called reality television show Survivor, the candidates posing the strongest challenges to others are the first to be voted *off the island* or relegated to the bottom-performing 10%

- Shabby corporate identification and directional signs

- Deteriorating facility, including roof, walls, foundation, windows, and doors

- Inadequate security

If you see an unpainted, poorly-lit parking lot, crumbling pavement and/or sidewalks, deferred maintenance, ignored safety issues, and evidence of failure to provide necessary *tools*, then the company is paying a high, albeit hidden, price for its increased productivity. For the excuses or explanations they can offer, sad to say, executive management simply may not care or is cheap. In this case, management bonuses are likely linked directly to monies saved.

- much covering of one's executive butt to ensure Jack Welch doesn't negatively call you out at meetings in front of others.

What can we learn from this backward system? **The main take-away is that GE does not trust its hiring process.** If the firm truly believed in the hires it made, then the percentage of folks who don't work out for whatever reason should be very, very low—at most 1 to 3 percent. Adding an extra 7 to 9 percent to arrive at the artificial level of 10 percent is wasteful—and backward—and counterintuitive to any organization's strategic HR goals. **Could we also say GE does not fully trust its employees? Could we say there was a military-like tiered employee structure? Might we say upward communications were carefully managed? May we add it was all about image?**

What else can we learn? Despite propaganda about strong executive development and decision-making at lower levels in the GE organization, **this corporate policy breeds an employee attitude of fear.** In fearful environments, employees make poor decisions. Fearful employees will focus efforts on minimizing adverse evaluations in performance reviews, rather than on doing their jobs to the best of their abilities. **Within the common employee ranks, expect considerable turmoil.** Turmoil includes acts such as sabotage. Co-worker sabotage includes hoarding/hiding necessary documents that are meant for use by another individual or small group; not sending colleagues emails conveying important information; snide comments to the supervisory manager or, if working in a matrix structure, the supervisor's manager; and, when meeting with clients, subtle digs at co-workers where the co-worker is unable to respond.

~~*

Organization Charts

At the most basic level, a company's organization chart can reveal a great deal. Here is what to look for:

First, count the number of CEOs!

Some companies have a dual-CEO structure. Royal Dutch Shell and Unilever, both with dual headquarters in London and The Netherlands, actually have two CEOs. It is fine for an organization to have a single CEO and, say, two lower-ranking presidents. However, an organization can have only one commander-in-chief or Chief Executive Officer (CEO). Two isn't good; a committee of three equal co-presidents or co-CEOs smacks of an inability to make any decision or, worse, the need for two of the three to manage the third. Imagine all the 2-1 votes on key decisions. What a waste! Such needless complexity!

Count the number of executive VPs (EVPs), senior VPs (SVPs), and VPs

A company needs to organize its functions and divisional/departmental interrelationships. It is fair to ask: Is this the best way to organize? Was this reporting structure established to build or maintain existing relationships among the executives? Did the board and/or CEO set this structure to provide better opportunities for certain executives?

It is also fair to count the number of people who report to every executive. An effective executive or manager generally cannot have more than seven or eight direct reports.

Compare number and level of EVPs, SVPs, and VPs with those of similar-size competitors

If a company has many more executives than its key competitors, then I expect to find a few substandard metrics. Operating expenses will be higher, communication will be impeded or ineffective, the company's reaction time will be slower than competitors with fewer executives at similar levels, more *empires* or internal silos will be built and zealously guarded, real decision-making authority will concentrate in the hands of a few executives, and the company will not welcome input from outside. **The number of VPs compared to competitors is critical—more VPs translates to slower event reaction, more time needed to coordinate, more empire building and protection, more concentrated decision making, and more exclusive acceptance of only those ideas which are internally generated.**

If no competitors of a similar size exist, then create a new metric called *number of executives per million/billion dollars in revenue.* The calculation is straightforward—divide annual revenue by the total number of executives listed in the annual report or SEC Form 10-K for each competitor. Compare the results. Companies with the lowest revenue per executive will exhibit the characteristics described above.

Look for any major changes to the organization chart

Note these specific items:

- More operating divisions, each with a separate division president

- Changes in key executive titles, such as adding the title of executive or senior vice president to a previously existing functional title. An example would be renaming the Director of Marketing as the Executive Director of Marketing without any apparent increase in responsibilities.

- Changes in the proportion of executive line positions to staff positions. Line positions include operations/production, engineering/design, marketing, and sales. Staff positions include finance, information technology (IT), legal, accounting, human resources (HR), any compliance-related activity, billing, and public relations. **A decrease in line positions and/or an increase in staff positions shouts of excess, bloat, fat, or confusion.**

Change, in and of itself, is okay. The challenge is to determine the nature of the changes or to identify the changes that most likely yield negative effects for the organization, the employees, or the customers.

Executive Titles

A person's title on his/her business card should quickly tell the recipient what the person does at the organization. Although advances in electronics and communications have changed many job functions, titles should nevertheless be clear. A confused sounding title reflects confusion in the organization.

An example of a high-level title with *fluffy-sounding* responsibilities?— *Managing Director, Diversity Strategies and Talent Development.* In the spirit of military acronyms, this title makes the person sound as though s/he is *RIP*— Retired In Place—and literally due to soon retire from the organization.

Unique titles may be functional. Guy Kawasaki held the position of *Chief Evangelist* at Apple Computer in the mid-1980s. At the time, Mr. Kawasaki's job was to convince third-party, or independent, hardware and software developers to create new products or write new programs for Apple's revolutionary Macintosh computer. At that time, the number and type of ancillary hardware products and third-party software programs that ran on a particular computer were key factors for success in the personal computer industry. Mr. Kawasaki was an effective sales representative for Apple; mission accomplished in four years.

The title, Fellow, is appropriate. In technology companies, a very talented senior employee with extensive technical knowledge is awarded this title. As a Fellow, that person remains involved in the technical workings of the company's products, but holds no managerial responsibilities.

Other interesting, questionable, or fun titles include:

- President and Chief Imagination Officer, Chief Sparkle Officer, Beervangelist (New Holland Brewing Company)

- Director of First Impressions (the receptionist; companies unnamed)

- Chief Fun Officer (Cohen Architectural Woodworking)

- Director of Culture Activities (Southwest Airlines)

- Director of Chaos (Berkshire-Hathaway Corporation, New Holland Brewing Company)

- Chief Troublemaker (web design firm, Matrix Group)

Sometimes jacked-up titles are compensatory for poor wages. Other unusual titles reflect a company's unique corporate culture—or the quirky nature of the individual holding the title. However, these unusual titles are equivalent to inside jokes—and, as such, reflect an internal focus.

Ineffective Business Card Layout and Content

A business card that overemphasizes the name and title of the executive and diminishes the name of the business or organization is a warning sign. As important as the executive may be, the fact is, s/he is part of a much larger business entity.

How Many Executives or Staff Members Report Directly to the CEO?

In some companies, as many as 15 subordinates may report to a more senior manager or executive. This is untenable. Even the most skilled executive or manager, and even the most experienced CEO cannot deal effectively with more than seven or eight direct reports. Beyond that, adding more fancy-titled executives or creating division-level presidents only increases operating expenses.

In some instances, companies may find it necessary to add an extra position in order to retain a well-qualified, experienced executive. It becomes a

---

A MOST REVEALING BUSINESS CARD DESIGN

I had picked up and analyzed a business card from a now-defunct ceramic studio, where customers bought green ware, smoothed it, painted it, and then fired it in a kiln. The store used a clever graphic—a circular pot with an artist's paintbrush sticking out the top alongside the name of the business.

What was the business card's most significant element? Front and center, the CEO's name, in 10 or 12 point semi-bold sans serif type, with *Owner* on the second line. The store name, street address, city, state, and ZIP followed on the next line in 6- or 8-point type. The store used a third sans serif type font, this one boldface, for the telephone number with the fax number next to its telephone number in 6- or 8-point type. The business card did not include a website link or an email address.

The messages were clear: **Everything revolved around the owner, not the business.** The confusing business card accurately reflected this person's scattered, incomplete approach to her business. When I looked into the business, I validated this observation. The owner had to control *everything*, reminiscent of the hub-and-spoke management style identified previously.

In addition, this person proved untrustworthy and unethical. She wanted to start a business selling ergonomic office furniture and accessories and needed immediate help with a business plan to present to lending institutions. Since I knew her as a dependable health insurance client and the project was on a very tight schedule, I waived my customary initial payment of 50% of the estimated project fee. In meetings, she, her father, her sister, and the operations manager praised the layout, flow, and content of the business plan. I worked extended hours to quickly complete this project, then delivered the final product. Jennifer claimed it was not what she wanted and refused to pay. I later learned that she pulled the same stunt with a second consultant. **It is not only about her; she does not value others' expertise nor deal with them as professionals. She is also a crook; she steals people's time and ideas.** I learned later that her ergonomic products business never got off the ground.

~~*

matter of degree—and functional efficiency. A company with seven operating divisions in similar lines of business, each headed by its own president and pyramid-shaped executive structure, shouts *corporate bloat* in seven languages.

Summary

This chapter examined in detail an organization's HR function and identified the many ways this seemingly innocuous department can contribute to organizational dysfunction. Look for employee backgrounds which do not fit the function for which they were hired. Consistently low employee wages will backfire on the company; paying low wages translates to shabby treatment of a company's supposedly most valuable resource. High turnover occurs for a number of reasons: an overly-challenging job, low wages, vague requirements, constantly changing hours, required overtime, lack of effective training, safety issues, poor management and supervision, a hostile environment, and lack of management support when dealing with customer complaints. Cheaply printed business cards and business cards that emphasize the name of the business owner over the name of the business also shout *misplaced emphasis*.

Other potentially dysfunctional aspects of HR include setting unrealistic or undefined performance measurements, forced employee ranking and low-rank firing, and withholding new hire moving expense payments. A key indicator of HR malfunction is the over-involvement by the HR department in decisions to hire executives or senior-level officers.

An organization chart reveals other signs of dysfunction. Compare the number and titles of executives with those of a couple key competitors; look at the number and level of persons who report directly to each executive. Weird titles and an excessive number of direct reports indicate organizational suckiness.

~*~*~*~

CHAPTER 13

ENRON—
MORE WARNING SIGNS

Thus far, we have examined mismanagement foibles at a number of companies . . . and how these can lead to dysfunction and disaster. Are these corporate disasters happenstance or predictable? Did Enron suddenly implode over a two- or three-month period? Or did the company provide subtle clues well in advance of its implosion that all was not right?

Indeed, the company provided many subtle clues about its culture of excess. The movie, *Enron: The Smartest Guys in the Room*, gave us a chance to play armchair detectives, observing and unraveling the thread of corporate dysfunction.

Many of the clues were available to the public during Enron's years in the 1990s as a corporate rock star. Wall Street financial analysts might have foreseen problems, but they apparently didn't. The business press fawned over the company and its leaders.

But the clues were there, fixed neatly in five categories:

- backgrounds and public actions of leaders

- political influence

- finance

- other observations, and

- ethical situations.

Backgrounds and Public Actions of Leaders

- The Chairman, Ken Lay, who had a PhD in economics, lobbied aggressively in Washington, DC for legislation to deregulate the less-than-fully-defined energy market

- In early ads for Enron, Ken Lay stated, "I am Enron."

- Skilling was basically a very smart nerd with thick glasses and a receding hairline; to change his image, Skilling had LASIK surgery, eliminating the need to wear glasses.

- In early interviews, Lay described Jeff Skilling as a "man with the biggest ideas."

- In interviews, Skilling did not know or would not provide answers to basic questions.

- Executives famously could not provide a simple answer to a business magazine reporter's fundamental question, "How does Enron make its money?"

- One of the executives who resigned early became the second largest landowner in Colorado and married a stripper after fathering a son. While he was at Enron, this executive's division lost $1 billion.

Political Influence

- Enron was the largest contributor to the presidential campaign of George W. Bush.

- Ken Lay had easy access to Bush; he also met with Vice President Dick Cheney.

Finance

- Enron created a market to trade *data communication and telecommunication bandwidth,* where excess bandwidth could be sold to other companies.

- The company used relatively conservative mark-to-market accounting practices for transactions with above-average economic and financial risk. Although the accounting practice was conservative, Enron's market valuations of securities and other assets were not.

- Its required cash flow statements did not make sense.

- The company's published tax rate was extremely low; no executive could easily explain why.

- Enron created many small companies and limited partnerships to add to the complex challenge to *follow the money*.

- The company used its inflated stock as collateral for loans.

Other Observations

- Macho culture—trips to Baja California where employees raced motorcycles and jeeps in the desert (one man was nearly killed).

- Enron's stock price was posted in the elevator.

- "Make Money" (to the exclusion of all else).

- Motivational posters emphasized four messages—respect, integrity, communication, excellence.

- Management *gurus* described Enron's corporate culture as "genius for innovation" and "capacity for revolution."

- Coffee mugs included the printed slogan, "Endless Possibilities."

Ethical Situations

- Traders involved in a 1987 Enron scandal about energy in Valhalla, NY, were neither held fully accountable nor punished.

- Investment banks that employed equity or fixed income research analysts skeptical of Enron's reported financial results were cut off from potential investment banking business.

Summary

It's not any single item or category of observations that reveal the nature and degree of dysfunction; it's the combination of factors that present a clear, convincing case. Here were two smart, highly-educated, somewhat geeky leaders who would not or could not provide answers to basic questions. These leaders, through political contributions, ultimately gained access to and protection through the president of the United States.

We identified five unacceptable finance-related practices including cash flow statements that did not make sense. We identified a corporate culture based on money and extreme risk; Enron posted its stock price in the elevator as a constant reminder to employees and visitors of the *most* important organizational culture factor, in spite of the more moderate messages on motivational posters. The motivational posters may have represented a diversion to visitors to the firm who would see responsible-sounding goals on the posters—not "make money." "Endless possibilities," imprinted on the coffee mugs, says only that the sky's the limit. The methods used to get Enron to where it was would indeed make the sky the limit.

Investors and the public received in advance the 23 clues listed above about Enron's dysfunction. Admittedly, one had to visit the offices to learn of the physical layout and scope, as well as the dysfunctional use of motivational posters. Nevertheless, until 2001, Lay and Skilling's elaborate Kabuki-like dance cleverly distracted investors, many equity (stock) research analysts, most fixed income (bond) analysts, a number of analysts at bond rating agencies, and the public from identifying signs of dysfunction and putting them together. In reality, Enron sent a steady stream of clues all along.

Unfortunately, this group of clues are offered in 20/20 hindsight. Enron is the perfect anti-organization to demonstrate the value of these tools and techniques.

~*~*~*~

CHAPTER 14

BUILDING EXTERIOR

Thus far, we have perused companies *from a distance*. Let's look at the up-close clues that will help you evaluate companies.

Your visit to the company, school, government agency, military unit, regulatory agency, or non-profit organization is the most important part of the evaluation process. Multiple inputs will bombard each of your senses. You may be anxious or concerned about your meeting. You want the meeting to go well.

At this confusing time, you *must* step back; take yourself out of the immediate situation and calm the associated emotions, then heighten each of your senses so you are better aware of your environment. Pay attention and make a mental or written note of your findings. It is indeed a challenge! Here are the evaluative factors to check, various ways to put them together, and how to interpret them.

We will discuss each topic in order . . . and in detail, working from the outside of the building to the reception area, kitchen or cafeteria, then restrooms, through the hallways, to the worker's cubicles, then into the executive offices.

But first . . . the exterior.

Exterior

Check the following:

- Location and elevation
- Guard house
- Signage and logo
- Appearance in front of building
- Appearance in back of building
- Company-owned vehicles

Location, Elevation, and Access

- *Is the location appropriate to the type of business?* If this is a retail business, is it located on a busy thoroughfare? Is a wholesale business located in a large building, in a warehouse, or in a light manufacturing district? Is a tax preparer, a personal and business service provider, located in a storefront, a house, or an office building?

- *Are there visual or physical barriers obstructing access to the front of the building?* The front of a business need not be barren. However, locations with constant commercial tenant turnover usually have one or more significant barriers that visually separate the business from the street. Barriers include:

  o   tall bushes

  o   an excessive number or height or density of trees; also trees located too close to the building

  o   a lawn space that is wider than that of neighboring businesses giving a literal and mental feeling of distance between the organization and its customers

  o   the building is located farther back than adjacent buildings. Although customers may have more parking spaces in front, the extra physical distance from the street creates an additional mental distance to the entrance.

  o   the main entrance driveway is off to one side or shared with an adjoining business

  o   a section of sidewalk in front of the business is *protected* against unknown vehicular threats by a two- or three-foot high metal railing

- *Elevation:* Street level or lower is preferable since you can look into the property. A higher elevation creates a visual barrier, since you must look up to see the property and, most likely, cannot see all of the property. Eye level or slightly below eye level looks best.

- *Entrance—style of door:* The choices include carved wood, plain wood, metal, or glass. Visually, glass provides the most open and welcoming look. This type of door may be clear, stained-glass, etched with a design, frosted, or sandwich glass with an internal wire grid. Revolving doors are a variation of glass door. Automatically opening doors . . . or ones with electronic handicap-access openers . . . are usually glass and are likewise welcoming.

Stand outside the building. If you can see into the building, either through glass doors or glass windows adjacent to the doors and the lights are on, the likelihood is, the company is open for business. Opaque doors leave the visitor guessing whether the business is open . . . or even if s/he has found the right door.

A wooden door outside an office building with security patrol or cameras sends a message of *closed off*. A stained glass insert may be a nice touch; however, the insert is most likely in a wooden door, with its implications of a closed, less than welcoming organization.

- *Practical additions:* An awning or overhang to reduce sun, rain, or snow is a thoughtful touch. If it is clean and in good repair, then add a point. Otherwise, if not in good condition, call it what it is—another sign of organizational dysfunction.

- *Accommodations for the physically disabled:* The business should provide sufficient designated parking spaces, wheelchair ramp or ramps, and an ADA-approved width front door. **If not present, this is a warning sign. Except in the case of designated historical buildings, Federal law requires certain architectural adjustments to accommodate the disabled.**

- *Smoking area:* Has the company established its employee smoking area just outside the front door? This practice ensures that visitors are forced to walk through an area where people are actively smoking or past an area stinking of stale tobacco . . . and indicates a total lack of regard for guests and non-smoking employees. The smoking area should be at least 25 feet from the front door; visitors should not have to walk through the smoking area to enter the premises.

Guard House

With this new era of security consciousness, the company may have a guard posted at the main visitor entrance.

- Does the guard ask you for a standard form of identification?

- If required, did your prospective manager or customer advise the guard of your visit?

- If the company required you to submit written approval to the guard, did your prospective manager or customer or the administrator send the required document to you well in advance of your visit? If you forget or misplace this document, how does the guard handle the situation?

- Is the guard professional in demeanor and appearance?
- Does the guard note the license number of your automobile?

If the answer to any of the above questions is "no," you have a quick and early warning of dysfunction. If the guard does not note your automobile license number, then why have a guard? You could just as easily drop off the admittance form at the receptionist's desk.

If the company employs a guard, then that person should be tasked with professional requirements such as verifying identification and documenting your time of arrival and departure, license number, and make of automobile. **If the company employs a security guard, this is a critical item. The act of having a guard implies both a sense of caution and the desire to look like a *real* company or, in extreme cases, a sense of paranoia.**

Sign and Logo

After you assess the building's elevation, location, and visual barriers, then look at the company sign and logo.

- Is the company sign freshly painted or in good repair?
- Is the company's sign surrounded by overgrown grass or weeds?
- Is the sign easy to read? Does the company use difficult-to-read letters and font sizes for its name? Remember, the name should be visible from a relatively far distance.
- Does the company logo reinforce the nature of its business? In an extreme example, I would not expect to see anything automobile-related on a sign for a beauty spa. More realistically, I do not expect a pest control service with lightning bolts in its logo, or a high-end, modern beauty salon/spa with its name shown in an old-fashioned type font, such as Times New Roman or worse, Old English.

In Front of the Building

Look around before you walk in to identify exterior clues about a company's dysfunction, values, and culture.

- Does the company provide reserved parking spaces for senior executives? In this outwardly egalitarian era, no one should have a reserved parking space near the building entrance. If you want a parking space near the front door, then arrive at the office no later than, say, 6:30 AM. **If you see reserved parking spaces for the executives, this is a significant warning of dysfunction, since it represents different treatment of a select class of employee.**

- Does the company provide sufficient spaces for disabled employees and visitors? Do the lines for each space painted comply with federal requirements? Is the required blue sign posted at the front of disabled parking spaces? Is each space sufficiently wide to accommodate a van with a side ramp for use by a wheelchair occupant? Is the ramp to the sidewalk conveniently located relative to the disabled parking spaces? Are these spaces located nearest to the front door? The Americans with Disabilities (ADA) took effect in 1990. Twenty plus years is plenty of time for organizations to comply with ADA requirements. Ignorance of the law is no excuse. This omission shows a cavalier disregard for a group of employees or visitors, shows the organization does not truly practice equal hiring, and is rigidly hierarchical.

- Has a non-disabled executive or visitor parked their car in a space designated for disabled persons? This criterion may seem unnecessary. However, I went to a meeting with the CEO of a local mortgage finance company. Two spaces designated for the disabled were located outside the front door. He parked his Porsche Carrera diagonally across the two spaces. Before we shook hands, I already knew with what I would be dealing. After our second meeting, I terminated our business relationship. **Any non-disabled employee, especially an executive, who parks in a space designated for disabled employees or physically challenged visitors sends a critical warning.** With this single act, the executive communicates:

o   The rules do not apply to me

o   I am better than others

o   I value my automobile more than I value others' abilities and/or disabilities

o   I cannot or do not keep my word

o   I do not return phone calls within a reasonable time unless I want something from you

- o I am an *operator*, looking to get something for nothing from others

- Is a parking space near the front door reserved for an *Employee of the Month*? That is fine. However, it should be the sole reserved employee parking space at an otherwise egalitarian, 21st century company.

- Watch for burned out or broken exterior lights, especially those in safety-related locations such as the parking lot, parking garage (especially stairwells), side or back of the building, or rear entrance. Once again, burned out or broken exterior lights evidence of a lack of caring for the welfare and safety of its employees. The company is certain to pay its liability insurance premiums, since such careless acts and others will likely lead to a greater-than-expected number of claims and a third-party helps pay the penalty.

- Is the grass cut? Do garden areas display freshly-planted, well-maintained seasonal flowers? How many weeds are in the flowerbeds and how high have they grown? A well-manicured landscape shows pride and provides a good first impression.

THE PHYSICIANS VS. THE HOSPITAL

On previous business trips to a large Midwestern city, one hospital chain stood out. With four hospitals, three outpatient clinics, four outpatient surgical centers, nearly 1,000 beds, and 7,500 employees including 1,300 physicians, this chain dominated the local medical scene. Prominently placed signs bragged that the hospital was one of the "Top 100" hospitals in the United States.

The sign at the adjacent medical building with offices for affiliated physicians emphasized the names of the physicians. It was easy to read the doctors' names in large, dark blue letters against the white background. At the bottom of the sign, in small letters and distinctive logo, appeared the name of the hospital chain and its distinctive logo.

During a recent business trip, I noticed a fresh coat of paint on the physicians' medical facility—and a new sign. This office building, housing the practices of doctors affiliated with the hospital, is not actually part of the hospital campus. Yet, the name of the hospital had moved from the bottom portion of the sign to the top and increased in size from 10% of the available space to 20%.

Does a good hospital make the physicians good or is it the other way around? Hospitals need effective medical-related operational procedures,

The company CHOSE its location, most likely with the intention of presenting a certain image. Failing to maintain the property shows the company:

- May be out of touch with reality—it fails to recognize when things are not *right*.

- May recognize things are not right, but is so arrogant it believes others are too ignorant to notice

- Is internally focused, not caring how outsiders perceive it

- Suffers imbalance—an unkempt property is invariably one where things are *out of place*

- Is cheap. Property maintenance costs money.

A company may be a tenant in a large office park or warehouse complex with a commercial/industrial property management company responsible for the maintenance of the buildings, grounds, and signage. However, a caring and progressive tenant company will notify the management company of deficiencies. There is no need to accept a second-rate environment when a company is likely paying first-rate rent.

---

caring and sufficient staff, the right facilities in the right amount of space, accreditation by the national agency, computers with software for patient care and finance, and a community-based marketing presence. Physicians provide expertise. Physicians also provide patient referrals. Done correctly, this is the perfect symbiotic business relationship. However, all the facilities, procedures, and technical installations will not make up for a lack of medical expertise or customers. There you have it. Good physicians make a good hospital.

Since the new sign on the physician's medical facility emphasized the hospital's name and not those of its affiliated physicians, the sign was backward. Patients coming to that building would be looking first for their physicians, regardless of the physicians' hospital affiliations. Many physicians have privileges at more than one hospital and some have more than one office location . . . so office location across the street from the hospital was probably more for convenience than for the (inaccurately) implied ownership suggested by the new sign. Note to medical, legal, and social service accreditation agencies: In similar situations, look especially closely at finance, marketing, management, and especially operational issues.

~~*

In Back of the Building

If you have the opportunity, drive around and look at the back of the building. This simple action will give you a far more complete idea of the company's health.

- Is the loading dock a mess? Or is it neat and organized?

- Is the area well-lit?

- Do you see a security camera trained on this portion of the building?

- If the company has a cafeteria, do you see food scraps or empty boxes with food outside a trash compactor or big dumpster?

- Is an unattended door propped partially open? This can indicate carelessness, a potential security breach . . . or less than loyal employees who have found an open door creates opportunity for theft.

- What evidence of scavengers do you see? Is this the local take-out for the population of birds, squirrels, raccoons, wild dogs, or feral cats?

The back side of the building is an especially revealing part of the tour. Since this is out back, few executives or managers expect anyone to look at this. In fact, you may wish to start future inspections at the back of the building, and then work toward the front. **If the business scores badly on more than three of the six counts listed, then the building exterior becomes a critical item for assessing the health of a company. Dysfunctional company characteristics include disorganization, lack of care for the health and welfare of its employees, and an all talk-no action attitude toward cost savings.** Again, do not to fight or intellectualize what you observed. Instead take notes.

Company Vehicles

Another subtle, yet often overlooked, factor for evaluation—the company's vehicle fleet—provides information about how employees treat the company's assets. As part of your evaluation, look at these aspects of a fleet car or truck:

- *Make/model of car or truck.* Is the vehicle from a U.S. or non-U.S. manufacturer? This is a more difficult area to evaluate, since many Japanese, German, and Korean automakers have manufacturing plants in the US. Is the vehicle an SUV? Although I do not expect to find many hybrid automobiles as company cars, it is certainly possible. Do you see any?

A smart company buys or leases cars or trucks that show minimal depreciation while in use. The most reliable or luxury autos and trucks depreciate at a slower rate than their less-reliable counterparts do. The makes of slower-depreciating vehicles are listed alphabetically, based on 2012 owner-reported reliability in *Consumer Reports* magazine. Acura, BMW, Ford Escape hybrid SUV, Ford pickup trucks, Honda, Infiniti, Lexus, Mercedes-Benz, Nissan, and Toyota tend to retain a greater percentage of their value when re-sold. The listed automakers offer sufficient model variety so an unusually tall or short sales rep driver can find a model that is comfortable to drive and stay within budget.

- *Signage on the vehicle.* If you see company trucks, what is the painted message on the sides, front, and back of the vehicle? Look at:

    o *Front:* Easy to read lettering displays the name of the company. It may read forward or be written so that the driver of the car in front may easily read the company name when looking in their rear-view mirror.

    o *Sides:* Easy to read name of the company, description of services or products offered, the state registration or license number, and an easy to read logo surrounded by ample white space.

    o *Rear:* Company name, short description of products or services, and the "How's my driving? Call a listed 800 telephone number." The vehicle number is listed.

    o *Warning sign(s):* "Now hiring: experienced plumbers, electricians, technicians, helpers, cable installers, warehouse workers, etc." The company must experience very high turnover; otherwise, it would not permanently paint *help wanted* ads on the sides and rear panels of its service vehicles.

- *Condition.* How good is the overall condition of each company vehicle? Scratches, dents, nicks, scraped paint, and broken lenses point to the lack of pride in the company.

- *Color.* Did the company purchase black or white vehicles? Or, did the company purchase vehicles of tasteful colors that a sales rep or delivery person would not mind driving? Do the colors tend to hide or magnify dirt on the car's finish?

- *Washed.* Is each vehicle clean? Are the windows clean, including the rear window? Are the headlights clean? Are the taillights and stoplights so dirty that it would be difficult for a driver following to determine if the brakes were applied?

- *Current or expired registration.* Does the vehicle display an up-to-date state license registration? This is not an automatic process. Someone must write a check, stand in line, or mail the form, wait for the newest sticker, then apply the sticker in the proper place on the license plate. An out-of-date registration or the lack of a Department of Transportation (DOT) registration for trucks if required tells you someone does not care about important legal details. Is the license plate clean?

- *Automobile interior.* Last step, look at the car's back seat. If it is messy, that screams of a disorganized owner/driver and states that person is uncaring about others' properties, is unable to make a decision, and is narcissistic. Rather than clean up the mess, that person wants someone else to take responsibility. S/he cannot be bothered spending time, getting dirty hands, or even thinking about which items to keep and which to discard.

Summary

Here is your up-close introduction to the organization. First review of the building exterior. Evaluate the location, the structure, the back of the building, and the infrastructure. Is the location appropriate to the type of business? Are the sign and logo readable? If the plant has a guard shack, is your interaction with the guard a professional one? Do you see physical barriers between the street and the front of the building? What can you learn from the material used for the front door? What did you find at the back of the building? Burned out or broken light bulbs? Vehicles with expired registration stickers?

The building infrastructure rates critical assessment. Can you identify a smoking area located at least 25 feet away from building entrances? Do you find reserved parking spaces for executives? Are spaces reserved for disabled employees and visitors clearly marked and located nearest the front door? Did you find a vehicle not displaying the required tag parked in one or more spaces reserved for disabled persons? If so, does that vehicle belong to the organization's CEO or senior executive?

First impressions count. However, don't let your first impression overwhelm you. Start building a mental or written set of notes of examples of dysfunction. Trust me. You are certain to find more.

~*~*~*~

CHAPTER **15**

INTERIOR ENVIRONMENT

When you enter the building, you will find more environment-related items for company evaluation, specifically:

- Temperature

- Odors

- Use of Space

- Noise

- Lighting

Temperature

Other than what you see and hear, the most likely inputs will be temperature and smell. Is the temperature in the lobby comfortable? Each of us has a different comfort level. Nevertheless, you can quickly tell if the lobby temperature is way too high or way too low.

A company's indoor atmosphere provides many clues about the company. Interior environments that are too warm promote sleepiness, serve as great breeding grounds for microorganisms, and reduce employee productivity. The company is wasteful of energy and is out-of-touch with its employees. As a Petri-dish-like space for culturing viruses and infections, this excessively warm office environment is toxic. Moreover, the company likely offers its employees a relatively limited number of sick days, which essentially means the very environment that fosters excessive absenteeism penalizes its employees for showing up and breathing! Of course, year 'round warm weather states are the exception; a slightly warm interior shows the firm is effectively using its cooling/heat pump system and is in control of its costs.

Up to a point, a colder office environment is better—boosted productivity, heightened alertness, better interpersonal interaction, and fewer trips to the water fountain or soda machine improve employee output. However, too cold is almost equally insensitive as too warm. In northern climates, too cold means the company is too cheap to properly heat the workspace; in year 'round warm weather states, too cold in summer months means the organization is wasting energy.

Odors

Odors, especially extreme odors, can be, at best, irritating or distracting and, at worst, dangerous.

Can you smell mold? If so, this is an unhealthy organization that, in turn, does not care about employees, suppliers, or customers. If the company is small and the founder/CEO has not recognized this undesirable smell, that person's judgment is limited. Think of this as the equivalent of personal body odor. If an individual is oblivious to being offensive, s/he will not be aware of how that stink is affecting relationships. Likewise, a foul-smelling business indicates minimal concern for suppliers and potential customers. This inattention to detail reveals poor communications between accounting and finance, marketing and sales, and operations and human resources.

Can you detect scents of berries, flowers, fruits, vegetables? The use of exaggerated artificial aromas creates an artificial work environment. Just as some people use too much perfumed scent to cover up poor hygiene, some companies attempt to hide reality by overwhelming it with purportedly pleasant scent. If the entry area smells good, it will likely look good. However, the employee break room/lunch room, restrooms, and copier areas will likely not be set up to be functional or efficient. The company may skimp on workstation/cubicle space for employees, including those of mid- to senior-level managers. Artificial scent is a cover for poor hygiene, whether personal or corporate.

Do you smell dust? This extreme aroma is similar to, but not as bad as, mold. Once again, the organization is an unhealthy one.

Can you smell disinfectant? Some work environments require or benefit from the use of disinfectants. If disinfectants are needed, they should be used during off-hours, when visitors and hopefully most employees are not in the building. The same goes for pesticides.

Can you smell paints, furniture polish, or cleaning solutions? Awareness about the short- and long-term health impacts of volatile organic compounds (VOCs) has increased in recent years. VOCs are found in disinfectants, cleaning supplies, pesticides, new carpeting and upholstery, and paints—and can cause headaches, dermatitis, nausea, and damage to kidneys, liver, and the central nervous system.

If painting is needed, low VOC paints are available and should be used
. . . both for the health of employees and for the comfort of visitors. (Note:
even low VOC paints have toxic chemicals in them, so painting should be
done when people are not around . . . with thorough ventilation of the area
before people come back into it.)

Cleaning solutions should have minimal odor. Many companies have
introduced a number of scent-free, *green* products which are far safer to use
and live with than their traditional heavily pine-scented counterparts.

If you smell paint, furniture polish, or cleaning solution, then the organization does not care about the health of its employees and visitors. Looked at differently, the company is always in a hurry to do something, often without planning and foresight, since after-hours janitorial work is crammed into the workday.

Can you smell ammonia-based window spray? Ammonia is highly irritating to some chemically sensitive individuals and should be used only when a minimum number of people will be exposed to the fumes. Once again, the firm does not care about employees or visitors. The *hurry up* operating mode pervades this workplace, too.

Bottom line: **If the reception area stinks, so does a part of the company.**

Use of Space

As you enter the building, note the use of space, both horizontal and vertical. Is the interior space appropriate for the type of business?

Hallways should be of reasonable length and width—they should not appear cavernous nor so long that a visitor might lose track counting the number of doors before reaching the correct one. This is especially noticeable and important when the building is located in **Class A** office space, the most expensive, usually in a city's downtown or an expensive suburb. The walls, ceiling, and floor should all be clean and in good repair.

Hallways should be free of obstruction, not used as storage space for boxes of files, discarded electronics, extra waste baskets, copiers or printers, and miscellaneous, apparently abandoned furniture. Room numbers should be clearly marked, and sequentially organized so unescorted visitors can easily locate the office they need to find. Winding halls with blind corners, dead ends, and hard-to-locate elevators and stairwells are not visitor friendly. **More than two blind corners, dead ends, or hidden stairwells tell you the organization has lost its direction.** A guest should not have to ask repeatedly for the location of a restroom or elevator.

Kitchens, coffee break areas, or rest rooms should be proportionate to the size and nature of the organization. In a production environment, more space is needed since relatively large groups of employees take breaks at the same time. In an office environment, only the lunch room or cafeteria need be sufficiently large to accommodate increased lunchtime traffic. **Overly large kitchens, coffee break areas, or rest rooms indicate poor decision making. If the company cannot effectively use its most visible resource, space, why would anyone expect wisdom in how it uses *any* of its resources?**

Noise

Is the space relatively quiet? While waiting, do you hear the hum of the ventilation system? Can you hear the humming from the fluorescent light ballasts? Does the reception area play neutral piped-in music? Does the receptionist have a radio set to play, say, international music at a loud volume? Does the receptionist's telephone make a muted sound or can it wake the dead?

In public areas, are people talking on cell phones about the organization's business? Do people talk to one another in loud voices? Can you hear shouting? Name calling? Do you hear an occasional laugh? Do managers criticize employees in public, not private, places? Are the floors carpeted? Are the floors covered in ceramic tile, linoleum, granite, or other hard surface, so everyone's footsteps and voices add to the cacophony?

Bottom line: **The quieter, the better. Relative quiet says "welcome to our place of business." Relative quiet is soothing. Relative quiet lets you gather your thoughts rather than expend effort trying to tune out unwanted blaring. Relative quiet lets you sit peacefully, relax, and even prepare for your meeting.**

Lighting

There is an expectation that an office will be appropriately lit. Light is necessary for employees to get work done, for everyone to see where they are walking, to accent something of value or importance, and to help maintain the body's natural biorhythms.

- *Natural light vs. artificial light*: Natural light is preferable to artificial light. However, the building design and cubicle location may preclude sufficient natural light. If this is the case, then the artificial light level may be increased. Fluorescent lighting is often used in large areas due to its high efficiency and relatively low operational costs. Flickering fluorescent light tubes need to be replaced since the flicker is hard on the eyes and can lead to headaches. The addition of incandescent, LED, or halogen lighting over work surfaces minimizes the potentially harmful long-term effects of fluorescent light.

BEHIND THE SCENES

In the 1970s, back before the existence of big box office supply stores, the son of the owner of an office supply store hired a woman I know as an interior designer. Ann's first assignment? Organize the second floor office furniture display, which was a dusty jumble of desks, credenzas, bookshelves, and chairs. Cleaning, vacuuming, and shoving the furniture around into logical, aesthetic office arrangements took a solid week. During the time, no customers showed up to even look at the furniture. Ann was then told that, until a furniture customer turned up, she would be working on the main floor, selling office supplies.

There, she found a filthy stockroom, with the journal and ledger inventory in total disarray . . . so, between customers, she cleaned the shelves and reorganized the inventory by product number so the correct items could be more easily located.

The owner's son was amiable and conscientious. The owner, as Ann soon found out, was cantankerous and mean-spirited. Almost daily, he yelled at and threw things at his employees. When Ann was sent out to measure for carpet for the local Democratic headquarters, she prepared a bid and showed the owner his cost and what a reasonable markup would be. The owner went into negotiation with the headquarters and, eager to get the business, quoted his cost as his bid. Naturally, he got the job . . . and blamed Ann for the fact he did not make any profit.

The owner then discovered that one of the men in the stockroom had been stealing inventory. The man's wife, the company's bookkeeper, was shocked . . . and worried that she was going to lose her job because of what her husband had done. She didn't. She lost her job when the son's owner discovered she had been fudging the books.

Ann quit when the owner, arguing that he didn't want to come between her and a customer, pushed her across the aisle into a shelving unit. The son tried to convince her to stay, but she, wisely, left this sick environment. A few years later, the son died from a heart attack. Ann told me she was certain it was from the stress of being under the old man's iron thumb. The "behind-the-scenes" grime and disorganization should have told Ann all she needed to know.

~~*

- *Direct sun vs. bright light vs. northern exposure*: Direct sun is not necessarily best for the work environment. Harsh bright sunlight shining directly on a workspace reduces productivity. Indirect bright light is best. Northern exposures, especially in locales above 42 degrees latitude, have less intense light than those in locales below 42 degrees. In more northern climates, a southern exposure will provide more light in the fall and spring months.

- Blinds should be installed on windows that receive bright, direct sunlight. Horizontal or vertical blinds reduce the glare and heat from direct sunlight.

An organization that does not help protect the eyesight for its employees is careless at best, negligent at worst. Executives' offices that face bright light are likely to have some type of shading, whether blinds, tall plants, or a screen. If workers' workstations with the same exposure are not likewise protected, then the company has a two- or three-tier structure, treats employees according to their relative rank, and is cheap.

Summary

An office environment that is too hot or too cold provides an additional clue of organizational dysfunction. Strong scents—fragrances, disinfectant, paint, polish, cleaner, and ammonia-based window cleaner—are distracting, and can compromise employee health. Subtle fragrances are fine. Mold, another health risk, signals poor internal communication and operational problems.

Look at the use of horizontal and vertical space. Hallways are horizontal spaces; ceilings are vertical spaces. Check the proportions of common spaces, especially the hallways. Make sure hallways are clear of clutter.

As far as noise, quiet is better. While seated in the reception area, make note of yelling, laughter, and small groups chatting at reasonable volume. Is the reception area carpeted? The use of ceramic tile, granite, or linoleum floors magnifies sounds in the reception area.

Light is good—up to a point. Direct sunlight that shines on a workstation hampers productivity; the long-term effects are unknown. Watch for a difference in the treatment of executives and individual contributors as far as the use of blinds, screens, or plants to shield workspaces from direct sunlight.

~*~*~*~

CHAPTER 16

RECEPTION AREA, DÉCOR, & WALLS

You completed the initial check of the temperature, smell, noise level, and use of space in the organization's entry. You need to next complete an in-depth evaluation of this entry area. Look at the:

- Reception area

- Furniture & décor

- Walls

Reception Area

Obviously, the reception area is the first interior space you will encounter. **The reception area sets the tone for the organization. First impressions count.** The reception desk should be near the front door, not 30, 50, or 100 feet from the front entrance. Is the reception desk clean, well-organized, in good repair, and free of dust? Is the desk professionally appointed, or is it covered with personal knick-knacks? Is the receptionist clearly visible? Is the front of the counter raised so high it hides the receptionist?

Is the reception desk at a start-up organization an elaborate, expensive workstation built by a company that specializes in elite corporate furnishings? **For a start-up, a very expensive workstation in the reception area is a clear sign of lack of a coherent business strategy.** If executives sufficiently misplace their priorities by purchasing an expensive reception workstation, then what other errors in judgment have they made?

Can the receptionist clearly see all areas of the reception area so that you may sit anywhere in the room and s/he will be aware of your presence? Since you are likely to speak with the receptionist before you sit down, we will begin with a discussion of the receptionist then move on to the décor and furnishings.

The receptionist is the first person at the company you will meet. Is the receptionist a man or a woman? Is that person young or old? How is that person dressed? Is the style of dress appropriate for the industry and city? The borough of Manhattan in New York City is more formal than downtown Los Angeles. How well is the person groomed? Is his/her appearance tasteful, or has the individual chosen an exaggerated style, with multiple, odd body piercings; excessive, inappropriate tattoos; overly suggestive clothing styles; or vintage/futuristic costume apparel, makeup, and hairstyle?

Does that person act in a mature and professional manner? Does he/she respond to queries in a thoughtful, respectful, and calm manner? Is the receptionist genuinely helpful to visitors? Is the receptionist genuinely helpful to fellow employees? How do others in the company address the receptionist—do they speak in gracious, condescending, barking, begging, or genuine tones?

If the receptionist also serves as a telephone operator, what best describes the nature of his/her interactions on the phone—does s/he sound helpful, friendly, standoffish, mechanical, curt, or bored? Does the receptionist's conversation sound professional, or is s/he using the company phone or a personal cell phone for an overly-long, overly-emotional, personal conversation?

Does the receptionist offer to bring you coffee, tea, soda, or water? Does the receptionist have a dish of candy or mints available for visitors? Do you feel comfortable with this person?

If you are hired, you will have to work together. Remember, too, the receptionist that management, or, more likely, human resources, chose represents the image and message the company thinks appropriate as its first impression. **The wrong person as receptionist sends a message of other wrong decisions at this organization.** Compare how you are treated by the receptionist to that:

- When you spoke with your prospective manager or potential customer over the telephone

- While you worked with your manager or the travel department to arrange for your on-site visit and interviews

- While you spoke and worked with administrators in different departments

- When you spoke with potential co-workers in other departments or potential customers

- When you spoke with the recruiter, if one was involved in your hiring process

Be alert for inconsistencies between the reception area and other departments. Inconsistencies include:

- Great treatment by prospective managers, customers, administrators, and peers and ungracious, even negative, treatment by the receptionist

- Great treatment by the receptionist and ungracious, uneven-handed treatment by prospective managers, customers, administrators, and peers

Furnishings and Décor

After you meet the receptionist, the person will likely ask you to take a seat while you wait to meet your party. First, inspect the furniture. Is the furniture relatively old or new? **If you see green shag carpeting or a Formica-topped reception desk, beware. The company is stuck physically and mentally in the 1970s.**

What is the furniture style? Is it traditional, modern, Art Nouveau, or English; French or Italian provincial; Oriental, modern oversized,contemporary, or ultramodern; or casual patio bamboo or rattan? No business, government, non-profit organization, or medical office reception area should be furnished in French or Italian provincial furniture. It does not fit. This space is not a person's living room, or worse, bedroom. Other furniture styles look good, are less delicate and formal, and make guests feel at home.

The use of provincial furniture is a minor, but not a critical, warning sign. Like ornate provincial furniture, executive managers in these companies are fussy, obsessed with looking good to the public, have dated management styles, have difficulty in reaching consensus decisions, have out-of-date views on key factors that influence their business, and are unfocused. The company is disorganized, with lack of clear reporting structures and accountability. But it looks good initially from the reception area.

What materials did the interior designer/buyer combine in the furnishings—wood, glass, Plexiglas ©, leather, vinyl, steel, iron, brass, ceramic, fabric? Fabric, leather, and wood provide the homiest, most inviting feeling. Steel, iron, brass, ceramic, and to a lesser extent Plexiglas ©, are not as warm. A good designer may tastefully combine accents of steel, iron, brass, or ceramic with the more traditional materials and create a different, yet comfortable, environment.

If the reception area feels artificial and unwelcoming, then the organization is likewise.

Are the furnishings in good condition? After all, this is a visitor's first detailed impression. Obviously worn furniture shows a cheap attitude. Furniture with broken springs or legs, threadbare arms, and chipped or scratched finishes belongs in the secondhand furniture store, not in a company's reception area. **Broken furniture also means a broken company.** Here is an early clue for you to keep searching.

Is the furniture correctly proportioned for the room? For example, modern oversized furniture does not belong in reception areas or executive offices. This massive style, with its heavily padded arms and deeply-cushioned backs, is designed to create a casual, comfortable feeling in residential great rooms, which can measure up to 20 or 25 feet by 30 or 40 feet.

The overstuffed upholstery (leather, or a facsimile thereof, seems to be the covering of choice) visually fills the space in a way that is most often interpreted as luxurious. However, the often unattached and loosely-shaped backs require babysitting to keep them looking their casual best; otherwise, they tend to end up squished at odd angles. In order to maintain proportions with the upholstered furniture, case goods—the end tables, coffee tables, lamps, and accessories—are also oversized.

Oversized furniture is designed for families and friends and is associated with relaxation, entertainment, and extravagance. The size dwarfs the individual. The goal is to impress. The style does nothing to suggest *business*.

If the company got a *great deal* buying these furnishings, it later paid a high price through its inappropriate initial public image. **The use of the modern, oversized style of furniture tells you: the organization's leaders have a limited boundary between home and work; the organization has grandiose, exaggerated goals; and the company's thinking is not aligned with what its customers require.**

Is the chair or couch comfortable when you sit? Does it provide good support for your back? Is it too hard? Do you sit perched atop a rock? Is it too soft? Do you sink into a pillow? If the seat is too soft, you have difficulty getting up when you stand to meet your interviewer or customer. You will automatically not be on an equal footing. If the seat is too soft, shift to another, more supportive seat. If that is not possible, you may want to sit with your weight shifted toward the front edge so that you may more easily rise. **If the chair or couch is too hard or too soft, then the company's focus is inward, not outward.**

This interior-related factor—upholstered couches or chairs that are too hard or too soft—is intriguing. What does a too hard chair or couch say about the company? What does a too soft chair or couch say about the organization? Your definition of *hard couch or chair* may differ from my definition. However, we could agree on the definitions of extreme situations—very hard or soft couches or chairs. How would we know these extreme situations? Sit down; your gluteus maximus will communicate the answer. Extremely hard or extremely soft is a surprisingly common denominator.

Metaphorically speaking, **an extremely hard couch, or chair represents an organization that literally will not let you in.** If the couch or chair is too hard, then the organization is closed; you cannot sink in or fit in to the level of peers and managers. Like the chair, this organization is rigid—innovation is not appreciated. You will be expected to conform, unquestioningly, to the way things are. Your assignments will be routine and unchallenging; you have little opportunity for personal and professional growth.

Key determinants for corporate success may include longevity; working in a certain department or business function (accounting, marketing, finance, operations, etc.); membership in a certain religious institution, social club, athletic club, or country club; being an alumnus of certain colleges or universities; moving in the same social circles as key executives; or athletic prowess in certain sports. Just as extremely hard chairs are not for everyone, this organization is not for just anyone to join and later succeed within.

An extremely soft couch or chair symbolizes an organization that definitely lets you in. In fact, it swallows or envelops you. The organization becomes your entire life—work, social, athletic, intramural or industry competitive sports teams, and attendance at spectator sports, religious affiliation, and college alumni activities. **Everyone does everything together.** Everyone is successful; the organization excludes no one—if you are willing to be absorbed. As you sink into a soft couch or chair, consider that, if you stay with this company, you will slowly lose your individuality.

It is also possible that the metaphors for hard and soft chairs and couches may apply in the opposite manner. That is, a hard chair or couch may indicate an organization that swallows you in the sense that you find yourself molding to the organization. Conversely, a soft couch or chair represents an organization that does not let you in because it provides no support. In any event, either extreme in furnishings is a sign of organizational suckiness.

An interior decorator, a designee in the purchasing department, or an administrator usually selects and orders furniture. That person's tastes may prevail. S/he may choose furniture scaled to her/his own body size. If the person is not trained in design, s/he may overfurnish or underfurnish the room, select furniture in clashing styles or colors, disproportionate sizes, or hard-to-maintain fabrics and finishes, or arrange furniture awkwardly. When the furniture arrives and is set up, I expect that others would sit down to sense the level of comfort.

Someone in a position of authority might *test* the chair or couch and make a judgment call — is this the right piece of furniture? In this way, someone in management tacitly or implicitly approves the purchase and, by doing so, allows the furniture to serve as an accurate metaphorical representation of the organization.

My comments and analysis intentionally focus on the extremes — extremely hard and very soft. Some executive or manager made an important decision — through their approval, they personally determined a visitor's first and accurate impression.

Does the condition of the furniture match the life cycle of the business? **In other words, is the reception area of a start-up company furnished with fancy designer or decorator furniture and art?** This is a definite warning sign. **The company's priorities are out of alignment;** a start-up company should spend its limited capital on people and technology-based devices to make everyone more productive in order to bring the product or service to market.

Is the furniture clean? Are accessories clean and shiny or dusty and soiled? Look at the cross members on the coffee table, look on the legs of the chairs or the couch, check out the plants, slightly move the table lamp to uncover evidence of dust. Make your search for dust and dirt a creative exercise! Barely shift the magazine piles, slightly relocate any decorative items on the table; drop your pen on the floor and when retrieving it run your fingers over the bottom shelf or legs of the coffee table. By now, you are likely asking, "Is this guy obsessed?" No, I merely turn my detective work into a quasi-fun exercise. So should you.

If the furniture is outdated, dirty, or in poor repair, the spontaneous excuse, "We are planning to remodel the entrance area," does not work. **It's far easier to sell what you plan to accomplish than to actually accomplish something. Any unprompted excuse is a warning sign of the dysfunction,** *all talk and no action.*

Are the live plants healthy? A very old cartoon suggested one could tell the quality of a doctor by the health of the plants in the reception area. This saw is true not only in doctors' offices but in corporate environments.

Healthy plants show a desire for a complete, positive image. Plants add life, especially in a reception area that contains stylish furniture, both upholstered and wood. The irregular forms and variegated shadings of green or flowering plants provide a balance to wall-mounted artwork, metallic or wooden sculptures, and corporate memorabilia.

It's easy to blame the poor condition of interior plants, trees, gardens, or fountains on the third-party service the company has retained to maintain them. However, the level of care reflects directly on the company's attitude. Poor maintenance may result from a company pressing for the lowest bidder and being willing to settle for minimal care. Live plants in poor condition also show management's lack of concern for its employees and visitors. If management is unaware of the problem, there are probably other, more critical problems management is missing. Yes, attention to detail even extends to plants in the lobby. If the facilities manager is not satisfied with the level and quality of service from the third party, then, without excuse or apology, s/he should change vendors.

If artificial plants are used, they should be the *silk* type. In this day, use of plastic plants is unacceptable. They look cheap and artificial because they are! Silk plants look far more life-like and, for only a few additional dollars, the organization can create a complete and appropriately appointed reception area. **Cheap plastic plants denote a cheap company that does not take the time to research alternative courses of actions — a *ready, fire, aim* mentality.**

What is the condition of the floor tiles and/or carpet? Floor coverings should be clean, with no more than reasonable wear. Carpets should have no obvious holes. Tiles or linoleum should have no cracks or gouges. A slightly dirty floor is acceptable, particularly in a heavily trafficked area; a floor covering that is dirty with holes or gouges is not acceptable. This is an important, but not critical, item. **Poor condition carpets or tiles imply the company is cheap and does not pay attention to details; i.e., lacks follow through.**

Do you see evidence of burned out light bulbs in the exit signs? According to any approved safety code, these lights must remain lighted. **If you see a burned out light, then this is a critical item. Personal safety, especially in the event of an emergency where one needs to be able to find an exit, is of paramount importance. The company's failure to maintain a critical although infrequently needed fixture shows it does not care about its employees or visitors . . . and is willing to violate legal requirements. Such an obvious clue tells you to look further.**

Is the reception area brightly lit? Natural light is best; metaphorically, sunshine suggests out-in-the-open company operations. Lacking daylight, overhead fluorescents, recessed or can lights, decorative strings of LEDs, or table lamps can provide needed illumination. **Dark, unwelcoming reception areas likely serve as a warning of darker activity within the organization.**

Do you see any burned out light bulbs? If so, how many? Where are they located—in the general overhead lighting, the table lamps, the accent lighting, or in the spotlights on artwork? This is an attention to detail item. **If the company does not pay attention to the initial image in its reception area, what else has it ignored?** Again, poor lighting represents non-compliance with a minor, but important, safety-related, government requirement (OSHA).

What kinds of magazines are on the tables in the reception area? In a technology-based business, I expect only technology- or business-oriented magazines. I do not expect, nor do I want to view, *Glamour, Fishing, Cosmopolitan, Golf, Ladies Home Journal, GQ, People, InStyle, Sports Illustrated, Popular Mechanics* or similar magazines.

The local daily newspaper, *The Wall Street Journal, Financial Times*, or *USA Today* are appropriate for a business environment. *U.S. News & World Report, Time*, and *Newsweek* are quite acceptable; they cover a broad spectrum of current topics. Exotic business-oriented periodicals such as *The McKinsey Quarterly*, Booz & Company's *strategy+business, Foreign Affairs*, or *Harvard Business Review* reveal a broader management perspective. In a service business, I expect industry-oriented magazines and business-oriented newspapers. Current magazine issues and business books reveal a timely, forward-looking mentality. Conversely, far out-of-date materials tell you the leaders are living in the past. Why would any company pay for subscriptions to magazines that send the wrong message to its employees and the public?

I would also expect to see relevant business- and industry-oriented magazines on the executive suite coffee table or credenza. Their presence shows the management knows where its focus should be.

The type and date of magazines and books in the executive suite is a semi-critical item.

Walls

Interior walls are a very important source of information for our company assessment. What is the condition of the wall surface? Is it chipped or cracked? If the surface has orange peel or other applied texture, does the texture require updating? On this textured surface, can you see areas that were repaired but the walls were not re-sprayed and matched to their original texture? If so, these symptoms indicate a lack of follow through and lack of consistency in the organization's operation.

Which wall treatments are used? Paint (usually on plaster), wallpaper, and wood paneling are most common, although decorative glass (beaded, molded, etched, block), plastic panels, fabric, stone, ceramic/pottery, and even metal may be part of the décor.

Is the wall treatment functional and appropriate for the area where it is used? For instance, a delicate grass cloth will soon look shabby in a heavily-trafficked location. Is the wallpaper color and pattern pleasant? Is it in good repair? Is the paint clean and professionally applied, or is it dirty and or sloppily dripped and spattered on the ceiling or floor? How well is the paint *cut in* at ceiling and floor intersections and around windows and doors? Is the paneling clean, polished, and free of gouges? Are the glassed sections or plastic panels clean and properly glazed? Is the stone in good repair?

Observe the artwork. Is it modern or is it traditional? Is it Americana/ Norman Rockwell, Native American, or 16th century Dutch portraiture? Is it French Impressionism or Art Nouveau? Is it a landscape or portrait or is it an abstract? Is it colorful or is it mostly monochromatic so that it matches the colors in the furniture? Does it exude a feeling of calm? Tension? Does the artwork consist of photos, whether new or old? Are colorful posters the foundation for wall decoration?

Are sculptures reproductions of famous works (I thought immediately of Remington's American West pieces) or are they originals? Does the sculpture convey a sense of restfulness or pent-up energy?

If the artwork matches the colors in the décor, then deduct one point. Artwork should not blend perfectly with its surroundings; it should provide an accent. **A monochromatic arrangement of art which matches the colors of walls, floors, and furniture shows a lack of imagination and stultified thinking.** This, too, is an important, but not critical item. However, if floor coverings are in poor condition and the monochromatic artwork blends with the furniture, then this combination of indicators becomes of semi-critical importance.

Do you see any motivational posters on the walls? If so, how many do you find? Where are they located—in the reception area, on the walls of cubicles, near (possibly in) the rest rooms, on the walls in the cafeteria or break room, or in the executive office area? How large is each poster? Does a wooden or metal frame surround each poster? How closely spaced are the posters? What are the topics or themes? **This is my number three critical assessment item.**

If a company cannot hire self-motivated employees, no matter the challenge of each position or the availability of well-qualified applicants, then surely the addition of one or more posters will not motivate.

No matter how tasteful or artistic, use of motivational posters reveals significant corporate dysfunction and serious suckiness. The question rightly becomes, *Whose motivation? Employees or management?*

Employees often recognize these motivational posters as exactly what they are—an attempt to dictate employee attitude by a management team which has little, if any, understanding of its employees. Management may be in search of a simple *solution* to complex people problems. One website offers fun-poking *de-motivational posters*. To maintain one's perspective in an environment of many motivational posters, take a look at: www.despair.com.

Evidence of adherence to a particular religious or spiritual philosophy is another critical negative item. Here are some examples:

- "We practice Christian (or Buddhist, Islamic, Jewish, Taoist, or other religious) values."

- Written evidence of adoption of L. Ron Hubbard's Scientologist-based philosophies

- Written evidence of adherence to *spiritual* (or Wicca-based) beliefs or philosophies

- Written evidence that all company or organization employees completed a specific type of training class, whether a class in diversity, interpersonal communications, personality types, leadership training, or process reengineering

A company transmits its values by its everyday actions, not with platitudes or slogans on a wall. Beware of any organization that links its core values with a specific religion or philosophy. This linkage has nothing to do with business. No business should promote directly or indirectly the founder's religious beliefs to others. **A murky church/business philosophy mix is as inappropriate as the blurring of church and state.**

If you encounter this situation in an interview, cut short your responses to questions and ask few, if any, questions when you have the chance. Then run, do not walk, from this so-called career or sales opportunity. Companies should hire employees based on their education, experience, skills, business and/or personal contacts, knowledge, ethics, hustle, and qualifications, not their religious beliefs. There is no middle ground. Stated differently, the identification with any religion usually hides some level of hypocrisy. Some folks treat their employees, suppliers, and customers a certain way – generally negative—for six days a week then feel exonerated because they attend religious services one evening or morning on the seventh day. One day's piety does not excuse or balance six days of unacceptable behavior.

Two exceptions to the slogan or specialized training evaluation factors are:

- ISO 9000:2000 quality training and certification
- ISO 14000 environmental practices and certification

These certifications indicate compliance with approved international operating standards and practices in the areas of quality practices and environmental policies and practices. Companies work very hard to meet and maintain the demanding standards for these certifications. Companies that meet the demanding ISO 9001:2008 quality standard may be especially proud of this accomplishment and have earned the right to display the certificate.

It is quite acceptable practice to display evidence of membership in civic associations such as the local Chamber of Commerce, Kiwanis, Rotary International, Soroptimist International, or ABWA (American Business Women's Association). This shows receptiveness to new opportunities and to meeting new people, an effort by the company or organization to reach out to and keep a finger on the pulse of the local community. **Through community-based associations, the organization maintains an outward, not inward, focus.**

Be sure to count the number of the organization's community affiliations; too many tell you the organization or its leader seeks a high community profile to the exclusion managing the business the leader is tasked to run.

One thing to note: membership in an organization is usually attained by paying dues, not by any level of activity. Financial support of an organization which does good deeds is always admirable, but posting membership without actual participation is posturing. From the organization's position, it may benefit from the financial payment and from being able to claim the executive as a member, but the executive's habitual absence will likely create a derisive attitude toward him/her—dumb enough to pay, but too arrogant to show his/her face. If you note such community affiliations, ask about them. If the response is dismissive, involvement is most likely minimal or absent and the executive is clueless.

Does the company display awards from the community, its suppliers, its customers, industry-wide organizations, or regional or international trade groups? Of what accomplishments is the company sufficiently proud to display these awards? Beware of awards from local magazines or quasi-legitimate sounding organizations which may recognize long-standing member companies or supporting advertisers. Unless the company displays proof that it accomplished something to earn the award, then the award is of limited real value. Claiming an unearned award provides evidence the company is desperate for recognition and unwilling or unable to put in the effort to earn it legitimately.

Is it possible to display too many awards? Absolutely yes! Awards from many community-based organizations during a short time period (say, one or two years) reflect one of two things:

- Executives may be too focused on outside activities and not paying sufficient attention to their business

- The company has very competent day-to-day operational managers who free senior executives to act as public spokespersons

I want to believe the latter reason is true. It may be. However, if executives are constantly on the go, it sends a message to first-line supervisors and rank-and-file employees that they are unavailable—and not concerned.

In addition, if a company has high-level, highly-paid executives with deep community involvement who contribute little or nothing to the company's bottom line, the company is carrying unnecessary bloat. Unfortunately, when more difficult economic times come, these companies tend to cut from the bottom—the jobs of those who are actually doing the work. This creates a highly dysfunctional organization with fewer of the true workers trying to carry a larger load. **Beware if you see a wall lined with memberships in many organizations over a relatively short time, say, a year or two. That executive-level company representative has become organizational** *bloat.*

Do you see customer "Thank You" letters displayed? These are one of my favorite indicators of good company health. Thank you letters show that customers appreciate the company—posting them shows the company appreciates its customers. Is that not what business is supposed to be about—a symbiotic relationship where a company provides goods or services that customers need?

Do you see "Thank You" letters from schoolchildren after they toured the plant? I applaud companies that find time to give presentations and tours to students, whether elementary, middle, high school, or post-secondary level.

Do you see plaques that commemorate key milestones? A good example is a brief description of the 10,000th unit of one product shipped, the date shipped, the name of the customer, and the customer's location. **If you see many current plaques, then the company is very proud of its growth and evolution.**

However, if all you see is out-of-date commemorative plaques on the wall, then the company is living off its past glory. It either has done nothing of note in the recent past, or it has lost its focus and no longer feels accomplishments are important to display. I vividly remember outdated commemorative plaques at Data General (DG) Corporation and Stratus Computer Company, both located in small towns along Route 128 outside Boston. Both

---

AN EMPLOYER INVOKES RELIGION-BASED VALUES

My former neighbor in Florida, George, worked for a local family-owned regional hardware distribution company. He spent nearly 25 years at a well-known national manufacturer and distributor of similar products, reaching a senior position in spite of a lack of formal education. His low-key west Texas/Oklahoma regional drawl makes him very approachable. He has a soft touch with people, is direct but friendly, and follows through on what he says he will do—a great combination for anyone in a leadership position.

George worked at this distributor for three years. One day, the company's new CEO dismissed him for "not working out as expected." In subsequent discussion, I learned that his new manager, the son of the founder and former CEO, had taken over as CEO, and had failed to communicate his expectations and measurable goals.

In our many front-yard chats while he was working, George never gave any indication of problems. After his dismissal, he confided that he was doubly disappointed. He said that, at his hiring interview, the new CEO's father, emphasized the company "lived by Christian values," as did George—a great match. The job dismissal slammed both his confidence as a highly capable senior executive, and his misconception that, as a Christian, he worked in an environment where that identification was valued.

~~*

DG and Stratus fell on hard times. Each was purchased by larger computer companies within one year after my visit.

If the company maintains an *Employee of the Quarter* or *Employee of the Month* award, then is it up to date? Does the plaque show the names of the latest winners? Does the company post photos of winners? If so, how current are the names and photos on display? I consider a two-month window as up-to-date. Ideally, the award is current, which indicates the company truly values its employees—this recognition is an important part of the organization's culture. Winning employees do what needs to be accomplished; similarly, winning companies do what they promise. **If the *employee of* listing is not up to date, then this is a sign of the organization's lack of caring, saying one thing and doing another, and lack of follow through.**

A PRETEND SENIOR VICE PRESIDENT

We toured the above-discussed Tampa-based technology-oriented facility. After lunch, some of us sat and chatted with one family member. I asked for his business card and learned he was the company's senior vice president. I asked what tasks were associated with his job. I expected a response similar to, "I work on strategy, mergers and acquisitions, major capital equipment purchases, training programs, corporate organizational structure, key hires," or a similar listing of responsibilities.

He instead replied, "I write job descriptions." He did not smile or give an indication that he was kidding. I asked if there were any other tasks. He said no; I believe he was serious. His audience consisted of four or five local educators and the purpose of this tour was to acquaint college faculty members with the hiring needs of his company. Armed with this knowledge, faculty members could recommend qualified and interested candidates to this firm. However, here is a major disconnect—the company's use of a temp agency to hire entry-level workers negated any real opportunities for our graduates.

The brief conversation confirmed my overall *dysfunction on parade* assessment of this family-run corporation with its Tampa Bay Buccaneers booster plaque. Why? I believe a competent, experienced human relations clerk or recent college graduate could accurately compose appropriate job descriptions. Why a senior vice president? Why did this senior VP not work on more strategic issues or do something to help increase sales?

~~*

A favorite sign of dysfunction is booster club plaques from local sports teams. I remember going on a tour of a St. Petersburg family-owned technology-based corporation. The only item on the wall in its 15-foot by 20-foot reception area was a booster plaque for the Tampa Bay Buccaneers dating from the Bucs' pre-Super Bowl winning days. At this company, the job of the lawyer-trained human resources vice president, who formerly worked for one of the largest family-held businesses in the United States, quickly became one of referee. Since the company paid for a skybox, this HR executive's job was to find ways to allocate use of the skybox among family members while avoiding internecine warfare. **The display of a sports team booster plaque was a critical, negative indicator of the organization's lack of focus on its core business.** Within five years of my tour, this business filed for Chapter 7 bankruptcy protection. The lone plaque revealed a great deal, namely:

- This business was all about the family. In fact, a family member held every office and executive title except that of CEO. After many unsuccessful years of rotating family members through the CEO position, they finally hired an outsider to run the business.

- Some family member, whether distant or family through marriage, held all key supervisory and department manager posts, sending a clear message to employees that opportunities for promotion were extremely limited or nonexistent.

- The company made major investments to automate as much of the production process as possible. The high level of automation changed the need for skilled *machine operators* to the need for unskilled *machine tenders*. The company hired these machine tenders through a temporary agency—not a good portent of employee longevity or growth opportunity.

- Whether this hiring decision was a first choice or not, it would eventually become institutionalized due to the lack of promotional opportunity, exhaustion of the local career-focused worker pool, and the company's poor community image. If the organization were truly a good place to work, then qualified local prospects would have identified this company as such and would have actively sought employment.

- Newer technologies rendered this company's technology obsolete. The aging family members did not remake the organization and update the equipment and processes in order to effectively compete.

Do you see evidence of company-wide sports leagues or teams? Does the company participate in a competitive or even intramural bowling, softball, baseball, flag football, soccer, or other leagues? Does the company enjoy sufficient employee participation that it can create its own sports league? I view this as a negative. Why? Teams with co-workers represent more time together, taking away from necessary down-time and family/ community/ and religious-based activities. If co-workers want to get together after work, that is fine. However, institutionalized camaraderie simply steals one's time or tries to link people who would not socialize voluntarily.

Worse, participants may feel coerced—after all, if they do not join in the fun, others may view them as non-team players. To demand increased face time and performance in activities not related to business productivity is to violate the boundaries a healthy individual needs to maintain. The attempt

---

EQUINOX SYSTEMS—AN OLD SPECIAL POSITIVE CASE

One visit took me to a small company in Sunrise, Florida. Years ago, as a Wall Street equity research analyst, I visited Equinox Systems, subsequently acquired in 2001 by Avocent Corp. of Huntsville, Alabama. Founder and CEO Bill Dambrackas and CFO Mark Kacer made a solid leadership team.

They were pleasant, circumspect, shared a wry sense of humor, were never hypercritical of employees or suppliers, and strived for constant product and process improvement. Bill and Mark were extremely careful not to reveal too much information, thereby inadvertently setting false future earnings projection expectations. They answered questions only to the extent of publicly available information. They were also consistent; Mark never volunteered more information than Bill and vice versa. It was an example of *Frick and Frack* at their very best. For me, the *Bill and Mark Team* represented my *platinum standard* for investor relations activities by a small, publicly-traded company.

Unfortunately, in late 1994, the company suffered a fire that caused extensive damage to its manufacturing and office facility. Employees voluntarily came in on two weekends and worked late every weeknight for two weeks to help the company transition rapidly to a temporary facility. In fact, the employees accomplished the transition with no loss of production.

I learned of this incredible accomplishment while reading the employee bulletin board. A copy of Bill's letter to all employees was posted at eye level in the center of the bulletin board and highlighted. Bill's letter congratulated everyone for two significant milestones.

to control employees' free time may result in resentment. That may sound harsh. Hell, it is harsh! It is a matter of respecting personal boundaries, honoring family time, and allowing individuals to set their own priorities.

Employee Bulletin Board

Did you locate the employee bulletin board? How large is it? If so, did someone neatly arrange the information? A disorganized bulletin board is a minimal sign of disarray in the human resources department.

How many square feet of space are devoted to posting required legal notices? **If the bulletin board is larger than 2-foot by 4-foot, and legal notices occupy the entire space, then beware—this organization is fearful.**

A preoccupation with legal notices shows that a company is fearful of new inputs and ideas. It is also concerned about employees beating it on a legal technicality, so it uses the legal notices to reinforce visually strong boundaries. I believe it highly likely that in this case company managers micromanage everything.

In reality, management may depend too much on such visual boundaries; smart employees are experts at working around the printed word. These employees may get management to say something in their presence that contradicts the organization's strongly written guidelines. And the employee will be certain to remind the manager of her/his comment when it is

---

First, for years, the company had unsuccessfully tried to win a contract to supply a key board-level serial input-output product for certain Hewlett-Packard (HP) computer systems. Second, the Equinox team moved the production facility in a couple weeks without a hitch—and prepared and completed a demonstration of the company's latest products for HP representatives. Because of the strong presentation, demonstration, and employee commitment, Equinox Systems won the contract to supply HP with board-level communication products, replacing one of HP's long-time suppliers.

Years later, I remember this wistfully. Bill's emotional letter to his employees told me everything I needed to know about the firm's character. The company could face short-term disruptions. However, the backing by management of its employees and the employees' strong commitment to the company's success told me this was a group of winners.

~~*

advantageous for the employee. Highly visible legal notices are indicative of a subliminally antagonistic cat-and-mouse game. **Executives and managers may claim a highly motivated work force but, beneath this façade, they trust no one. The favor is returned.**

What are the dates of the company notices posted on the bulletin board? What is the date of the most recent posting or memo? Is it within the past few weeks? If not, **old information on a bulletin board means the company's thinking is likewise outdated.** What does this say to the potential employee or business partner? You can expect that the managerial staff communicates poorly with its employees, the company maintains a pervasive attitude that employees are lazy and unmotivated, and the HR department manager does not care or is incompetent.

The employee bulletin board is also a critical indicator of the health of an organization. Why? The date, tone, and words management uses to communicate with employees in internal memos reveal management's true attitude and beliefs. Companies can easily become two-faced, especially if they use outside agencies to produce professional-sounding external marketing materials, on-line or print-based help wanted ads, and financial press releases. Internal communications may differ substantially—and reveal the truth. In internal memos, management's tone may be condescending, reproachful, blaming, or accusatory. Conversely, in the same memos, management's tone may be grateful, appreciative, encouraging, accepting, forward looking, and laudatory.

Had I not stopped to read the contents of the employee bulletin board, these two self-effacing men would not have voluntarily shared details of these incredible accomplishments. I strongly suggest you look at the employee bulletin board and search for anything beyond the required employment-related legal notices. Do not deprive yourself of any opportunity to learn about the inner workings, motivations, and *real* character of a company or organization.

To gain a different perspective, try to find published company rules. Generally, an organization with more strict rules takes itself more seriously. The rules may be posted on the bulletin board, listed prominently in a company handbook or new employee orientation package, or maintained on a regularly updated internal website. They may also be disseminated informally through shared stories, water cooler chit-chat, organizational or departmental gatherings, celebrations of key milestone attainment, or at retirement or going-away luncheons or dinners.

I fondly remember one prominent technology-based market research organization. There were only a couple published rules: (a) be conservative in forecasting five-year growth rates; and (b) check with other industry groups to ensure data and forecast consistency. The most important rule was not published: analysts were asked to do more than the customer asked for so clients would renew their annual program subscriptions. In a short but memorable discussion, the firm's sales vice president explained the difficulty of re-signing a past client, who, dissatisfied with the company's products and service, had chosen to sever the business relationship. Simple and straightforward—and Dataquest maintained a solid 98% client renewal rate and its number one reputation in high-tech market research for many years.

Summary

As a visitor, you have now entered the building. Welcome to the reception area. What you see, including the receptionist, the first person you meet, provides your first impression of the organization. If you arrive early for your appointment, you will have a chance to evaluate the style and condition of the furnishings, artwork, plants, displayed periodicals, and floor coverings. Don't forget to take a good look at the walls to gather more clues.

Three factors which provide important clues are the presence of motivational posters, the relative hardness/softness of the seats or couch cushions, and whether you see evidence of the organization's adherence to a particular set of religious or spiritual philosophies or beliefs. You may be able to find the employee bulletin board. What information is posted? What is the tone of management's communications with employees?

The walls in the reception area reveal more necessary information. Do you see up-to-date lists or plaques that commemorate *Employees of the Month/ Quarter/Year*? Do you see plaques or other evidence of organizational milestones? If so, what is the date shown on the most recent plaque? Can you find evidence as corporate booster for one or more local sports teams? Does the company field one or more teams in competitive leagues? Has the organization formed a sports league for intramural play? Do you see any trophies?

The final evaluation tools link the executives to civic/charitable/industry associations. You may find neatly framed certificates of membership by executives in various organizations. To how many organizations does each executive belong? What is the nature of the membership organizations?

~*~*~*~

CHAPTER 17

FLOORS, CEILINGS, HALLS, LIGHTING, ELEVATORS, & ADA REQUIREMENTS

We are inside the building. We will walk away from the reception area and explore the interior spaces in detail. Our assessment focuses on these six factors:

- Floors

- Ceilings

- Hallways and hangouts

- Lighting

- Elevator

- ADA requirements

Floors

Dirty floors are a metaphor for a company focused upward—and onward. By not looking downward, the organization ignores its base—whether the base of operations or customers. Such an organization does not devote sufficient resources to complete day-to-day tasks in a timely manner. Operations and customer service suffer.

Look for worn carpets. Worn carpets can result from improper and inadequate cleaning—dirt in the fibers causes them to break down. Worn carpet can also be the result of poor installation or failure to install an adequate carpet quality for the level of traffic. Or it may just be old carpet. Slightly worn carpet is not a problem. Carpet which is rippled or ripped is a safety hazard. Inattention to the danger of torn or irregular carpet surface is a warning sign: **Ripped or torn carpets or flooring with an uneven or rippled surface tells you the** company does not pay attention to details, misses key deadlines, and is not concerned about the safety of its employees, vendors, and customers.

Can you see *dust bunnies*? An occasional dust bunny is not cause for concern. After all, these things practically run away when they see a vacuum cleaner coming. New carpet is notorious for shedding copious amounts of loose fiber as a result of the manufacturing process. Dust bunnies or far larger *dust elephants* in older installations are often the result of inadequate cleaning efforts. A good number of dust bunnies and dust elephants show the organization does not pay attention to details. **In the worst case, dust creatures reveal dirt — ethical, financial, product quality, treatment of employees, or treatment of customers — at the root of the organization.**

Do you see piles of paper? Paper stacked on the floor is paper that has not been properly processed and filed. This paper may contain confidential information . . . which either needs to be stored in a secure location or destroyed properly.

Do you see evidence of insects or rodents? Insect droppings, or even the actual scurrying creepy crawlies, do not belong on office floors. These are difficult to control in open warehouses, but cleanliness procedures need to be in place in the office to prevent infestations, particularly if the company deals with foods. If you see evidence of rodents, then management shows it is unable to take action in a timely manner and it is facing major problems in operations or other customer-facing activities.

I long ago heard of a company which brought a computer system into a computer store for inspection by a technician because it smelled funny. This ancient carry-on suitcase-size Compaq computer had sizeable access slots for the 5-1/4 inch floppy disks. When the service tech opened the case, he discovered the source of the smell. Mice had nested inside the computer . . . and fried. I doubt this was the first evidence the company had that rodents were in the building.

Ceilings

How high is the ceiling? Is it proportionate to the space? Is it proportionate to the building and the size of the company? **A ceiling which feels** *too high,* **can indicate uncertainty about goals — they are hard to see and grasp. A ceiling which is** *too low* **feels oppressive and shows limited** *vision.* **There is no room for** *reaching.*

Do you see ceiling stains? If a ceiling is stained, something bad happened. The stain may be the result of roofing failure, improper air conditioning duct maintenance, or plumbing problems. Left too long, the moisture buildup can result in ceiling collapse or the growth of toxic mold.

Does the ceiling look unpainted? If a company repaints the walls, but not the ceiling, the company is focused on growth (vertical plane), not on stability and structure (horizontal plane)

Does the ceiling have an uneven surface and texture? An uneven surface or texture can result from building settling (instability), or poor and unprofessional maintenance and repair. Poor maintenance indicates instability and unevenness in the organizational structure.

Does the color of the ceiling blend with the color of walls and carpet/ floor? Do you see sloppy transitions from wall color to ceiling color? **Unblended colors and sloppy paint transitions indicate poor balance or lack of boundaries between growth (vertical plane) and stability and structure (horizontal plane).**

Is the ceiling color and type appropriate to rest of the interior architecture and design? Just as you would not expect a cheap drop ceiling in area with high-fashion or antique furniture, silk screens, or Oriental rugs, you would not a expect lofty, coffered ceiling in a room sparsely furnished with medical clinic waiting room vinyl and chrome chairs. The ceiling must blend with rest of interior—in color and style. **A ceiling that clashes with the interior design and décor represents an organization where many departments are unable to work together.**

Hallways and Hangouts

A building's hallways reveal minor clues to corporate dysfunction. Think of hallways as blood vessels that symbolically link a company's organs. As blood flows between various organs in the body, people flow between various departments and functions in a company. **Poorly designed hallways represent literal organizational bottlenecks.**

Observe the interior floor plan. Do hallways allow traffic to flow logically? If the building exterior and reception area are square or rectangular, do the interior halls mirror this design? Or does a rectangular or square building contain curvilinear interior walls, creating odd, marginally-functional corners? Can you see evidence of a logical traffic flow? Can employees and visitors easily access busy functional areas such as human resources (HR) or accounts payable? The HR office should be located relatively close to the front entrance; there is no logical reason that a prospective employee should require escorted access through an entire floor to find the HR department . . .

nor that employees should have to come down from some obscure corner of the third floor to fetch job applicants. **An illogical floor layout reflects a lack of direction as well strategic planning failure and wasted tactical effort.**

If offices are numbered, did the company establish a logical numbering scheme for the offices or workstations/cubicles? For example, the numbers for offices located on the second floor down one hallway begin with 2A (or 21−) followed by the office number. Offices on the same floor down a different hall-way begin with 2B (or 22−) followed by the office number. This is a small de-tail. However, done properly, an efficient numbering system minimizes wasted time and searching for the right location. If each floor is large, maps posted in conspicuous locations with the basic floor layout and the designation "you are here" help visitors—and fellow employees—find their destinations.

An illogical or non-existent numbering scheme reveals the company is stuck in the past. Its belief that a numbering system is not needed was estab-lished when the organization was small. **Has this larger organization reached a point where it has no vision for growth or its vision is self-limited or con-strained? The lack of attention to detail also contributes to poor internal communication, missed deadlines, and lack of a well-defined strategy.**

Are fire extinguishers and first aid kits available as required? Is each fire extinguisher or first aid kit easy to locate by a consistent easy-to-read sign or symbol? Do you have easy access to all fire extinguishers? Does each fire extin-guisher tag show a current inspection date, usually within one year of the most recent past inspection? Do you see any burned out lights in the exit signs?

Since each criterion is safety-related, this is critical. What do these ob-servations about fire equipment tell us about the organization? If the orga-nization shows negligence in fire equipment maintenance, someone in man-agement apparently believes in *Mad* magazine character Alfred E. Newman's famous brush-off, "What me worry?" or "No problem." It is a problem.

The company is reactive—not proactive. A proactive company would have everything in place before an emergency. A reactive company waits for disaster, and then notices what is not working. Its reactivity is mani-fested through lack of planning, whether in daily routines, unexpected business challenges, or emergency situations. To compound its lack of planning, the organization works from unrealistic assumptions about its customers, suppliers, creditors, regulators, and competitors.

Does the company maintain an AED—automatic electronic defibrilla-tor? Does the company have at least two employees trained in its proper use? Can you quickly identify the name, office location, and telephone extension for each trained person? If so, this company is forward-looking, although selectively.

Are the hallways clean? Is the carpet clean? Is the tile shiny, spot-free, and streak-free? Do you see or feel Braille indicators for the floor number and office numbers? If so, this is a positive action and sign of equal treatment. **This organization is outwardly focused; cares about its employees, suppliers, and customers; and is community-minded.**

Do you see easy to understand symbols for emergencies or emergency exit routes? **Do you see a map of evacuation routes, one that shows all exits?** In some states, this is required. **If required by state law and not readily visible on walls, then consider this a critical omission; the organization is poor at planning.**

A hangout is a place where people gather, usually on an informal basis. The coffee room, copier/network printer area, water cooler, receptionist's desk, and the cubicle or office of an informal organization leader are all potential hangouts.

- Look at the layout of the interior space. Did the architect and interior designers provide any built-in areas where a group of employees, and to a much lesser extent an employee and visitor, could meet informally?

- Hangouts are good. They encourage employees to get to know one another and informally exchange information and ideas. If the CEO's reception area is an executive hangout, that's a good sign—this is a space for open communication, exchanging ideas, and building camaraderie. If the layout and location of CEO's office discourages interaction, that's not a good sign—you can expect the organization to be run by an inwardly focused, standoffish, and possibly insecure CEO who prefers a large degree of separation from other leaders and may want to be in total unquestioned control.

Executive Hangouts

Carefully evaluate the executive office suite. Look for *hang out clues*, spaces where other executives are welcome to congregate. Like staff members, executives cannot work all day with little personal interaction.

You want to look for clues that help identify a suitable, convenient place for executives to congregate. Do you see an executive break room with a table with magazines surrounded by easy chairs, or a conference room with a wide selection of beverages and an executive kitchen or kitchenette?

Offices with little space to meet are a strong clue of individual fiefdoms, little face-to-face communication, excessive reliance on impersonal electronic communications, and a lack of trust and cooperation to ensure the organization moves in the same direction. An office with a sofa or a table and chairs allows more people to meet together, although private offices do not work well as regular hangouts because the resident executive needs enough private time to get his/her work done.

Executive hangouts work well, but with a caveat. If executives spend all their time in their own offices, in meetings, and hanging out with other executives, they are likely to lose touch with rank-and-file employees. The result? A two-tiered company of *the rulers* and *the ruled*, the rulers having insular perspectives and elitist, heads-in-the-clouds reputations and the ruled being well aware that the rulers rule in absentia.

Does the company post the daily price of its stock in plain view of visitors? This information is useful only to employees and should be kept in a place with restricted access. On second thought, why would a company post its stock price *anywhere* in the building—particularly with today's dramatic volatility? Whether a stock is up or down from the previous day can vary many times daily from market opening to its close.

Posting the stock price in the elevator, lobby, or anywhere it can be seen sends the wrong message to a visitor. This says the value of the holdings of executives and few employees is worth constant reinforcement—for better or worse. The effects on stock prices are many—from quarterly reporting, interim analyses of the stock, results of annual and portfolio manager meetings with company officials down to the level of body language and belches, rumors, and even intentional lies designed to send the stock price up or down.

Posted stock prices clearly show a link between the haves and have-nots. Employees may externalize stock market gains and losses, particularly losses. After all, it's easy to claim gains as a result of outstanding performance, but losses? It's easier to blame customers who failed to purchase the company's products. Thus, higher stock prices may improve employee attitudes toward customers—because everyone is on the same team. Conversely, lower stock prices may adversely affect employee dealings with the public. It's not the employees who failed. It's the consumers . . . demanding, cheap, and disloyal.

When an employer regularly posts the previous day's closing stock price, some employees may shift their focus from critical day to day business operations to align with the employer's interest in "the numbers." Other employees may be tempted to spend work hours "tracking" management activity, theorizing about the company's direction, and "second-guessing" the market price . . . hardly a productive use of time.

Changes in the daily share price should not affect morale, but if posted, likely will. An *up* stock price day may lead to more cooperation and a less tense work environment. A down stock price day, especially if the drop in price cannot be attributed to actions taken by the company, may put that day's activities in a tailspin.

Although stock prices can be influenced by a number of factors beyond the control of management or the employees, **the act of posting stock prices tells the visitor, "This is all about us" or "Although this is a lousy place to work or the company has 100% control over our time, we can at least make a few extra bucks if the stock goes up."**

Lighting

Has the company installed energy efficient light bulbs wherever possible? Energy efficient bulbs are available in spotlights, floodlights, standard light bulbs, and three-way light bulbs. **An organization with up-to-date energy efficient lighting can be characterized as appropriately thrifty, not cheap, since the initial cost of the replacement bulbs is far greater than standard incandescent lights. If the company installed LED (light emitting diode) fixtures, then the firm shows it is forward-thinking, environmentally responsible, electricity-saving, and community-minded.** Since many of the newer LEDs emit different colors of the light spectrum, the firm could be viewed as having an artistic flair.

Do you see burned out light bulbs in the ceiling or in wall-mounted fixtures? Proportionality counts. If you find many burned out bulbs, the company reveals its inattention to details. On a different level, the company may figure no one will notice; it haughtily believes it is such a superior operation that it does not need to pay attention to such minor items as burned out light bulbs.

If one or two bulbs among fifteen are burned out, then the organization is not paying attention to its fundamental business; it may be on the prowl for acquisitions or may be an acquisition target. If twenty bulbs out of fifty are burned out, the resulting relative darkness tells us the firm is hiding something. Are spotlights working properly, especially those aimed at artwork or awards? They should be; you want to see an organization that is proud of its taste in art or awards. **Unaccented art means the company**

has its focus on something new — new markets, new organization, new HR initiatives, new business partnerships — and is choosing to ignore or minimize its current operations.

Elevator

Two elevator-related observations are critical in the assessment of supreme suckiness. Do you see burned out lights for any floor numbers? This is a small detail. However, it is part of the all-important initial impression. The elevator is likely under a maintenance contract. Similar to vendor/management negligence when green plants in the lobby look shabby, a number of burned out elevator car lights is another example of management choosing to accept second- or third-rate work from its vendors. **Second- or third-rate work will permeate the firm's operational and regulatory-related functions.**

Does each elevator car show a current operating permit or inspection certificate? The certificate posted may be a photostatic copy. On the other hand, you may see a reference that the certificate is on file in the maintenance or operation manager's office. Either is fine. In some states, this is a required posting. If you do not see it, then **the lack of a posted operating certificate becomes a critical item.** Once again, **management has chosen to accept incomplete or shoddy work from its staff. Management may have limited tactical and strategic vision — this omission is readily observable, yet management has not bothered to ensure the maintenance department corrects the problem.**

Do you see or feel Braille indicators for floor numbers in the elevator? This is a small detail. However, it reflects on the organization's commitment to a lack of discrimination and visitor-friendliness.

Do you notice burned out lights in the ceiling of the elevator car? Do you see or feel loose elevator wall panels? Are the floors and walls clean? These are minor points. **Once again, this shows a lack of attention to detail,** and possible safety issues if enough lights are burned out or wall panels are demonstrably loose. Alternatively, burned out lights or loose panels may reflect an attitude of, "Let someone else report and/or take care of this obvious defect."

Does the organization post important notices in the elevator car? If the message is something that all employees, visitors, suppliers, and clients should see, then this shows an attempt at good communication. **If a *blast* broadcast method is used and the message reaches a far larger audience than intended then this reflects a lack of boundaries and respect between**

departments. Blast broadcast also reflects: departmental one-upmanship, laziness on the part of the sender who did not carefully identify the intended message recipients and use an appropriate communication method, and *pointy haired boss* cluelessness by the overseeing supervisor or department manager since this was not quickly corrected. **If the communication is appropriately targeted, that's great. Good communication is both an indicator and a precursor of good departmental cooperation, minimal politicking, and semi-enlightened management.**

Compliance with Disability Act Requirements

Modern building codes provide for equal ingress, egress, and mobility by disabled persons. Are the hallways sufficiently wide for use by wheelchair occupants? Does the company have push-button, electrically-activated doors into the building and in any interior areas where the doors would be difficult to handle? If the company does not use electronically activated-doors, are the manually operated doors lightweight or heavy? Are door openings sufficiently wide for wheelchairs? **This is a critical item.**

Congress passed the Americans with Disabilities Act (ADA) and President George H. W. Bush signed it on July 26, 1990. This law mandates equal treatment of disabled persons by private employers and government agencies. Ignorance of the law is no excuse; affected organizations have had more than 20 years to learn the requirements and comply. Unfortunately, this is a good/bad, over the line/not over the line issue. **If the company or organization fails to meet these long-established minimum requirements, it sends these messages:**

- **We do not treat everyone equally**

- **We hire only the physically able, thereby eliminating the pool of talented, capable employees whose only issues are physical disabilities**

- **We're better than everyone else since we're not trying to hide our non-compliance**

- **We are an insular organization, focused inwardly not outwardly**

- **We talk a good game; we do not practice what we preach**

- **We use a top-down management style; we don't really want to hear from the employees who deal with the day-to-day operational issues**

Summary

Our evaluation of common spaces continues with a look at floors and carpets, ceilings, hallways, lighting, and the elevator. Compliance with requirements of the Americans with Disabilities Act (ADA) completes our examination.

What is the condition of the floors and carpets? Are they clean? Are the carpets ripped, torn, slightly worn or threadbare? Do you find dust bunnies or dust elephants, the larger relative? Are hallways clear of paper and boxes? Do piles of paper sit in unused but visible corners? Can you find evidence of rodents?

Stains on the ceiling tell of far larger problems, as do ceilings that are unpainted or painted a color that does not blend with the color of walls. The architecture of the ceiling space needs to blend with the architecture of the surrounding walls.

Are offices numbered so you can easily locate your designation? Do you see first aid kits and fire extinguishers placed throughout? Can you easily find the signs that show the emergency routes and locations of emergency exits?

Is the lighting diffused or focused where it needs to be brighter? Does the type of lighting save energy? Count the number of burned out bulbs relative to the total number.

Does the organization post the operating permit in the elevator car, if required by state law? How many burned out lights for floors or in the ceiling can you count?

Does the organization's office space comply with the federal requirements established in 1990 by the Americans with Disabilities Act (ADA)? Electrically-operated, lightweight, or counter balanced doors are a good sign; a rest room that lacks a stall meeting ADA requirements is a bad sign.

~*~*~*~

CHAPTER 18

COMMON AREAS

I have lumped together a number of interior building locations under the heading *common areas*. By definition, common areas are shared spaces. Since everyone uses them, it is often the case that no one feels responsible for addressing issues or advising maintenance of anything that requires attention. Thus, negligence may be the result of failure to report safety, cleanliness, and maintenance issues. Or, perhaps these issues are reported, but the maintenance department is understaffed or underfunded—or, due to poor morale, under-motivated.

In any event, these common areas, which would also include the restrooms (which will be discussed in the next chapter), provide some of the most telling clues about organizational problems. Clues about organizational dysfunction can be found in the mail room, copy center, conference rooms, and around water fountains. Kitchens, break rooms, and cafeterias provide even more conclusive information.

Mail Room

You are highly unlikely to receive a grand tour of the mailroom during your visit to the company. If you are able to get a glimpse of the mail room, consider this a bonus. The key factors demonstrated by the condition of the mailroom are organization, timeliness, and service.

- Do you see clearly labeled pigeon holes for individual or departmental mail?

- Are there adequate horizontal work surfaces for efficient sorting and processing?

- Does the room have a designated storage space or closet set up for oversized packages? Or are oversized packages cluttering the floor so that workers find it difficult to move around the work space?

- Can you identify a logical, organized structure for delivery to each department? Is the organization consistent? Mailbox organization may be based on physical location of each department, by alphabetical order for easier sorting, or by department alphanumeric code or number. Each is fine as long as it is consistent. Is the mail for branch offices kept separate from mail for the main building?

- Does the company use special envelopes for internal mail? Is the outgoing mail basket marked as such and located away from the internal mail basket?

- Do the mailroom's responsibilities include charging each department for postage? If so, has the company established a standard marking system for each envelope to ensure proper charges?

- Does the mailroom supervisor post the times for incoming mail pick-up and outgoing mail distribution? Is this schedule accurately followed?

- What procedures are in place for last minute or emergency mailings or packages or shipments through FedEx, UPS, DHL, or local courier? What procedures are in place for regular and expedited delivery to overseas destinations?

- Is the mail cart neatly organized? An efficient mailroom with an inefficient mail cart makes no sense. A poorly managed mail cart wastes time and results in mail not getting delivered, landing in the wrong department, or not delivered in a timely manner.

- Do mailroom personnel help employees send personal packages and collect the necessary funds, if required? Are these collected funds tracked? If so, how?

Violation of basic mailroom operating standards indicates more dysfunctions—poor quality and untimely communication, missed deadlines, and lack of follow through on commitments.

Copy Center

Companies do not offer special copy center tours for prospective employees, suppliers, or customers. However, try to take a peek at the copy center on the way to your prospective manager's office or the rest room.

- Is the copier a newer or older model? Do you see staples or paper clips in the feeder, on top of the machine, or in the sorter? Is the glass copy surface smeared with dried white correction fluid or peeled correction tape?

- A more obscure measure of corporate dysfunction concerns the *copy rating* for the copier. The number of copies per month provides the basis for copier ratings. Simply put, copiers with higher ratings are more durable than those with lower ratings. Some companies will try to save money through leasing a copier with a lower copy rating than they need. Since the copier is overworked, it will break more often than one rated for the greater actual number of copies run per month.

The use a lower-rated copier than required is a sign of false economy, imprudent planning, and a penny-wise/pound-foolish attitude. Viewed at extremes, the company takes advantage of its employees, suppliers, customers, and financing sources.

Which options have been installed on the copier? Options include sorter, stapler, three-hole punch, enlarge/reduce, two-sided copies, set up for multiple jobs, and interrupt capability. The most sophisticated copier should be in the copy center. Departmental copiers may be less complex and incorporate only basic features. Is a system in place to restrict access or track usage of the copier by department? Some machines require a four-digit code; others require the swipe of a copy card through a reader. The code is much easier; and far easier to change and control than copy cards.

- Is colored paper available at the main copy center? Report covers, important memos, and posted company-wide notices may require use of colored paper.

- Does the main copy center stock different sizes of copy paper? Is the stock of 8-1/2 by 11 inch, 8-1/2 by 14 inch, and 11 by 17 inch paper sufficient?

- What is the typical turnaround time for copy jobs? How does the department handle rush jobs or special requests?

- If used, is the copy request form complete? Does it allow for exceptions to standard copy practices such as reduction or enlargement percentages, two-sided copying, and copy margin changes from the original document?

- Can you make your own copies if you wish or must someone from the copy department complete all the jobs submitted?

- Are the copies readable? Do you see dark lines on copies caused by a dirty platen?

- Can you see a backup toner cartridge? One of Murphy's Laws prevails in the copy room—when doing a rush job the copier will invariably run out of toner.

- Are binding options for documents available through the copy center? Do you have a choice of types and colors of bindings or does the company offer only one option?

Bottom line: **The copy center reflects the company's investment in people, processes, professionalism, and saving time.** An understaffed copy center—with the combination of low capacity copiers, lack of built-in copier options, lengthy turnaround times, limited sizes and colors of copy paper, an inability to accept rush jobs, dirty copiers, and outdated departmental copy charge assignment protocols—represents an extreme situation. **This less-than-inspired combination equals a solid warning that the company does not value its people, is characterized by empire-building, is wasteful, is not professional, and places little value on the employee's time.** Unfortunately, you would not likely spot this until after you have been hired.

Work and Conference Rooms

Work rooms and conference rooms are intermittently-used spaces which allow employees to meet to focus on targeted projects or tasks, to consult with clients, and for meetings of management and Boards of Directors. Except in the case of a CEO, these spaces are not usually owned by a specific individual. More often, they serve a specific department or are available company-wide by appointment.

Work Rooms

Depending on the industry, does the company offer quiet spaces for employees? Management consulting, investment banking, insurance actuary, market and investment research, teaching, architecture and engineering planning and design, high technology engineering, and production planning and scheduling are examples of jobs where employees need some quiet space. These quiet work rooms allow individual employees to work uninterrupted or two or three to confer without distraction. Can employees easily use a quiet space, if available? Can employees easily reserve this space?

Conference Rooms

Conference rooms provide subtle, but highly accurate, evidence of organizational impairment. We will explore the *approach* to conference rooms by examining the:

- Location, access, and scheduling

Then, we will step inside the rooms to evaluate the:

- Interior structure, furnishings, and equipment

Location, Access, and Scheduling

Many modern office environments are cubicle cities or cubicle farms, a core of row upon row of cubicles, with managerial and executive offices located on the periphery (usually where the windows are) or on a separate floor. If this describes the layout of the interior office space at your current or prospective company or customer, where are conference rooms located? Are they convenient for the groups which will need them? How many conference rooms serve a group of, say, 100 employees?

Depending on the nature of the business, at least one conference room per 50 employees is reasonable. One conference room per 25 employees is better. These conference areas may be relatively small. A 10-foot-by-15-foot room with a table and up to six chairs, a small hutch or credenza, a projector and small screen, a wall-mounted whiteboard, and sufficient room for an easel serves well for small group discussions

How far in advance must an employee reserve a conference room? Is the reservation process straightforward and easy? Do you have to go through Dilbert © administrative hell in order to reserve a room for a one- or two-hour time block? If you do, this is an obvious sign of dysfunction. Is the administrator using a complicated reservation process to wield power? Is the demand for conference room space sufficiently great that reservations must be made far in advance? Does your failure to use a reserved space and not provide advance cancellation notice result in a penalty? If so, what is the penalty? If not, how prevalent is this behavior?

Furnishings and Equipment

The appearance of the main corporate conference room, which serves as meeting space for larger internal groups, or corporation/client/vendor meetings, helps a visitor or prospective employee gain a better understanding of the corporate culture and possible dysfunctions. **The main conference room tells how the company sees itself—or wants to see itself.**

First, consider differences in décor—including the quality, style, and level of detail. Is the conference room furnished with extremely elaborate, expensive furniture and artwork when the reception area and employee workstations have relatively simple, functional furniture and bare walls? The opposite extreme mixes plain, almost hand-me-down, or used furniture in a conference room surrounded by nicer offices, workstations, and reception area. Of the two extremes, the fancy conference room in a plain office environment is far more likely.

What does the discrepancy between conference room furnishings and office furnishings communicate? **A fancy conference room in a relatively pedestrian work environment says, "We're a 'wanna be' company." This firm is most likely a start-up or a few years old in an industry where image or years in business is important. This company took the image part too far too fast. It views itself as a big player when, in reality, it is not. The key word is** *unrealistic*—**unrealistic expectations, unrealistic plans, and unrealistic schedules likely followed by disappointing deliverables to the client.**

As the largest piece of furniture in a company's suite of offices, the conference table communicates a strong message. Essentially, an organization may have a conference table; a C-O-N-F-E-R-E-N-C-E T-A-B-L-E; and, in an exaggerated visual metaphor, a C—O—N—F—E—R—E—N—C—E T—A—B—L—E. Most are appropriately large and functional. Some are very large and, while functional, are overly elaborate or ornate.

A table is too large for a room if the passageway behind the chairs around the table is not at least three feet and preferably more. Is the style of the conference table compatible with that of the chairs and other furnishings in the conference room?

An oversized conference table is the first clue that the company's executives or founders are *wannabes*, **aspiring to a level of professional and community respect or recognition that comes only after years of dependable and ethical work. The oversized table is a visual shortcut to respectability.**

An inappropriate mix of furniture styles (ultramodern with traditional, or custom wood pieces with 1970's vintage chrome and steel) is also a warning sign. **If the room furnishings appear unbalanced, the company or organization leadership lacks a sense of unity or unified vision. Internal** infighting characterizes this environment. **The company puts off decisions or debates an issue endlessly; the result is a compromise that does not really address the issue. The issue must be addressed again.** Carved tables, those made of exotic woods, or those built in four or six large sections reveal an oversized ego or set of egos.

What style of chairs surround the conference table? Do the chairs have arms or are they armless? Are they comfortable, with good lower back support? Do they roll, swivel, rock, adjust height, or some combination? Is the material leather or fabric? Chairs with arms are more professional and businesslike than those without, but also require more space behind them. Administrators use chairs with no arms.

Chairs must fit around the conference table in a room designed for serious business discussions. Since discussions may extend for hours on end, the chairs should be comfortable and offer firm support, especially for the back's lumbar region. If the chairs rock, they should be designed to do so safely; today's office chairs have five or six wheels and supports rather than the traditional four. The height should easily adjust so that both the user's feet are flat on the floor when the person sits. **Uncomfortable chairs, which may indicate lesser quality, may highlight cost saving. In the worst case, chairs for visitors are intentionally somewhat uncomfortable, giving the members of the firm an advantage in negotiations.**

Although leather is often associated with quality, it is not the best choice for chairs in a conference room. **Leather looks good, but does not breathe sufficiently. (Vinyl or naugahyde is worse.)** After people sit for a long time in leather chairs, the chair occupant can sweat. The chairs' leather-covered arms may actually become sticky from perspiration from hands and wrists. Fabric chairs do two things: breathe, allowing evaporation; and absorb residual sweat, making those who sit in them far more comfortable.

Can you see a voice amplifier in the center of the conference table? These devices are necessary for telephone discussions involving meeting participants in remote locations. It is difficult to imagine someone in the role of information relay person in a serious telephone-based conference discussion. If you see a voice amplifier, then that's a healthy sign. If you do not, then it is appropriate to wonder how a group of employees communicates with another group of employees or clients at an office connected only by a telephone line even with speakerphone capability. It is also appropriate to wonder about the quality and speed of decision-making at this company or organization.

Do conference room furnishings include a credenza? The style of the credenza should match the style of the conference table and chairs. The goal is an integrated look. A credenza can easily store couple of reams of copy paper, pads of easel paper, marker pens, white board erasers, remote controls, and company literature. The organization may also use a closet, storage cabinet, or open shelving unit. **A credenza in the main conference room is a sign of a grown-up, sophisticated, planning-oriented company. However, the presence of an oversized, overly-elaborate, or unmatched credenza, like an oversized conference table, indicates a *wannabe* company and one that wastes space and money.**

Many conference rooms include built-in projectors mounted on the ceiling. Newer technology provides connectors between the projector and a personal computer. The presenter attaches his PC, or loads her PowerPoint presentation, Word document, Excel spreadsheet, or flash drive with photographs into the projector's PC. Alternatively, do you see an older slide viewer or small video monitor near the conference table? Although not as fancy as the ceiling mounted projector, a monitor will work for smaller groups.

Is the tightly rolled projection screen electrically operated or is it a pull-down model? An electrically operated screen is classier. However, does it blend with the rest of the furnishings? Do you see an electrically-operated screen with a manual projector setup on a plastic, metal, or wood shelving unit or cart? Are a plain conference table and basic wall unit paired with a sophisticated, electrically-operated projection screen? This is not an appropriate combination. This combination shouts, *incongruity*, and provides clues of organizational dysfunction.

Which specific organizational dysfunctions do these incongruities illustrate?

The company does not understand what is appropriate in terms of internal conduct and external appearance. Potential internal conduct problems include poor employee relations, possible discrimination, and unequal treatment of women and/or minorities. Potential external appearance problems include brochures with incomplete information, a visually unappealing and uninformative website, and the dissemination of out-of-date information.

Wall Furnishings

Many companies make effective use of the main conference room walls to impart a desired atmosphere/impression or to communicate information about the company, publicize its values, and provide a record of company history, awards, and global outreach. Every few years, the organization should change artwork and poster art.

First, note the artwork, if any. Does the art blend with the style and scale of the room and with the furniture in that room? An obvious style mismatch would be ornately-framed Dutch Masters portraits in a room furnished with sleek, modern furniture. Likewise, loose and bold abstracts would not work well with formal, traditional furniture.

Is the artwork an appropriate size for the wall space and room? Relatively large wall art should hang on a large wall in a very large room fitted with relatively large pieces of furniture. A small clustered arrangement of framed art may occupy the same visual space as that of one large wall sculpture or framed painting, drawing, or poster. The objective is not mono-style or mono-scale, but a visually pleasing environment that facilitates, rather than distracts from, business. Native American—also called Southwestern art, Asian art, or Art Nouveau posters are surprisingly colorful and versatile.

People display artwork in their homes which they feel reflects their interests and who they are. A corollary would be to ask, "What does the artwork in the conference room say about the company's interests and what the company represents?" This raises the question of whether strictly decorative artwork belongs in a business environment. What is its purpose? Does nice artwork strengthen employee morale, attract better quality customers or clients, improve vendor relationships, or provide a better return to the bottom line? When the company is not getting the results it wants, does it need to buy or lease more expensive artwork to improve its operations? If so, what kind of artwork? Might the problem be solved by trying a different style of artwork?

For instance, the only company appropriate for high-quality portraits of the Dutch Masters might be a certain cigar company. For other companies, the likelihood is that these pictures would be lithographs or mass market posters. **Unless the company is in the art investment business, purchasing extremely high-ticket artwork means it is spending an inordinate amount of money on non-business *frills*. This would likely be the result of an egocentric, high-level executive more interested in appearances and accumulating *things*, rather than in bottom line performance for the benefit of shareholders.** Additionally, this particular type of artwork would suggest that the company is stodgy and not focused on the future. **Investment banks and private client banks may be the only two acceptable exceptions to this guideline.** Both want to create comfortable, almost home-like environments which suggest traditional values. The objective? To build customer confidence in businesses that work with large sums of money.

Dutch Masters aside, any attempt to impress with recognizable, original masterworks indicates the company is focused on appearances, not on its primary business. Perhaps the company feels more safe purchasing artwork or copies of that artwork which have recognized value rather than risk purchasing something of less *known* value.

Art, being highly subjective, is one case where *you get what you pay for* does not necessarily hold true. Excellent original artwork by lesser known artists is available at far more modest prices. At the same time, a higher price is no guarantee of quality. Many popular artists are not necessarily *good* artists. Thomas Kincaide, America's self-described *Painter of Light*, was a master at marketing yellow paint, but his perspective was painfully inaccurate. For the aesthetically-educated, there is little more irritating than seeing poorly-executed artwork prominently displayed day in and day out . . . and questioning, "If the person who selected this could not see the errors, what other errors is the company not seeing?"

In contrast, Tom James of investment bank Raymond James & Associates in St. Petersburg, Florida, displays his and his wife Mary's personal art collection of more than 1,800 works not only in conference rooms but throughout the firm's four-building campus. Mr. James' collection focuses on Western and Southwest U.S. art. The collection also includes contemporary, Pop, figurative, sports art, and landscapes. Although Mr. James's background was not one of investment research and analysis, he takes pride in doing his own research and buying art from undiscovered artists. The firm has a full-time curator who rotates and maintains the art. The public can enjoy the James' art collection through pre-scheduled tours.

Wall Displays

Aside from establishing "atmosphere, the second, and more important, purpose of wall decoration is to communicate the company's values and philosophy, How does a company make the intangible tangible? Easy. The values and philosophy can be read in the corporate history. A company's history is the main component of its organizational DNA.

Wall art is a crucial vehicle to communicate this history.

If you get the chance, peek into the conference room. The walls in this important setting will provide information beyond what you may have learned from the art on the walls in the reception area. Look for:

- photographs or, more traditionally, oil-painted portraits of the company's founders

- statements of philosophy

- mission statements, statements of purpose, organizational goals

- photographs, drawings, or patent applications for early products or services

- community and industry awards

- letters of appreciation

- published articles about company activities and accomplishments

- links with sports or political figures

- milestones

- donations to community and arts agencies

- relevant maps or photographs which illustrate the company's global presence

One of the items likely to be displayed prominently on a conference room wall is the organization's mission statement. As an aside, a Google search under "write a mission statement for a business" yielded 8,600,000 results—in only 0.21 seconds! Hundreds, likely thousands, of websites provide free assistance to organizations wanting to create a meaningful mission statement.

Despite this readily available, free, good-quality advice, most organization's mission statements suck. Most mission statements are *motherhoods* (conventional social allegiances), are non-specific, praise God/apple pie/the military/freedom, do not relate directly to the firm or company (could relate to any organization), and do not mention suppliers, customers, creditors, regulators, employees, and/or shareholders.

Read the mission statement. What does it *not* talk about?

Water Fountains

The lowly water fountain may be divided into five areas for evaluation: overall condition, cleanliness, noise level, water temperature, and the location of the fountain.

- *Overall condition.* Is the unit shiny, with no rust or hard water stains?

Is all fountain hardware attached and working? Is the stream set so one can drink from the fountain without one's lips or cheek touching the spout or protector?

- *Cleanliness.* Is the stainless steel shiny? Is the drain opening clean and shiny? Is the unit polished with no grime build up around the base of the spout, handle, or protector?

- *Noise level of fountain.* Do the pump motor and compressor make a lot of noise when water is dispensed or the compressor is cooling?

- *Temperature of water.* Ice cold, cold, room temperature, lukewarm, hot. A water fountain with a compressor should not dispense room temperature, lukewarm, or hot water.

- *Location* – Is it conveniently located?

Kitchen/Breakroom/Cafeteria

Organizations vary in their accommodation of employees' need for breaks and meals. Very small organizations may provide nothing more than a coffee pot sitting on top of a small, unstocked refrigerator. Larger organizations may have multiple break rooms and fully staffed, on-site cafeterias.

In any area where food is prepared or served, evaluate:

- *Cleanliness of walls, floors, and ceiling.* Has food been left smeared or splattered on the walls or ceiling? Is the floor clear of food debris? Do you see signs of insect or rodent infestation?

- *Condition of paint.* Is the paint chipped? Is the color scheme pleasant and harmonious?

- *Condition and cleanliness of counters and serving areas.* Are the countertops and serving areas clean or dirty?

- *Condition of the sink.* Are the sink or faucets rusted with built-up lime scale on the handles and debris at the base of the handles or along the edges where the sink meets the countertop? Is a soap dispenser available at the sink? Is it full and functioning?

Kitchen/Breakroom

The kitchen which is used by employees in a smaller company (as differentiated from that used by professional food preparers in larger organizations) is one of my favorite places for evaluating an organization's health.

Why? The kitchen can look great one minute. After an unmotivated, uncaring employee enters the room, the degree of overall sloppiness following in his/her wake mirrors the health of the organization.

If the company's manufacturing process requires use of a continuous line, is the kitchen sufficiently large to allow the entire production staff to eat lunch together in that room? Is the room furnished with long, rectangular tables or with small round or square tables? Smaller tables encourage discussions of up to four or five co-workers. With longer tables, employees create defined areas for group interaction. Communication is impaired because each person can only clearly see (and read) the faces of the people on the opposite side of the table.

Do you see a jumble of electrical plugs jammed into a single outlet? Do the wires connect to major energy-drawing appliances—microwave, toaster oven, toaster, electric kettle, and, in the worst possible case, the refrigerator/freezer? The use of a surge protector is irrelevant; this circuit is overloaded—and dangerous.

Is the Formica or laminate on the countertops or tables chipped, worn, dirty, or discolored? The time of day you inspect the kitchen does not matter. Dirty countertops reveal employee attitudes. During or just following the busy lunch rush, someone could wipe the countertop—preferably the person who made the mess in the first place. However, if no one bothered, the lack of pride in cleanliness is obvious.

Employee Accessible Refrigerator

Is there a refrigerator for employees' lunches or snack foods? In larger organizations, the employee-accessible refrigerator may be close to, but separate from the professional cafeteria refrigerators. In smaller organizations, the employee accessible refrigerator, if there is one, will be in the break area, or tucked into a corner of the storage room. Evaluate:

- *Condition of the outside of the refrigerator.* Is it clean and rust free?

- Is the cold storage space large enough to hold everyone's lunch and beverages?

- *Condition of the walls, shelves, and drawers inside the refrigerator.* Are they clean? Or are they dirty, broken, or rusty? **The overall cleanliness of the refrigerator tells you about employees' and management's real attitudes toward the company.** I expect small spills or crumbs; I do not want to see mold growing, hardened beverage spills on the bottom, or weeks or months out-of-date dairy products.

- *Condition of the freezer.* Do you see chunks of built-up ice? A dirty, rusted, or broken shelf? A dirty or broken freezer door shelf? What about the freezer's contents? Do you see half-open containers; spilled, now frozen, beverages; or evidence that food items have been thawed and refrozen? An unreliable freezer is a health issue.

Do you see the ubiquitous sign: *All food items must be cleaned out before Friday afternoon at 3:00. Otherwise, we will throw out those items. Signed, Management?* Despite the sign, when you open the refrigerator door, do you see outdated food inside?

If the refrigerator appears neglected, the message is conclusive: A bunch of uncaring, unmotivated, lazy employees works here. Interestingly, management generally does not empty the refrigerator and throw out the old items as stated. **This is a critical item.** Such idle threats show a lack of company management commitment and follow-through.

If you are able to snoop around, you can observe the refrigerator in as little time as it took to read this. Pop the refrigerator door open as if to see whether there would be space for your lunch. You can quickly check for mold, outdated dairy products, and major spills. Elapsed time: 15 seconds.

Check the sink. **If you see dirty coffee mugs, dishes, glasses, and silverware in the sink, then this is additional evidence of poor employee attitudes.** If the company is good enough to provide free coffee (including decaffeinated), creamer, sugar, and artificial sweetener, then the least the employees can do is keep this area clean. This is common courtesy—not an expectation of holier-than-thou behavior.

A dirty sink exposes a lazy subset of employees—those who fail to keep their commitments and meet deadlines, who do not communicate well with other employees, and some who expect someone else to clean up their messes, whether in the kitchen, on paper, or in the production process. Some not-so-subtle one-upmanship may be at play since certain employees or managers will always expect someone else, generally a subordinate, to clean up the mess the offender made.

You may see handwritten signs communicating expectations posted on the cabinet over the sink. Look for the infamous message, *Your Mother does not work here. Clean up after yourself. Signed: Management.* Or an equivalent. This adds fuel to my lazy employee fire. Not only is a subset of employees lazy, the group does not respond to written requests. This naked display of management's frustration further highlights the traits of lazy, unmotivated, uncaring, non-responsive, non-team players—habitually late employees who miss deadlines and need someone to cover for them so their incompetence remains hidden from management.

Look for signs (literally) that complain about stolen food. Stolen food means one or more miscreants have no respect for private property and, more importantly, believe they won't get caught. **Evidence of stolen food also represents stolen ideas, clients, and time.** This organization has a war-zone-like work environment—individuals are forced to respond defensively. Operating in a defensive mode increases stress and distraction, which stalls creativity and cripples initiative. An organization plagued with internal theft is running nowhere near 100%.

Does the company sell sodas, fruit juices, bottled water, even foods through vending machines? These machines can be located in the employee kitchen, break room, cafeteria, or sometimes even within departments or in hallways. If vending machines are used, how fairly priced are the beverages and food items? Alternatively, does the company excessively mark up the items for sale to its captive customer base? Do the profits go to a fund for employee activities or personal assistance, if needed?

Does the company offer coffee or tea? If so, is it self-serve in the kitchen or break room? Does the company charge for coffee or tea? Has the company established an honor system, where employees pay per cup? Does someone collect a nominal amount each month from participants to pay for coffee, tea bags, creamers, cups, and stirrers? If the company uses a vending machine to dispense coffee, tea, or hot chocolate, what is the price per cup? Do the profits go to a fund for employee activities or personal assistance, if needed?

Does the organization provide non-refrigerated single-serving half-and-half or non-dairy creamers? Are flavored creamers an option? Real dairy products and flavored creamers are a plus; the company is willing to go the extra mile for everyone's benefit. Does the organization provide packets of refined sugar, raw/turbinado sugar, Equal ©, Splenda ©, or Sweet 'N Low ©? Alternatively, do you see only powdered creamer? **A variety of fresh creamers and sweetener packets shows a variety of thinking and is one means to provide a variety of small benefits for staff members.** The use of powdered creamer means the organization wants to just get by, doing the minimum for its employees and customers. If the firm previously provided fresh milk, half-and-half, or creamers and switched to powdered creamer, the firm's business is not healthy.

Excessive markups on all beverages are a critical item. Keeping the money and not rebating it to employees in some impartial manner is unforgivable. Taking advantage of a captive audience translates to only one thing—greed.

Selfish, passive-aggressive behavior builds on itself; bad behavior leads to more bad behavior. As employees consciously or subconsciously observe organizational dysfunction, they will respond consciously or subconsciously with their own negligent or purposely destructive acts. It is difficult to turn an organization around when employee attitude is reflected by a dirty refrigerator, spills on counter tops, and a filthy sink. Posting clean up signs is not going to get the attention of the most egregious violators. From the tone of my discussion, **this is a critical item. Why?**

The messy kitchen reflects lack of teamwork, lack of individual and corporate responsibility, not-so-subtle employee rebellion against perceived internal requirements, and insubordination against a management that preaches economy yet flies first class, stays in four- and five-star hotels and dines in the most expensive restaurants.

Let us step back for a moment and think more about the behaviors associated with a dirty kitchen. Generally, employees use kitchen equipment one at a time. If someone makes a mess, how likely is another, clean-oriented employee to point out the mess and ask that the offending party to clean it up? Not very.

Unless an individual wants to be ridiculed as a *Mr. (or Ms.) Clean*, the fictional character with the same name as a liquid cleaning detergent, s/he will watch—and, perhaps, glare. The offending employee may defensively ask the critical employee. "What are you looking at?" as if the behavior should be acceptable. If requested to wipe up a spill, the miscreant may try to shift the responsibility or blame by saying, "It was already a mess when I got here—I'm *not* the janitor." The offenders are also likely to respond with an attack, as if the observer were out of line in making the request: "Leave me alone," "Mind your own business," or, "If you don't like it, then you clean it up." And if Mr. or Ms. Clean doesn't volunteer for the job, the messmaker uses that as justification—the mess wasn't that big a deal.

Bottom line: No one has much incentive to intervene and tell messy co-workers to clean after themselves.

Look at the wastebaskets. Are they full or overflowing? Or has someone taken the time to empty the baskets or tamp down the trash? If the wastebasket fills during the day, then common courtesy dictates tamping down the contents to make more room or taking the trash to the dumpster. This is more subtle. However, once again, mess overflowing the wastebaskets shows two things: Employees do not care about the company's success and management is not paying attention to potential health-related issues.

The kitchen problem is seldom limited to a single appliance or built-in. Objectively, the refrigerator, stove/oven, microwave, counter tops, and sink are clean—or they are not. The wastebasket is full or overflowing—or it is not. One sign of dysfunction generally accompanies a second, third, or fourth sign of aberrant behavior. Similar to never finding only one cockroach in the kitchen or one ant at a picnic, you never find only one sign of organizational dysfunction, especially in the kitchen.

Not only are these kitchen indicators consistent, they are reliable indicators of organizational dysfunction. Due to ingrained cultural and organization-specific practices, the kitchen indicators remain solidly in place, unmoved by the addition or subtraction of a few employees.

One other food-related benefit can quickly morph into a problem. Some companies boast of a snack closet in the kitchen, where employees help themselves to any of a number of free snacks. Some organizations may go so far as to provide fancier snacks—gourmet cookies, truffles, popped popcorn or the highly addictive kettle corn. Other fancy snacks may include healthier foods—granola bars, refrigerated hummus, pita or naan, and vegetable and/ or fruit trays.

At first glance, this is a wonderful benefit. What you may not realize is the company expects its employees to work long hours, likely including some weekends. The easy availability of food minimizes time away from the office to get a breath of fresh air and buy food or mingle with fellow workers who are also working late or on weekends. In short, beware of organizations bearing food!

Employee Cafeteria/Break Room

The Eating Space

A larger company often has an employee cafeteria or good-sized break room. Many of the evaluation criteria are similar to those for a smaller kitchen, although there are differences.

Does the facility accommodate most or all the production staff at a single sitting? The latter is rare, since it is not the most efficient use of space and requires stopping the production process if everyone leaves the production floor at the same time. However, a single lunch period enhances the opportunity for informal production staff interactions. This space can also be used effectively for company-wide informational meetings.

Many manufacturing companies have small cafeterias or break rooms capable of serving a limited number of employees at a time. Staggered lunch and coffee breaks enable a company to maintain a continuous (albeit, perhaps slowed) production process over the break times and to stay within safe break room occupancy limits. However, production staff with different lunch shifts will not be able to use that time to brainstorm production line improvement strategies or build interpersonal relationships that enhance teamwork.

Do the company's managers and executives eat in the same cafeteria as rank-and-file employees? Do they have a different lunch schedule, a designated separate section or, through tradition, do only executives and managers eat at certain tables? If so, are the tables for managers identified as such? If so, this visually emphasizes a rigid hierarchical structure and resistance to change. Do the executives and managers select from different menus?

Executives and managers eating in separate dining facilities or dining from separate menus are significant warning signs of dysfunction.

Why? When managers, through corporate tradition, refuse to mix with non-managers, they are reinforcing a class distinction—that they are above the common worker and do not need to socialize, let alone communicate with or get to know those who actually carry out the day-to-day activities.

Does the organization operate the facility or does a third-party manage and operate it under contract? I believe self-managed food services are evidence of corporate distraction. Unless the company is in the food service business, it makes little sense for it to manage this no-win function with its myriad of equipment, safe food storage and handling, ventilation, worker safety, and health and nutrition requirements. **If a large company that is not in the food services business manages the cafeteria, the company does not know its limits, lacks boundaries, imagines company strengths, lacks flexibility in relation to new inputs, and focuses on the past if the organization has always operated its own food service facility. The company should stick to its main business.**

Additionally, since corporate cafeteria bashing is always in style, it makes little sense for a company to put itself in line for culinary criticism. In the eating area of the cafeteria, note:

- Are the walls, floors, and windows clean? Are the tables and chairs clean and in good repair?

- Is there sufficient space around the tables for people to comfortably walk with their trays? Is the room well-lit? Is the atmosphere pleasant?

- Are there touchless hand sanitizer stations available at the cafeteria's entrance?

- Has the company installed effective sound-dampening technology in the cafeteria? Large open spaces with hard surfaces can reverberate with unpleasant noise levels if soft materials are not used somewhere. The clank of silverware on plates, conversation, and the scrape of moving chair legs can result in jangled nerves.

- Have immature employees plastered sandwiches on or planted fork tines in the ceiling? This is behavior more often associated with junior high school students. In the organizational environment, it is a sign of extreme dissatisfaction and rebellion.

Do dirty dishes on trays remain on the tables after workers have left the room? **If the cafeteria operation expects everyone to bus her/his dishes to a conveyor or rack, then a large number of tables with dirty dishes and trays is a clear sign of dysfunction.** When are these dirty tables cleaned and wiped? By whom? Does anyone wipe the table down between seatings? Are disinfectant-towelettes available so employees may wipe down the tables? Remember, you are highly likely to find multiple signs of dysfunction. If one table is dirty, you will surely find other dirty tables. Dirty table tops loudly proclaim:

- "I do not bus my dishes; I am far more important than anyone else." This is not the sign of an egalitarian organization where everyone pitches in as expected. This special person is a credit taker, not a genuine contributor. Be careful if you must work together on a project or serve together on a committee.

- "My time is more valuable. I do not bus my dishes. One's sense of self-and community-respect, and common courtesy is more important than this bad boy's valuable time. His priorities are not straight; his values are not aligned with those of the company. Chances are good that her work is substandard, sloppy, or late. She does not care.

She may be a short-timer, one who plans to soon leave the company, or was never fully integrated. He may have been an error in hiring.

Other things to note in the eating area of the cafeteria:

- Neatness, spelling, and pricing accuracy on the menu board, if one is used

- Does the company use china, plastic plates, or high or low quality paper plates?

- Does the company use silverware, or high or low quality plastic ware?

Food Handling

As with the kitchen, any health-related violation is a warning sign. **Food safety-related warning signs are critically important, since they relate to health and ultimately to employee absenteeism.**

If you get to tour the breakroom or cafeteria food preparation area, apply the same guidelines as those for employee kitchen facilities. Watch for:

- Dirty ovens and stovetop burners

- Grease-filled vent hoods (actually a fire hazard)

- Dirty refrigerators

- Dirty serving counters

- Dirty utensil and napkin holders

Realistically, one cannot see inside the commercial refrigerator or oven. You can't get close enough to inspect the stovetop burners. However, timing may be in your favor. A cafeteria worker may open the refrigerator door when you are standing in a place where you can quickly observe. Since you cannot easily and consistently look inside the refrigerator or oven, then you should place additional emphasis on the factors you can observe, such as:

- Burned out lights

- Condition of ceiling tiles

- Condition of walls and baseboards

- Floors

- Food slicing machines, if used

- Glass sneeze panels on the serving line

- Menu lettering and spelling

- Utensils, seasonings, condiments, and napkin holders

From this list, the key factors, all items that touch food, are:

- Food slicing machines

- Tops of dining tables

- Utensil and napkin holders

The three items listed directly above are critical items. Germs on this equipment or these surfaces may also spread to people—a potential epidemiological nightmare.

Summary

The common areas offer extensive clues to organizational weirdness. In the mail room, look at the logic of the setup and the organization of the mail cart. In the copy center, the all-important number of copies per month rating becomes an important indicator.

In the conference room, wall displays of mission statements, photographs, milestones, employees of the month/quarter/year, letters of appreciation, and community support add to your storehouse of information about the organization. Although no single indicator in the conference room is critical, certain combinations of décor and furnishings provide strong clues to dysfunction:

- The combination of an oversized, overdone conference table with a manual screen and portable projector.

- The combination of small conference table with electrically operated screen and built-in projector.

- An electronically-operated screen and a fancy table which does not match metal or wooden shelving used for office supply storage.

- The use of leather or vinyl chairs which communicates that the company does not like to hold long meetings.

- With the exception of investment banks and financial services firms, expensive artwork does not belong in the conference room.

In short, when analyzing the conference room, **look for things that do not fit together.** Too much emphasis on a firm's early history tells you the firm is living in the past or cannot move forward. Excessive emphasis on community activity tells you the firm is spread too thinly. Autographed pictures of sports figures scream loudly, "This is a group of emulators or wanna-bes. The presence of too many pictures of the organization's executives with politicians reveals either a lack of operational boundaries or that the organization feels its actions are protected by its strong political links. Check out the mission statement, if visible. Does it really tell you the organization's mission? Items of furniture or wall furnishings that do not fit together indicate policies, customer relations, or people not fitting together within the organization.

Water fountains should be clean and operate quietly. Rust stains and tarnished metal indicate bigger problems.

Dirt is the enemy in the kitchen/breakroom/cafeteria; specifically, dirty counter tops, *clean up after yourself* signs, filthy sinks, and dirty refrigerator shelves and door compartments. Employee and corporate attitudes are clearly expressed and amplified in the cafeteria . . . as well as in the next common area we will explore—the restroom.

~*~*~*~

CHAPTER 19

RESTROOMS

No evaluation of corporate dysfunction would be complete without a visit to the restroom. In fact, **the restroom provides so many clues about organizational dysfunction, we may be tempted to call it the number one (pun intended) source.**

Sad to say, the appearance of the restroom at any time of day reflects simultaneously the corporate culture and employees' attitudes. Stated differently, **"The restroom does not lie."** You or I could provide advance notice of our planned visit to the organization's offices. Just before our visit, everything would be re-cleaned and the organization would feel 100% prepared. However, the condition of the restroom during our visit will reveal employees' true attitudes. **Of all the assessment tools used, this one is most consistent.** Restroom evaluation criteria are divided into the following categories:

- Sanitation requirements, cleanliness, and environment

- Ceilings, walls, and floors

- Stalls, toilets, urinals, and sinks

- Accommodations for women, disabled employees, or visitors

Sanitation Requirements, Cleanliness, and Environment

Is the handle on the outside door to the restroom fastened securely? Is this handle clean? Is the entrance door hung properly so it closes completely? Is the door adequately wide for disabled access? Restroom doors often open inward. If the doors are heavy and do not have electronic assistance, disabled or elderly employees or visitors could end up trapped in a restroom. In the event of a fire, the result could be tragic.

What is your first impression? How clean is the restroom overall? Do you see trash or paper towels scattered on the floor? Is the paint in good condition? Is the wallpaper peeling? How many burned out lights do you count? Do you see graffiti on the walls of the stalls? Are any mirrors dirty or streaked?

What is the temperature of the room? Is it colder or warmer than the offices, kitchen/cafeteria/break room, and hallways? A small difference in temperature is acceptable. However, a significant difference in temperature reveals inattention to employee welfare and morale, lack of concern for employees' health since hotter environments are incubators for germs, an imbalance in the efficient operation of the organization, and lack of attention to detail. Lack of attention usually results in missed key deadlines.

How does the restroom smell? The use of strong-smelling disinfectants and air-fresheners, some of which have been proven to be carcinogenic, in the restrooms, particularly units which release their scent according to motion or on a timed basis scream one thing—the restrooms are not properly cleaned. Proper ventilation with powerful but quiet restroom fans can keep the air clean and free of smell. However, sewer gas may leak in from improperly maintained plumbing. Water leaks behind the walls can promote the growth of mold. A busy restroom may retain a definite odor if the wastebaskets aren't emptied and properly sanitized. Too many urinal cakes in urinals leave a lingering odor. If the place consistently smells badly, then the company does not care about its image or the health of its employees. The organization is cheap.

The restroom is *not* the place for a company to save a few dollars.

What do you hear? Do you hear flushing or running water noises or conversation from the adjacent gender-opposite restroom? If so, then this reflects cheap building construction or installation of cheap plumbing fixtures and valves. These extraneous noises are particularly a problem if they exist in newer buildings, which are built to more stringent building codes. Good insulation, quality equipment, plus use of high quality valves should equal a quiet operating environment.

Many department stores, discount stores, and supermarkets post a form adjacent to or on the back of the main restroom door. If the company uses such a posted checklist, is it correct and timely? If you visit the restroom five minutes after an inspection was completed, you want to see an item checked off as okay after a previous inspection identified the item as a problem.

From a different perspective, the use of this form assigns accountability. However, if the person who must periodically check the condition of the restrooms has other required public-facing tasks, then these inspections will not be completed and the employee has a legitimate excuse for not doing the required inspection. If a company fails to monitor the condition of the restroom as required, then this lack of follow-through is indicative of lack of attention to details with resulting missed key deadlines, a culture of internal finger-pointing, and an environment where management responsibility and accountability are not equal. In this work environment, managers are responsible for certain tasks or processes but are not held accountable for failure or success.

Do you see burned out light bulbs? Once again, this indicates poor attention to detail. It is a matter of degree. If you note many burned out individual incandescent bulbs or two or three fluorescent bulbs, then this is a clear warning sign of major corporate dysfunction. Any burned out LED or halogen bulbs are cause for concern, since these new technology lighting devices rarely burn out. The combination of lack of attention to detail, lack of concern for an environment used by employees and visitors, and lack of follow through reveals an "I don't care" attitude on the part of management. Admittedly, some managers ignoring these problems may have a short-timer's attitude—they have a short time remaining before they give their notice to quit.

The task of replacing burned light bulbs is generally the responsibility of one person or one department. Why attribute major dysfunction to an entire organization based on the overlooked actions of a busy department with significant operating responsibilities? Since management sees the situation every day; *some manager, any manager,* should realize its impact on employees and visitors. Someone in charge should ask for the relatively simple remedial action—replace the bulbs and, while you're at it, please wipe down the fixtures.

If the restroom has decorative items placed around the sink or atop a shelf, are these items in good repair? Do they shine? Do they show a layer or two of dust or dirt? Plants, stone or sand arrangements, knick knacks, or tops of pictures should be clean as should built-in architectural restroom features. In restrooms at four- and five-star hotels or resorts, you should expect nothing less than everything being *perfect*.

Ceilings, Walls, and Floors

Is the ceiling smooth, clean, and well-maintained? Is it stained yellow from years of cigarette smoke or less-than-white from a build-up of dust and dirt? Most businesses have not allowed smoking in the restrooms for the past decade, so if the ceilings are stained in this way, either company employees are ignoring the "no smoking" mandate, or the company never bothered to repaint the ceiling. Is the paint blistered and stained from water damage, either from a leaking roof or from bathroom or kitchen leaks on the floor above? Are there mold stains or cobwebs in the corners?

What is the condition of the painted walls, wallpaper, paneling, or tile? Is the paint faded, chipped, worn, or cracked? Do you see chipped paint on corners, exposing white wallboard? Is the wallpaper clean, and free from rips and bubbles? Is the paneling properly maintained? Are the moldings dusted? Is the wall tile free of chips and evenly grouted? Is the grout clean? This is not a major item. However, teamed with other indicators, what emerges is a picture of whether or not the company pays attention to details.

If there are mirrors over the sinks, are they spattered with water stains? Are they cracked, chipped, or corroded? Has the reflective silver finish chipped away, especially in the lower corners? Silvering on a mirror chips away due mainly to age. If you see a small section of unreflective surface, that's okay. If the bottom two-to-three inch width of the mirror has no silver, then the organization is not accurately or fully reflective of its mission. In addition, the organization and its leaders do not consciously acknowledge good deeds done by employees—employees are taken for granted.

Does restroom equipment, in men's as well as women's restrooms, include a baby diaper-changing table? If so, this is a thoughtful touch. However, before adding a point, ensure the table is securely fastened to the wall. It should also be clean, in good repair, and have a functioning safety restraint (belt).

What is the condition of the floor? Most commercial and residential restrooms have tile floors because tile is durable and impervious to water. Older buildings may have old-style linoleum, which can be an asbestos-containing hazard. Are the floors reasonably clean and stain-free? Are the tiles broken, badly-stained, or missing, and the hard-to-reach floor areas (corners, under toilets and sinks, behind the door) thick with a buildup of dirt and debris? Is the grout free of dirt and stains? Broken tiles and deteriorating grout can be a safety hazard and filth is just that—filth.

Another lesser-known cleanliness indicator is the floor drain. Nearly all commercial restrooms include a drain for water drainage after mopping the floor or cleaning the walls. Look at the drain. Do you see lint or dirt caught in the drain cover? Extensive build-up shows the lack of thorough restroom cleaning. **In essence, people in this organization do only enough of their jobs to meet minimum standards.** If cleaning occurs frequently and completely, then someone would remove the lint or dirt from the drain grate.

One more clue brought to you by the Duke of Dysfunction, Sultan of Suckiness, Prince of Prattle, Consigliere of Crap, Demon of Doubletalk, Commissioner of Claptrap, Lord of Lies, Baron of Baloney, Marquis of Mendacity, Umpire of Untruth.

Stalls

Does a shared restroom offer sufficient privacy? Do all the stalls have working doors? Do the locking handles on each stall door work properly? Are the stall walls bolted securely to the floor and walls? **Loose stall walls and doors indicate an organization that is unstable, in flux or, worst case, literally coming apart at its foundation.**

Do women's restrooms offer a receptacle for convenient, hygienic disposal of feminine hygiene products? These receptacles, for discretion, are usually located within the stalls. Are the toilets clean, properly aligned, and in good repair? Once again, this relates to health, safety, and convenience. **Unbolted toilets and toilets in need of repair show that the organization is in need of repair.** Since this is safety- and health-related dysfunction, the organizational problems start with operations.

Graffiti tends to proliferate more on the walls of improperly installed stalls as opposed to properly installed and maintained stalls. The presence of *any* graffiti is not good. The words, whatever they are, might as well read: inattentive management, poor communication, poor follow through, lack of caring. Why?

- The company could have purchased a graffiti-resistant surface for its stall walls. However, for whatever reason, it did not. The most frequent reason is cheapness since graffiti-resistant surfaces cost more.

- The graffiti could indicate a lack of attention by the maintenance and custodial staff or its manager. If senior managers use the same restrooms and they do not report the lack of maintenance, then managers fit in just fine—they don't care either. Surely, no one could miss this obvious indicator of corporate illness.

- The maintenance staff could be diligent and remove or paint over graffiti soon after it is discovered. Some graffiti means dissatisfaction; more graffiti is an obvious sign of rebellion. By responding promptly to extensive graffiti, a company sends a message: We need to talk to learn the nature of the extreme dissatisfaction; we can then deal with it. The maintenance or janitorial staff can repaint using, if necessary, a different color. The object is to keep up with the aberrant behavior and not let it multiply. It's not the graffiti, stupid; it's the amount of time that passes before management does something about it—if at all.

Toilets

Do you see a commercial grade toilet? Commercial toilets use a chrome-plated handle pointing to the right mounted atop a vacuum valve. Some commercial toilets use a self-flush mechanism with a built-in sensor module. Household-grade toilets use the regular flush mechanism usually mounted on the left side of the toilet tank. Commercial grade toilets are designed to meet heavier usage in factory, office, retail, convention center, airport, or sports venues. Use of a household-rated toilet in any high-traffic environment screams, "cheap, cheap, cheap."

How securely is the toilet bolted to the floor or the wall? A loose toilet tells you of a loosely run organization failing to pay attention to details. A very loose toilet shows signs of organizational imbalance or, at the very worst, the organization is falling apart, i.e., nearly out of business.

What is the toilet's gpf (gallons per flush) rating? Some newer, water saving toilets use no more than 1.3 gpf; the current federal standard for urinals is 1.0 gpf. Waterless urinals, with no moving parts, cost between $250 and $500 apiece. However, since they don't use any water, they don't require urinal cakes, and never need maintenance—no matter how heavily they are used. Cost savings can add up quickly. An added benefit? They are quiet. **Penalize the business one point for use of older water-wasting toilets or urinals. There is no excuse for not installing water saving toilets or urinals.**

Many local water districts gladly reimburse up to $150 to help pay for the purchase and installation of water saving devices. The business payback is measurable—gallons of water saved, lower water bills, and lower sewage bills.

Is the toilet seat clean? You would expect that someone who made a mess, even a small one, would wipe away the evidence. Unless someone were totally unaware of her/his infraction, this person is unhealthy. This unhealthiness will be reflected in the substandard quality and lateness of his/her work, an inability to communicate clearly, and disrespect of others. (kind of goes together.)

It may be difficult to discover the culprit when the activity goes on behind closed doors. Eventually, the miscreant will err and leave the stall, only to be followed by someone s/he knows. When the co-worker makes his/her less than fortunate discovery of the wet seat, the victim *will* remember. S/he may never say anything, but the affront will be ever fixed in his/her mind.

In some businesses and small medical offices, men and women share the same restroom. In this case it is especially important that the toilet seat be kept clean. A package of disinfectant wipes or spray disinfectant adds a thoughtful touch.

Is the underside of the toilet seat clean? How about the rim? And under the rim? The outside of the toilets and the urinals may be spotless. However, dirt on the underside of the toilet seat or in these less accessible and less seen areas may be the source of that offensive bathroom smell—and unwanted germs or viruses. Lack of diligence in keeping these areas clean further highlights the organization's lack of attention to details, cheapness with resources, and poor internal coordination and communication.

Are all the toilets properly flushed? Clogged toilets are either a result of poor maintenance or an employee who won't take the time to flush the toilet twice if that is what is required. If employees do not notify maintenance that a toilet needs repair, maintenance cannot fix the toilet—no matter how diligently the department operates. If the toilets are self-flush, a clogged toilet is more likely a maintenance issue . . . but one, which, if the employees were working as team-players, would have been promptly reported and corrected. Like dirty toilets, clogged toilets reflect poor internal communication and coordination.

Toilet Paper and Seat Covers

What is the quality of the toilet paper? Most businesses or organizations use a relatively thick single-ply paper. A minority uses the nearly-useless, thin, single-ply paper. This is false economy! The employee or visitor uses far more than twice as much of the poor-quality paper compared to the quantity of better quality paper required. **This is a subtle warning sign. Since this is false economy, what else does the company do that reflects a penny-wise, pound-foolish attitude?** If they make bad choices for relatively small decisions, what quality of decisions can we expect about bigger issues?

A second minority uses the high-quality two-ply paper. What does this tell you? Management of this organization truly values its employees. This positive attitude toward employees may be necessary. For an organization that provides business or personal services, the employees are the face, heart, and soul of the company. Characteristics for this successful organization include good communication, lack of hierarchy, a possible *fun* work environment away from clients and customers, and sound attention to financial detail.

Does each stall include one or more backup rolls of toilet paper? The transparent dispenser with two large commercial/industrial rolls saves many hours of labor for staff who otherwise would have to more frequently check and replace the much smaller household-size rolls. The key is the visible presence of a backup capability, whether with a fancy two-roll dispenser or simply an extra roll sitting on the toilet tank. The presence of backup toilet paper tells us the organization operates with sound plans in place, is efficient, and is always on the lookout for better ways to improve operations or the customer experience.

Does the company provide disposable toilet seat covers? Literally and figuratively, this is a nice touch. While not essential, toilet seat covers significantly reduce wet toilet seats. Some women, too lazy to put strips of paper on a seat and too fearful to sit on a seat that might be germy, will squat and hover, invariably missing their target. Some men, too lazy to lift the toilet seat and too private to use a common urinal, will aim at their target . . . and invariably miss. In either case, the paper cover either protects the next sitter from germs or provides advance warning that the seat is wet. Thus, the popularity of this *extra*.

Toilet seat covers are a nice idea, but the dispenser should be stocked. **An empty dispenser tells you the company wants to look good and do right by employees and customers but does not want to do everything it must in order to actually follow through.**

Urinals

Standing at the urinal, the first thing you will see is the chrome valve and handle. What is the condition of the flush valve? Is the chrome finish shiny and bright? Do you see a discolored or pitted finish? I believe the condition of the chrome finish is the more important factor of the two. Whoever is responsible for the maintenance of the restroom walls, stalls, fixtures, and installed equipment, should also clean and shine the chrome-plated fixtures. The shiny chrome completes the image; pitted chrome plainly shows ongoing neglect or intermittent care. **The presence of dull, pitted chrome is a semi-critical item.** Once again, the organization is too lazy to find a suitable cleaner and thereby chooses to ignore the hygiene of its employees and visitors. The organization misses a great opportunity to present a complete, positive public image.

Is the round cover to the urinal's brass adjustment valve missing? These covers, often stolen for their brass content, are then sold to scrap metal dealers. If not replaced, the company does not follow through on its commitments to suppliers, employees, and customers.

What is the condition of the caulking and paint around the urinal? Is it smooth and filled in or is it full of gaps with rough edges? Is it cracked? Has it peeled? Is it chipped? Is it dirty or mildewed? Caulking should last for years. If caulking has deteriorated, this is a warning sign of a *rough around the edges organization*, one where the trend is negative, not positive. The negatives translate to internal politics, confused reporting structures, poor project management, inaccurate budgets, poor planning, and lengthy and involved approval processes.

Urinal dividers. The use of dividers between urinals shows the organization respects the privacy of its suppliers, employees, customers, and visitors. I expect to see dividers in public restrooms located in hotels, airports, shopping centers, office buildings, convention centers, sports venues, and the like. No divider translates to no respect for privacy and a cheap, impersonal attitude.

Has someone left cigarette butts in the urinals? Since many states and/or companies prohibit smoking indoors, I would not expect to find any. However, there are always one or two employees who want to *sneak a smoke* rather than go outdoors. Unless one works in Minnesota, the Dakotas, Michigan's Upper Peninsula, or northern Maine and it is the middle of winter, it should not be a problem to go outside for a cigarette. This is a minor warning sign. It shows one or more rebellious employees who will not abide by basic rules and observe common courtesy. One cigarette butt a trend does not make! However, two or more tells me that the company has problems with employee morale and motivation. The company is not likely to be a market leader. Employees have a cavalier attitude. Taken a step further, evidence of many cigarette butts in urinals and on the floor indicates widespread evidence of poor hires.

Does a plastic or rubber screen cover the drain hole in a urinal? The screen prevents cigarette butts from disintegrating and spewing pieces of tobacco when the urinal is flushed. Cleanup is easier—for the lucky employee who gets to pluck the butts from the bowl. Since most company or government rules do not permit indoor smoking, why install an unneeded item? In this case, I look at common practice. For years, the installation of the plastic or rubber screen was common practice—possibly considered a suitable *tar-*

get for guys. Today, this practice continues, although it is not 100% necessary. Is the company's thinking stuck in the past?

Can you see the original product sticker with bar code or agency certification affixed to the top of a new urinal? The sticker confirms that the installed urinal complied with required Federal and/or state plumbing standards. Frankly, this is not common; most plumbers or the janitorial staff will have removed this sticker. If the company has not removed this sticker, the organization does not pay attention to details and shows incomplete or untimely follow-up on projects or customer commitments

Most men's restrooms do not post signs over the urinals. Any sign to encourage *accurate aim* is a humorous, albeit equally accurate, indicator of employee citizenship. If many male employees choose to miss the urinal target, one must ask:

- To what degree are male employees dissatisfied and use poor aim as a symbolic gesture of dissatisfaction?

- Do some of the male employees dislike the custodian and want to make that person's life miserable?

- Does a disproportionate share of the male employee population suffer from prostrate-related problems?

- Does the company hire a greater than average proportion of jerks?

Whatever the exact reason, I interpret this sign in a similar manner to the sign in the kitchen that tells employees to clean up after themselves. Common courtesy should prevail. However, people's real character shows when no one is looking. **If the area around the urinal is a mess, few employees or visitors care.**

Men's restrooms in some restaurants permit third-party companies to provide advertisements above each urinal. This is distracting; one cannot even do one's business in peace without visual bombardment. Does the restaurant or store receive money in return for providing the ad space? By doing so, that business sees itself only as a revenue source, not as a source of escape and enjoyment for its customers. Alternatively, some restaurants place the sports pages from the day's newspaper above each urinal. That's fine.

The new water-free urinals mentioned above have been available in other countries since 1991; two major U.S. manufacturers introduced U.S.-specific models in 2001. For high traffic areas such as airports, sports venues, museums, main library locations, high occupancy office buildings, class A resorts, hotels, conference centers, and spas, these new urinals are a must. From an environmental standpoint, they save water; in so doing, these urinals immediately reduce water bills. My favorite museum, in fact I joke it's the ninth wonder of the world, is the Getty Museum in Los Angeles. This amazing award-winning museum complex, designed by Richard Meier and completed in 1997, uses standard low-flow urinals. I am astonished they have not installed water-free urinals. The Getty complex is *always* busy; the Getty is forward-looking on matters of art, architecture, and aesthetics; and since this is LA, water is *always* an issue!

Sinks

Are the sinks firmly attached to the walls and at a proper height—especially for disabled clients who may be in wheelchairs or use walking aids? Are there enough sinks and enough counter space for the number of stalls/urinals? What is the condition of the sinks and any adjoining countertops? Are they reasonably clean, dry, and in good repair? Wet, soap-slopped countertops mean that employees or visitors do not clean up after themselves. A buildup of lime scale, soap scum, or rust stains indicates long-standing poor maintenance practices.

What is the condition of the faucets? Is the chrome finish shiny and bright or discolored and pitted? The chrome-plated fixtures should be clean and well-maintained. Shiny chrome shows the company pays attention to details; pitted chrome plainly shows on-going neglect or intermittent care and reflects the same in the organization.

Does the hot water handle deliver hot water? You would be amazed how many businesses do not provide hot running water for hand washing. **If there is no hot water, then this is a warning that the business or restaurant takes other shortcuts.** Moreover, the organization is not customer-focused and may not follow ethical behavior rules.

For restrooms with hot water, has the company or restaurant installed a hot water restrictor to prevent scalding? To test, turn on only the hot water spigot. Let it run for a few seconds. If the water is not scalding hot, then the company has a restrictor or a separate hot water tank with a setting for warm, not scalding, water. This is positive! The company is safety conscious, considerate, and litigation conscious. **It may want to avoid a lawsuit resulting from extra-hot water. If a company permits the flow of scalding water, then this is a critical, safety-related item.** The firm just doesn't care and may take unnecessary risks in other aspects of its business.

As an exception to temperature-controlled water requirement, touchless, motion-detection faucets or floor, step-bar-activated faucets do not have temperature or flow control options—and are usually set to deliver warm water. Touch-free operation reduces germ transmission, but does not help healthwise if the faucets don't work . . . there is no manual override.

Are all the faucets in good repair? Do any of them leak or drip? The wonderful Getty Museum has not installed hands-free faucets, instead continuing its use of the separate hot and cold faucet handles originally installed. In fairness, these old-fashioned faucets have worked fine every time I needed to use them.

Soap

Are the soap dispensers conveniently located relative to the sinks, with at least one dispenser for every two sinks? Are they clean or do they have a gummy soap buildup? Older, liquid hand soap dispensers are quite adequate. The newer, touchless, foam dispensers provide the same disease prevention advantage as touchless faucets and toilet flushers . . . with the same caveat about tech-failure—no override.

Are the dispensers full, nearly full, nearly empty, or empty? The level of liquid soap will vary with the time of day. However, someone should check once a day to ensure the dispensers are full and functioning—as well as to restock the paper towels. Empty soap dispensers are unacceptable; **this is another hygiene and safety-related item.**

You should see a dispenser of liquid hand soap or foam soap. Bars of soap work fine, but have a tendency to get messy—plus people have an aversion to picking up a dirty bar, not knowing whose hands were on it previously. Common timely practice dictates the use of pump dispensers. **If a company does not offer liquid or foam hand soap, then it is a definite warning sign.**

The company may consider itself avant-garde and above the hum-drum fray of day-to-day activities and behavior. Why should this company use a different standard for health and safety? In the case of public health and hygiene, conformity is necessary. **The combination of dull, pitted chrome faucets and insufficient or poorly located liquid soap dispensers is a semicritical item. This combination shows the company, like the chrome faucets, is pitted. The company is pitted against its partners—suppliers, bankers, creditors, and to a lesser but negative extent its customers.**

Towels and Hand Dryers

Did the company install paper towel dispensers or electric hand dryers? Or both? If paper towels are available, does the dispenser operate by motion, pull, wheel, or lever? The newest, most sanitary towel dispensers are motion activated; your clean wet hands do not touch anything other than the new paper towel. The newest electric dryers also operate by sensing the presence of your hands. Both of these touch-free alternatives eliminate the need to make contact with something someone else may have touched. However, since washed hands are clean, this should be a relatively minor issue.

If the company uses paper towels, is the dispenser full or empty? This observation will depend on the time of day and the use of the facility. A busy airport restroom is far more likely to run out of paper towels than a restroom in an office building. Nevertheless, someone should periodically check the level of paper towels and replenish as necessary. **An empty paper towel dispenser signals that the company does not care about the health and hygiene of its employees or visitors. An empty paper towel dispenser is a warning sign. It becomes a critical warning sign when the dispenser remains empty for longer than overnight.**

Brown vs. white paper towels. White implies clean and pure. White also requires the use of chlorine bleach. A white paper towel may look clean and pure, but it is an environmentally unfriendly product. Brown works fine and sends a message of a socially conscious yet money-saving organization.

Type of paper towel dispenser—pre-measured sections on a roll vs. individual paper towels. Pre-measured towels save time, labor, and money. However, if the pre-measured towel is very small, the user will need three to five towels to do the job of what one good-sized towel would accomplish. Here is a great example of penny-wise, pound-foolish thinking. On the positive side, a quality roll dispenser seldom jams and does not dump wads of towels. Again, a touch-free option prevents disease transmission.

Most men's restrooms offer paper towels to dry hands. Some guys like to crumble the towel and pretend it is a basketball and the wastebasket is the hoop. They fade back or make a small jump, take a shot, then . . . miss the basket. If the man picks up the paper towel and places it in the wastebasket, that is fine. This is considerate of the next user. If you find many crumbled paper towels lying on the floor at the base of the wastebasket, then:

- Some employees do not care about the company

258 WACKY, WARPED, & WICKED

- A few employees think they are too good to bend over and pick up their errant paper towel/basketball shots

- The culture is based on *it's all about me*, extreme competition, lack of interpersonal or interdepartmental cooperation in spite of talk of cooperation, or one group having a feeling of superiority.

This undisciplined group, often sales, is in charge. Measures of individual or group success do not pertain to this *country club* within an organization—and someone high up in the organization protects them. Whether protected or not, **this is a critical indicator, arguably one of the most important. Many crumpled paper towels on the restroom floor reveal the heart and soul of an organization.** An organization's employees either care and act civilly toward one another or they do not care and act accordingly. It hardly matters which department is the informal leader or gets away with most everything. What matters is the unequal attitude and treatment within the organization.

Location of the wastebasket. The ideal location for the wastebasket, health-wise, is by the door. This allows people to use the paper towel they dried their hands with to grab the door handle, and once the door is open, discard the towel as they depart. An additional thoughtful item often found outside the door is a touch-free dispenser of antibacterial foam or liquid. This allows people to treat their hands after they have left the restroom and touched the door handle.

From a sanitation perspective, dispensed cloth towels in a cabinet are not acceptable, since users share the bacteria with reuse of the towel. Mechanized cloth roll towels require pulling down a dirty section of towel to get to a clean section or touching the wheel that moves the towel to the next clean section. The only exception to the issue of cloth towels are very up-scale hotels, restaurants, and country clubs, where individual cloth towels are used once then dropped in a wicker basket or receptacle for laundering—hardly a practical alternative for a standard business or organization.

Installation of the relatively new powerful motion-operated Dyson Air Blade is the best of all hand dryer worlds—fast, very effective, environmentally sound, and economical, unless the electrical power fails. Triple the price of most other hand dryers, its noise level can reach 90 dB. OSHA stipulates that continuous exposure to 90 dB for an 8 hour period might require ear protection. The XLERATOR brand hand dryer, similar in price to traditional hand dryers, also offers powerful, effective hand-drying capabilities. However, the rush of air can produce a deafening roar—up to 95 dB! OSHA stipulates that continuous exposure to 95 dB for a 4 hour period might require ear protection. That's a cruel tradeoff for quick drying . . . and definitely distracting for someone whose workspace is close to the restroom.

An electric hand dryer reveals the company wants to save money and janitorial time, while lessening maintenance chores. Unfortunately, this tradeoff has a price—the user's time. The user must stand and wait while the dryer dries the water on their hands. Thus, a built-in electric dryer with no option for paper towels is a conundrum. Paper towels save time for the user, but cost time in the labor involved in filling and maintaining the dispensers. Electric hand dryers cost more than paper towel dispensers, but are more reliable, and electricity costs far less than paper towels. Throw in the noise factor for electric hand dryers, and I'd call this a wash (or a dry—pun intended).

Do you see exposed or loose wires connected to the hand dryer? If so, this is a serious safety issue. To be fair, I have never seen an exposed wire for a hand dryer in any restroom. **If you see exposed or loose hand dryer wires or any electrical component in a restroom, the organization is loosely run, likely by someone whose likes or hobbies include physically dangerous activities. The lack of communication to individuals responsible for fixing this hazard is symptomatic of broader dysfunction at the company.**

Is this sign visible, "Employees must wash hands before returning to work," located either near the sinks, or on the back of or adjacent to the bathroom door? **The lack of this required sign in a food-handling or food-serving establishment reveals that the management is not following government requirements. If management missed such an inexpensive easy-to-find item with which to comply, what less obvious infractions are committed every day? Cleanliness of the food storage, handling, preparation, and cleanup areas is likely lacking. Might we also include a cheap attitude by management?** Why wouldn't management spend less than $5 to buy a readily-available legally-required sign?

Accommodations for Women and the Disabled

Ladies, does the organization provide a separate area, generally part of the ladies room, which contains a couch, table, a chair or two, and soft lighting? If so, this is consideration is a very positive sign—the firm cares about its female employees and visitors. If not, the company does not treat its female employees as well as its male employees. Taken one step further, this omission could be a sign of latent misogyny.

Does the company, firm, or organization provide good restroom access for those in wheelchairs? Is the main door to the restroom heavy? If you see an electrically operated door, that's great. Is one stall sufficiently wide it can accommodate a wheelchair? Is the entrance to that stall easy to access? Are the heights of grab bars, sink, paper towel dispenser, liquid soap dispenser, and waste container set at levels that someone in a wheelchair can access? **This is another critical item.** The Americans with Disabilities Act of 1990 specifies the requirements for this accommodation. It is not sufficient to install the equipment; the equipment must conform to specific requirements. A company that chooses to ignore longstanding legal requirements demonstrates a cavalier disregard for disabled employees, visitors, or guests as well as an attitude that the company is above the law or stuck far in the past.

Summary

One of the key concepts is, "The restroom never lies." A thorough review of the restroom evaluates the overall sanitation—ceiling, walls, and floor; stalls, toilets, urinals, and sinks—and observes accommodations for the physically disabled. Is the main door heavy? A heavy restroom door presents a major challenge for disabled employees or visitors. What is your overall impression of room temperature, smell, noise? It is easy to detect loosely installed stall dividers and stall partitions. Inside the stalls, do you see graffiti? Are the toilets rated for use in an office or factory environment? Is any toilet clogged and overflowing? Does the organization pay more for two-ply toilet paper? Does each stall have at least one backup roll of toilet paper within easy reach? Are the urinals clean—no cigarette butts, paper towels, or other litter? Ideally, the urinal should be of the no-flush water saving type.

What is the condition of the sinks? Do you see chipped porcelain, rusty stainless steel, or lime scale, scum-coated glass or porcelain? Does the faucets dispense warm to hot, but not scalding, water? Is the soap dispenser activated by hand motion? Is the hand dryer activated by hand motion; is it one of the high-performance models? Is the paper towel dispenser full, nearly full, nearly empty, or empty?

Is there at least one large, easily accessible, wide-doored stall, fitted with grab bars, a wheelchair accessible sink, and a higher-level toilet? Accommodations for the disabled have been required since 1990. Accordingly, any organization not in compliance with the requirements of the Americans with Disabilities Act (ADA) is not living in the present.

~*~*~*~

CHAPTER 20

WORKERS' CUBICLES

Most of the analysis going forward focuses on office workspace. In this chapter, we will address worker's cubicles, today's solution for what in the past were rows of regimentally-aligned desks spanning large, open workspaces. Often, several departments shared the same open space—managers could look out over a whole room and observe every employee. Today, steel, modern plastics, sound-muffling synthetic fibers, and easily-erected, modularized workstations provide a semblance of privacy, enable companies to isolate employees by function, pack them in more tightly (desks are now separated by inches instead of feet), and in a high-tech environment, control distractions.

To discern signs of organizational misalignment, our analysis of employee workspaces examines:

- Common areas
- Furnishings
- Storage spaces

Common Areas

Describe the lighting in the work area. Do you see rows of uncovered fluorescent bulbs? Do you see plastic light diffusers as covers over fluorescent light fixtures? If employees must work long hours at PCs or workstations, then lighting is important. Lighting experts prefer diffused lighting over uncovered fluorescent tubes or glaring incandescent lights. Newer technologies such as light emitting diodes (LEDs) and compact fluorescent lamp (CFL) bulbs are cost effective means to produce light that is less harmful to one's eyes than fluorescent tubes. Does each workstation have additional, personal light? It should.

Lack of light implies workers are kept in the dark—you'll see untimely and poor communication, possible company shenanigans, and lack of personal interactions and friendships.

Does natural light diffuse to the workstations? Where are the managers' offices? Do they occupy the windowed periphery of the floor, claiming all natural light? Designing office space that maximizes available light and space for all is a difficult challenge. However, the resulting layout reflects the executives' priorities. If the workspace for managers claims all available natural light; individual contributors work either in dark *mushroom farms* or under bright lights with excessive glare.

Note, too, the *difference* in lighting; it is telling. If executives work in a bright, plush, country club-like environment, managers work in natural light, and employees work either in the dark or in an environment with excessive lighting glare, then you have immediate evidence of a strongly hierarchical organization. Everyone knows his/her place. Communication is largely formal and mainly top down rather than bottom up. Everyone knows and purportedly respects the established employee stratification. Although everyone works for the same company, the corporate culture has established a physical environment that emphasizes differences, not similarities. **Beware. Differences in lighting provide a strong warning: This company functions under the weight of excessive corporate hierarchy and limited communication flow.**

Are the main aisles in the employees' work areas relatively wide or narrow? Are the secondary aisles in the employees' work areas relatively wide or narrow? The answers to these two basic questions reveal a great deal. Narrow aisles, especially the main ones, in a cubicle-based office layout tell you the company or organization is cheap and takes a narrow approach to its business. The use of cubicles in and of itself saves an incredible amount of floor space and cost. A design that shaves a few extra feet from aisle space, barely permitting two people to pass safely, shows an extremely penurious position. **The combination of small cubicles, narrow aisles, and poor or excessively glaring overhead lighting identifies a cheap outfit with a very narrow approach to its business.**

Cubicle Furnishings

As you walk through the employee work area, look into each cubicle. What is the nature of the furnishings? Can you identify the following components?

- High quality armchair with five wheels for safety

- Locking compartment above the work surface for pseudo-security

- Ample space and connectors for a personal computer, monitor, and printer (lack of sufficient space leads to a messy workstation)

- Single work surface, ideally in an L- or U-shape

- At least one built-in file drawer, preferably locking

- Storage shelf for books, manuals

- Wall surfaces where the employee may hang photos, calendars, poster art, lightweight hanging sculptures, personal mementoes, Dilbert © cartoons (!), announcements, or memos. **If many of the cubicles display Dilbert cartoons, then this is a sign of poor employee morale. It's a matter of degree—one or two Dilbert cartoons pokes fun at the situation; an entire cubicle wall of Dilbert cartoons or cartoons from New Yorker magazine screams: (a) I need a lot of attention from my co-workers, manager, or both; (b) I have a bad attitude and this is my way of thumbing my nose at the organization and its higher-ups.**

- A built-in fluorescent, incandescent, halogen, or LED lamp for light focused on the main work area

Ideally, the workspace permits use of its back wall for additional work or storage space. Some cubicles may include a small table and chairs for informal conferences that do not require the privacy of a conference room. However, only relatively quiet-speaking persons should use their space in this manner. It makes no sense to allow a loud person to conduct informal meetings in his/her cubicle, disturbing people in the neighboring cubicles. Loud guests of a soft-spoken employee will provide the same kind of disruption. The noise disrupts employee productivity and instigates long-term resentment.

What is the quality of the cubicle and its furnishings? Every employee does not require a Herman Miller- or Knoll-designed cubicle. Indeed, Herman Miller and Knoll products are elegant and functional with improved sound-proofing. However, few companies can afford this luxury. Office planners can recommend alternatives from many reputable manufacturers. If management has determined that the workspaces will be based on cubicles, what does that tell you? A legal, CPA, management consulting, market research, insurance actuary, investment research, real estate research, insurance sales, or similar business should have private offices. If not, did management choose a higher grade of cubicle? People, not furniture or equipment, are service organizations' main assets. The investment in higher quality cubicle furniture is a relatively small one compared to the overall investment in its employees.

Is the style of cubicle furniture in harmony with the building? Do you see a modern, sparsely furnished cubicle in a renovated Victorian house? Surely, someone could locate and install more appropriate furnishings than a series of small cubicle farms in each of the rooms. **Such a design mismatch indicates significant organizational dysfunction. This mismatch points to a lack of planning, a rush to move forward, a lack of organizational and executive self-knowledge, lack of understanding of community perceptions, and cluelessness about the organization's workflow and internal processes.**

Let us return to an important topic—the office chair. Each executive, administrator, or employee spends more time in this chair at work than in any seating or sleeping furnishing at home. The chair must be comfortable; provide good support for legs, thighs, and lower back; and adjust for height and tilt. Is the chair of high, medium, or low quality? Does the chair have arms? Secretarial chairs typically do not have arms. From a functional standpoint, arms on a secretary's chair impede movement . . . from the desk, to the file cabinets, to the executive's office, to the supply storage cabinets or closets. If an administrator prefers a chair with arms, then the company should supply one of good to excellent quality. This is a reasonable accommodation.

If you see only inexpensive chairs from a mass merchandiser, big box office supply store, furniture store selling only low-quality products, or ones that look badly worn or in poor repair, then this is a sign that the company treats its employees cheaply.

Storage Space

Companies do not always have large built-in closets for storage. Rapid organizational growth, special project requirements, odd-shaped item storage needs, and storage of required, sensitive documents add to the continual need for space.

Do you see boxes stacked in the hallways? Do you see boxes stored under the kneeholes of desks or workstations? Boxes in a hallway are a safety hazard—one to be avoided in our too litigious society. More importantly, such obstruction is a fire code violation. **Stacked boxes stored in a hallway is a critical warning item—the organization does not care about safety and, indirectly, its employees.**

Do you see exposed wires at workstations? Modern workstations have built-in troughs or panels to keep wires out of sight. Do you see bundles of communication and computer wires leading from the workstation to the ceiling? Do you see bundles of wires protruding from any workstation? If the office's design requires clusters of wires extend from workstations or copiers to the ceiling the wires should be hidden behind a covering.

Exposed wires expose a cheap organization, one with increased exposure to or operating on the edge of legal or regulatory requirements.

Do you see excess equipment, especially personal computer-related, lying around the office? Copy rooms and mailrooms are favorite equipment-dumping grounds. If the equipment is out of the way, it is not a problem. If storing excess equipment obstructs people's movement into or within a room, limits the operation of the high-speed copier's sorter, or slows the sorting and delivery of mail, then this is a problem. Remember, you have 10 to 15 seconds to look in, consider the intended use of the space, evaluate the amount of equipment stored in this space, and determine if this is a good or bad situation.

The obvious *sucky* situations will present themselves as that. If the situation is less obvious, then trust your intuition. If the room gives you the claustrophobic creeps, that is exactly the feeling those who work there experience. Too much junk is stressful, and increased stress leads to irritability and accidents. Logically, you may argue that the overcrowding is not that important. However, make a mental or written note; it's a matter of degree. **Too much visible junk is merely another piece of the corporate dysfunction puzzle falling into place.**

What does this lack of storage space tell you? If the items in storage are odd-sized—such as architectural drawings—and used frequently, the seeming disorganization means the company is customer-oriented—timely easy access to current customer information is important. Someone stored the information to facilitate easy retrieval.

If the items are not in current use and could be boxed, why has the firm not done so—then transferred these lesser-used items to off-site storage? One person's workstation with many scattered boxes and files in the open shows only that person's work style. If the habit of mess is pervasive within the organization, then the likelihood is that more than one critical file is missing . . . somewhere.

Once again, the conclusion about organizational dysfunction is not reached through a single observation. If you see many storage boxes or rolled blueprints or diagrams, whether or not labeled, scattered in aisles, near copiers, or throughout the organization, the message is clear. Organization and leadership at this office is a myth.

Executive Administrators

Evaluate the workstation, cubicle, or office of the executives' administrator. What is the quality of the furniture? What artwork, degrees, certifications, mementoes, books, knick-knacks, awards, office supply items, and photos do you see?

Compare the quality of furniture in the administrator's workspace with that in the executive's office. Are the administrator's furniture and furnishings similar to those of other non-executive employees? Are the furniture and furnishings similar to those of the executive? The administrator's furniture may be a little nicer than that used by other employees. A small difference is fine; a significant difference is not. **Significant differences in furniture quality imply significant differences in status.** In some businesses, the CEO has granted her/his executive assistant considerable latitude to deal with issues and permissions as they arise. If the executive assistant is indeed powerful, then that person's furniture may appropriately reflect this.

However, look for evidence that this furniture is made by an exclusive manufacturer, designed and built to fill an irregular space, includes a number of expensive built-in features, or incorporates an unnecessary, fancy feature such as a marble shelf or is constructed of a rare, exotic wood. If the administrator's furnishings appear more similar to those of the executives, this is further evidence of corporate elitism. **Not only are the executives removed physically and in the sense of furnishings from the employees, so is the administrator. This is a clear sign of "country club-ism," that this group is different from and superior to rank-and-file employees. Overall, this is a relatively minor item.**

Summary

In the world of cubicle farms, let there be light! Diffused sunlight, not direct light on one's workspace is ideal. A dark work environment metaphorically shows the dark side of an organization. If executives and their administrators have access to plenty of natural light but individual contributors are kept in the dark, the contrast reveals a structured, hierarchical environment with strict reporting and information sharing requirements.

Other indicators of organizational misalignment include narrow aisles between cubicle rows; boxes stored in the aisles; and unused or obsolete equipment stored in empty cubicles, corners, the copy room, or aisles. Compare the quality of workstations used by executive administrators with that of rank and file employees. A slightly higher grade for the administrator is appropriate and reflects the powers delegated to the administrator. A significantly higher quality workstation, equal to that in the executive offices, reveals a status-oriented organization set up in a rigidly hierarchical structure.

~*~*~*~

CHAPTER 21

EXECUTIVES' OFFICES

A visit to the executive offices of a company, professional firm, government agency, military unit, or organization nearly guarantees the addition of strong clues to your assessment of corporate dysfunction. In order to analyze the executive office suite, we need to evaluate the following components:

- Location
- Reception area/hallway/restroom
- Layout
- Electronics
- Furnishings
- Décor
- Walls
- Desk/workspace/étagère/bookcase
- Administrators' desks/workspaces

Location

First, on which floor is the executive office suite located? For a service business, the executive office suite may be located on the top floor of the main headquarters building, particularly if the office is located within a group of high-rise office buildings. For a discrete- or process-manufacturing, wholesale or retail distribution, or agricultural product business, or a government agency, a better location for the executive suite may be near the main production area. I fondly know the executive director of a luxury hotel who moved his office from the second floor to the basement so, in his words, he "could be closer to the action."

Such a location ensures more efficient communication and recognizes that the executives are an integral part of the business. They are not mere

268   WACKY, WARPED, & WICKED

overseers. Moreover, the close physical location sends a message that the CEO is actively involved in the prevention of problems or in keeping problems small after early identification. If the CEO maintains a heavy travel schedule, then the lieutenants should be physically close to the production area to answer questions or provide guidance.

If the executive office is located on the top floor of the headquarters building, is the CEO in the corner office with the best view? A tranquil view of trees, water, bushes, grass, seasonal flowers, and even concrete or asphalt provides a visual contrast to an office interior. The Chief Executive may subconsciously look differently at problems based on which way the chair faces and what he or she sees.

How does a visitor reach the executive suite? In the post-9/11 era, it is difficult to balance protection and privacy for executives with a reasonable level of access to them. Is a guard stationed at a desk at the building's main entrance? Does the guard phone the executive suite to announce a visitor? This would be a very professional situation. However, it may not be realistic or cost effective, based on the nature of the business, its usual visitors, and the physical location and layout of the building. If the building sits in midtown Manhattan and shares office space with other companies, then the use of a security guard service makes sense. If the headquarters is located in a suburb or small town away from a large metropolitan area, then this security arrangement may be unnecessary.

To reach the executive suite, must someone enter a code or scan an identification card in a reader in the elevator? Is the executive suite accessible only via private elevator from a lower floor? Does the CEO employ a dedicated personal security guard while in the building and a bodyguard when outside the building?

The more elaborate the measures to protect the CEO, the more inbred the company's thinking and problem-solving capabilities. The organization, as well as the executive staff, values its insular thinking and wants its privacy.

Reception Area and Hallway

Evaluate the executive reception area using the same factors you did when evaluating the main reception area. I will repeat each and add pertinent observations:

- Describe the receptionist or administrator. Is that person genuinely helpful? Did that person offer coffee, tea, soda, or water? Is a candy dish located near the receptionist or administrator's workstation?

- While you waited, did anyone walk by? If so, did they say hello or acknowledge you with a nod or smile? A lack of acknowledgement indicates snobbishness, a class-conscious attitude, or employee dissatisfaction.

- Describe the furniture. What is its style? Is it new or old? Is it in good condition? Is it plain or fancy? Is the furniture proportional to the space? Is it upholstered in leather or fabric? Does it feel comfortable when you sit? Does the chair or couch provide good support for your lower back?

- How much nicer are the furnishings in the executive suite than the main reception area? The key is the level of difference. A little nicer is not a concern; a significant difference in quality and appearance indicates a significant difference in valuation of an individual based on company position. **This executive management team places itself in a different class. Executives have lost touch with the average worker.** The difference in salary is not sufficient; the difference in work environment makes a private perception public.

- Does the condition and style of the furniture match the life cycle of the business? Is the furniture clean and in good repair, the wood polished, and metal hardware firmly attached?

- Are the plants or trees healthy? **Are they well-dusted?** If either is artificial, are they the nicer silk type, rather than cheap plastic? **Unhealthy plants are a harbinger of an unhealthy organization.**

- What is the condition of floor tiles and/or carpet?

- Do you see burned out light bulbs in the exit signs or table lamps? **If you see a burned out exit sign light, this is a critical item, since it represents health and safety.**

- Can you easily find the fire extinguisher or fire hose? If an extinguisher, is the equipment inspection up to date?

- How bright is the light in the reception area? Is it adequate for reading? Is the lighting intentionally subdued? Reception area lighting may be subdued. In contrast, an office should be well lit—it is not the place for mood lighting. Dim lighting tends to obscure what should be seen.

- What kinds of magazines or newspapers are on the coffee or end table? Are they appropriate to the business and the industry?

Walls

Describe the artwork. Do you see signed, original works of art or signed numbered lithographs? Is the quality of art in the executive suite significantly better than that displayed throughout the building? If so, then this states that executives treat themselves far better than they treat employees. Alternatively, they are showing off for their guests.

Executive Restroom

If possible, use the executive restroom. Apply same restroom standards as before. However, please add two important criteria. Does the rest room have a private shower, bath, sauna, or Jacuzzi®? Second, does the executive suite have its own well-equipped room for physical training? A "yes" answer to either indicates further distance from the average worker and manager. **A separate shower, bath, sauna, or Jacuzzi® is a warning sign that elitism at this organization is alive and well. Work is to be done at the office; recreational activities should be done elsewhere. If the firm offers an exercise room for employees, then this needless executive suite extravagance further amplifies the distance between executive and worker.**

Other Observations

Do you see an atrium or aquarium in the executive reception area? If so, how does this compare with the main reception area? If the executive reception area is significantly nicer, then the degree of difference provides a clear representation of how the organization perceives the social status difference between executives and staff.

Do you see any dogs (other than those to assist disabled persons) in the executive suite? This is generally not the case at a large organization. However, at smaller companies or in retail businesses, executives and workers may have more flexibility in bringing their dogs to work. Is the dog friendly toward people? A snarling, growling, jumping, or yapping dog directly contradicts the pet owner and business executive who wants to create a positive environment. If dogs are permitted in the executive suite, are the rank-and-file employees also allowed to bring their dogs to work? If only the big boss may bring a pet to work, then this is a sure sign of executive elitism.

Do you see fresh flowers in the executive suite? Since flowers are a sign of a genteel, civilized society, flowers represent a classy welcome to visitors to the executive offices. Do you see flowers at the main reception desk? If you don't, then the missing welcome sign for visitors and employees at the main reception desk signifies lack of a generally open, welcoming environment—plus the usual executive elitism.

Do you see a candy dish, especially one stocked with favorites of the executive staff? Is the dish full or empty? Is it clean? Is the dish plain or fancy? Are the candies individually wrapped or loose? Individually wrapped candies are obviously more sanitary. If possible, find out who pays for the candies. In most cases, it is the administrator, not the executives. A candy dish is the equivalent of a neon sign or flashing light that says "Welcome" or "Hang out here"—both positive messages for employees and visitors. Good. Who pays for the candy? If the administrator pays without reimbursement, then shame on the cheapskate, self-serving execs. Not good.

Does the executive suite offer a wider range of beverages than offered in other departments? Does the executive suite offer coffee, tea, regular or diet soft drinks, plain bottled water, lightly or heavily carbonated bottled water, fruit juice, or even alcoholic beverages? Once again, the *difference* between what the company offers in the main reception area versus that in the executive reception area reveals elitism and whether or not employees are taken for granted.

Does a relatively wide hallway link executive offices? If so, this is a symbol of open communication. Building design and construction may place certain limits on options. Space in the hallway limits space in individual offices. Once again, it is a trade-off. If you see a lot of open space in individual offices, then the hallway could be wider.

While you are waiting, note if the door to each executive's office is open or closed. Some executives may have loud, booming voices that carry; others want a quiet workspace or are in meetings. An open door physically reinforces an organization's positive open door policy.

Do you hear background music from a radio or syndicated music channel? Is the music soft or loud? You'll easily know the difference. Despite the presence of piped-in music, does the administrator listen to different music on a personal radio or CD player? Is the administrator listening to music or voice through earbuds, headphones, or earphones? I hope not!

What is the aroma in the room? Is it subtle or strong? Does it smell earthy (wood or metallic), floral, citrus, or neutral? Does the aroma match the type of business? I would not expect the executive offices of an automobile manufacturer to smell like citrus or flowers. An earthy, leathery, or neutral smell matches my image of a company in that industry. It is a real estate axiom that a house for sale is made more enticing to buyers with the smell of baking bread or simmering cinnamon sticks. Although one person's aroma may be another person's stench, the aromas of baking bread and simmering cinnamon seem relatively neutral and non-offensive. **Strong odors mask ethical issues, and reveal that the organization faces at least one major issue, lacks openness, and does not have a positive learning environment.**

Layout

Does the company have a separate conference room used exclusively by the high-level executives? If so, is it located within the executive office suite? Does the CEO have direct access to the conference room from his/her office? The CEO's ability to enter or leave the conference room without outsiders being aware suggests secrecy. At the very least, this is a warning sign that the CEO may be a control freak. It also suggests that not everything of importance in the company is visible. The direct attachment also symbolizes a less-than-egalitarian truth: that the CEO believes the conference room is for his/her primary use. Most people would not mind a short walk to a conference room. A conference room detached from the CEO's office implies equal access for all members of the executive staff.

Does the CEO's office include a small table and two or three chairs for informal meetings? Or, does the CEO's office include a couch and two or three armchairs or leather chairs for guests? The option does not matter as much as that the CEO has the space available and gets a choice of room layouts when meeting with employees, executives, or visitors.

Does the CEO have a coatroom or closet to conceal overcoats and larger items? A single small hook on the back of the main door should not be the only option for a CEO to hang an overcoat, scarf, hat, clean shirt, or extra necktie. The hook is literally and figuratively a small point. However, use of a coat closet ensures appropriate privacy—the office area is for work, not storage, and personal items belong out of sight. Most executives' offices have a credenza or tall finished cabinet for storage of papers, brochures, and small electronics. An executive office without a credenza, cabinetry, or functional built-ins requires open shelving for storage. If the office has open shelves, are they well-organized, clean, and polished?

Does the CEO's office include a wet bar? If so, is the bar located prominently within the CEO's office or in a separate alcove? Does the bar contain alcoholic and non-alcoholic beverages? In a litigious era, on-premises serving and consumption of alcohol is not wise or appropriate. **A wet bar in an office is a warning sign of a possible problem with alcoholism. Alternative** explanations for a wet bar? The executive wanted to be in a more glamorous industry so may not be 100% committed to the current one, the boss is a *wanna be*, the CEO falsely thinks this home-like addition in an office will make a guest feel more welcome and may possibly open up more than s/he normally would, the executive wants to show off rare brands of liquor or wine to supposedly reveal the executive's good taste.

Does the CEO's office include a coffee bar? Can you get a cappuccino, espresso, or latte? If so, this is a nice touch. The choice of decaffeinated or regular coffee is a thoughtful extra. The question is now, "Does the executive or the administrator make the coffee for guests?" If the executive is the barista, then that is notable—the executive is not above personally providing for the comfort of his/her guests.

Do you see an unmarked back entrance/exit to the executive office suite? This may prove a handy escape route if the CEO is pursued by journalists or television crews. In other circumstances, the CEO's personal safety may be at stake. However, I view the use of a back door as evasive. Someone who attains the position of CEO should be in a position to deal directly with the media or whomever. **The presence of a back door** *escape route* **for the CEO is a minor warning sign.**

Electronics

An executive's choice of electronics reveals additional aspects of the person's character. Do you see a personal computer (PC) or video monitor on the executive's desk? We take for granted the proliferation of computers in today's office environment. In fact, we expect to see one on the desk, workstation, or credenza of every employee. I believe this is a reasonable expectation. **If you do not see a PC or monitor in the executive's office, then this is a warning sign. If there is no PC, the executive expects all employees to communicate and share information with one another, yet refuses for whatever reason to be part of the broader group.** Perhaps, the executive views the computer as a menial tool to be used by administrative assistants and staff. This executive's *better than* attitude is usually not shared by the staff who, for the most part, will see the executive's technology avoidance as laziness, elitism, or ineptitude.

The executive may have never taken the time to learn basic keyboarding skills and the fundamental programs required in today's business environment. **Failure to understand the technology can result in the executive being unaware of its capabilities and shortcomings . . . and not knowing how to set**

realistic expectations. How long should it take to draft a letter? What kinds of reports can be generated from a spreadsheet? What does s/he need to do to make a last-minute correction to a presentation slide?

Possibly, the executive had a bad experience with a PC when s/he was inundated with copies of irrelevant e-mail correspondence. If this is the case, then the executive needs to establish guidelines on the type of correspondence s/he wants to receive. S/he may ask the executive assistant to screen e-mails, respond to those requiring standard answers, and forward those which require a more critical, executive response.

In any event, an executive office without a working terminal (I've seen terminals on executives' desks that were not connected to a computer), especially in a technology-related company, reveals the individual:

- Is not a team player

- Is willing to make decisions based on information that may get sanitized before it is delivered

- Makes the rules but does not have to follow them

- Feels s/he does not need to continually learn new processes or technologies

- May consider his/her time too important to spend it learning new technologies

- May be fearful of asking for assistance in learning new technologies

Does the CEO use a Research in Motion (RIM) Blackberry, Apple iPhone, Sony Treo or CLIE, SmartPhone, Samsung Galaxy, Palm Pilot, or other personal digital assistant (PDA), tablet computer, or media tablet? Small, portable devices integrate a variety of functions: cell phone, email, and web browser capabilities; address book, memo pad, and personal organizer storage functions; and sound and visual (digital camera) recording. An executive actively using this device tells me that s/he wants to stay connected with what is going on in the company. That person is a team player, since s/he is willing to be connected to the corporate umbilical cord on a 24 X 7 basis. While underlings may always need to be available, this executive is also available to subordinates.

Cell phones are ubiquitous. The challenge is discerning whether their use is healthy or obsessive. The executive sets the limits on contact via cell phone; therefore, any overuse is that person's fault. **If the executive answers** any cell phone calls during your meeting, this may be symptomatic of a lack of planning or a clear sign of a person who operates in *interrupt mode*, where the executive compulsively deals with the most current interruption. Unless the call is critical (in which case, the executive should have informed you at the beginning of the meeting that s/he might be getting a critical phone call), responding to it during a meeting is disrespectful.

An electronic Rolodex © is relatively outdated, but remains an effective means to store and transfer personal or business contact information. Its presence indicates a very basic outdated use of technology to gain efficiency and improve organization. More effective are the business card scanners, notebook or tablet computers, or cell phone applications which gather and store business card and personal information.

An executive who refuses to adopt current electronic technologies to the point of not using at least a personal computer, personal digital assistant, tablet computer, or cell phone is an executive living in the past. Operating in the 21st century requires at least a personal computer, Apple iPad or similar, or full-function cell phone to send and receive email messages. **Failure to adapt to these now-standard communication methods indicates inward-focused thinking or limited strategic vision, a lack of openness to new ideas or different approaches to conducting business or solving a problem, and an *I-know-better-than-you-do* attitude.** If the leaders do not use reasonable technologies to improve productivity, then it follows that employees have little incentive to improve productivity, except through rudimentary process or paperwork improvements. The absence of electronic devices is not a healthy sign.

Furnishings

An evaluation of the furnishings in the executive suite is interesting and involves a number of important tradeoffs.

As you walk by each executive's office, note the style and specific pieces of furniture. Do you see the same pieces of furniture in each office—desk, chair, credenza or wall storage unit, a small conference table and two or three chairs? Is the style of furniture in each office identical to that in the other offices? Conversely, is the style in each office distinct from that in any other executive office? Specifically, do you see a mix of executive offices furnished with Oriental, traditional, Danish modern, contemporary, Provincial, and Shaker furniture—purportedly in response to different preferences? **The same furniture in every executive office reflects stifled, herd-like think-**

ing or that the most senior executive is obsessed with standardization—to his/her standards.

The U.S. military is different. For officers, the person's rank and job title dictate the size of her/his desk. Only the base/fort/port commanding officer (CO) is allowed to have the largest desk.

How many pieces of furniture are in each executive office? Is the furniture oversized for the space? Either **too many pieces or pieces that are too large can restrict movement, thereby showing stifled thinking.** Furniture needs to be compatible with the length and width of the office, the ceiling height, and the size and placement of windows.

Describe the window coverings. Are they massive velvet-like, floor-length draperies or are they slim vertical or horizontal shades? Massive, thick curtains with tie backs over light-filtering sheers imply outdated thinking. The heavy window treatments reveal the inappropriate desire to create a home-like environment (from decades past), a throwback for the office holder to feudal days and the strong reinforcement of class, or a fantasy recreation of scenes from old movies. The common theme? **These thinking patterns look backward, not forward.**

Green or, less likely, flowering plants are extremely important in an executive's office. Plants provide oxygen and thereby signify life. They also add color, texture, height, irregular surfaces, and decorative containers to balance the furniture, wall coverings, window coverings, and bright or indirect lighting. Unless the person is allergic to green or blooming plants, an executive office without plants is devoid of life. **In an executive's office, the lack of green plants indicate a lack of balance in the executive's life, an overemphasis on work, a lack of appreciation of and respect for Nature's beauty and goodness, a lack of appreciation for co-workers, and a lack of openness.**

Some level of standardization is necessary to reinforce the idea that everyone is on the same team and works from the same base. Executives may customize the furniture in their offices, varying the style or substituting, say, an open wall storage unit for a credenza. However, no executive should use major pieces of personal furniture in their office. It is possible, but not likely. If the organization permits or subtly encourages wide differences in how executives furnish their offices, then this is a subtle warning sign. People need to work from a common base with personalized modifications, rather than work from an uncoordinated base. **If you observe disparate and uncoordinated furniture styles or furnishings, this is a sign of corporate dysfunction.**

The specific dysfunctions are:

- Decentralized operations, with lack of planning and coordination

- Lack of shared corporate vision, exacerbated by poor communication

- In the absence of strong leadership, excessive, often nasty, internal politics

- Difficulty in agreement on strong, clearly written policies

- Uneven enforcement of corporate policies, which depend on the executive in charge of the function

The contrast in furniture styles may not be all bad. One executive may be very strong-willed and decisive at a time when the organization requires such intervention and leadership. From the perspective of style versus need, this may be the right person to lead a long-overdue corporate restructuring initiative. Your research into the corporate DNA and current challenges facing the organization will help you determine if this is the right person at the right time.

Once you are in the executive's office, note the arrangement of furniture in the executive's workspace. Is the PC monitor located on the credenza or on a separate stand next to the desk? Is the stand at desk height or is it set for the executive to stand while working on the computer? Some individuals, particularly those with back problems, find it more comfortable to work at their computers standing up. Is the PC monitor located on the executive's desk? Newer flat-screen technology monitors occupy minimum space on the desktop. An item that previously could not fit easily on the desktop now fits. Moreover, it looks as though it belongs in this space.

The addition of a small round table with two or three chairs away from the executive's desk creates a neutral environment for meetings. Simply stated, **a desk creates a barrier;** a round table creates a sense of equality among participants.

Note the relative positions of the desk and the file cabinet or credenza. Are they located at a 90-degree angle to one another or does the file cabinet or credenza occupy a space behind the desk chair? Or does the executive work at an L-shaped workspace with file cabinets or credenzas located near this main space? The efficient layout of the CEO's workspace tells of good organization, quick paperwork turnaround, and true open-door accessibility.

In order to get to the executive suite, you probably will pass by employees' workstations, offices, or cubicles. Note the type, style, and layout of employees' workstations. Compare the level and type of employee workstation with the type, style, and layout of furnishings of executive offices. **The important factor is the degree of difference or contrast.** I do not expect executives' offices to be furnished in a style similar to those of rank-and-file employees. Conversely, I do not expect lavish furnishings in executives' offices and hand-me-down furnishings in employees' cubicles.

What is the physical setup of the executive office suite? Do you see solid walls with solid doors? Do you see instead solid walls with glass doors or wooden doors with small windows which allow observance of individual offices? Do you see long glass walls? Each style reveals something about the organization.

The combination of solid walls with solid doors, particularly if the executive keeps the door closed, tells you the executive values privacy. S/he prefers to work uninterrupted, occasionally emerging from the office cocoon to check for telephone messages or other information. Of course, that person is just as likely to check email messages in the comfort and privacy of their personal office. **Communication with peers and subordinates is restricted, possibly overly-controlled.**

The combination of solid walls with a glass door or a door with a small window tells you the executive is approachable and open. A few interruptions are okay; the administrator will know the person's limitations on interruptions. **This executive manages lateral and downward communications well.**

A solid door with a door-height strip of glass next to it is also a sign of openness. The solid door signifies privacy; the long strip of glass adjacent means someone can easily look inside and see the executive before interrupting a discussion or phone call. Importantly, this strip also allows the executive to look out and feel connected to peers and the administrators. **I view this narrow strip of glass as a sign of effective teamwork.**

The combination of glass walls and glass doors is ideal. **That executive is, of course, highly visible, implying that person is also highly approachable and available. I expect timely, direct communication with peers and subordinates. Just as this person is on display to peers, subordinates, and visitors, they are equally on display to this executive. While this person is open and approachable, the large amount of glass indicates transparency.** Aside from openness, this same transparency may enable the executive to become meddlesome—and able to watch their staff. Could this person be a control freak? Does every piece of information need to pass through this office in some manner? What appears as a positive setup may actually be a warning.

Last of all, look at all executive offices. Look for differences in doors and walls. Do vice presidents' offices have a solid door or a solid door with a small window while the CEO's office has a glass door? Conversely, does the CEO have a solid door while VPs' office doors include a small window or a strip of glass adjacent to the solid door?

A difference in one area, door or wall, is a healthy sign. However, if you note differences between the walls and doors of the chief executive's office and that of every other senior executive, then it is a definite warning sign. The interior view is not a balanced one; the executive staff is not balanced in its approach to strategy, operations, dealing with the employees/ clients/suppliers, and management of unexpected events.

Does the executive suite have its own kitchen? Do you see a sink, refrigerator, microwave oven, or coffee maker? Does the executive suite serve hot beverages in bone china cups and saucers, coffee mugs, or paper or Styrofoam™ cups? Contrast this with the employee kitchen. How does the employee kitchen serve hot beverages to guests? Although bone china in the executive suite is an elegant touch, its exclusive use places symbolic distance between the executives and the rest of the company.

We may evaluate the use of fancy china versus disposable cups from another perspective. Specifically, what is the company or organization's main business? It is reasonable for a corporate law, public accounting, or management consulting firm to use bone china to serve its guests—these guests are almost exclusively organization board members, executives, or senior managers.

It is not reasonable for an electronics manufacturing firm, fitness center, medical office, or non-profit organization to use bone china to serve its guests. This affectation damages an organization's credibility—both externally, between the organization and its customers or clients, and internally, between employees and management within the organization.

Thus, if the use of bone china does not match the type of organization or its customer base, then it is a sign of dysfunction—another *wannabe organization*. The organization has grandiose plans, maintains a carefully cultivated public image representing itself as more powerful and involved than it actually is, and relies mainly on its network of contacts rather than working to create lasting community buy-in.

Obviously, bone china is an extreme example, but one for which there are many corollaries. The key concept is whether a particular element—from

wall décor to furniture to writing instruments—is appropriate and functional for its environment. If it doesn't fit, what is the message?

Office Furnishings

Office décor—your choice of desk accessories, artwork, books, mementos, and plaques—leaves a bread crumb trail of clues for coworkers and clients about your sociability, efficiency, and competence. In an article written
by Larry Buhl on www.monster.com, *What Your Workspace Says About You*,
Professor Lisa Marie Luccioni of the University of Cincinnati was quoted as
saying that *everything* in your workspace communicates a message, whether
intentional or not.

I largely agree with Professor Luccioni's observations and assessments
and in a few cases, have added my own observations and analyses. Visual
examples of symbolic office décor dysfunction include:

- Too many pictures of the person's hobby or interests: the person
  would rather be engaged in that activity

- A flimsy guest chair, a chair covered with files, or no guest chair: the
  person is more likely an introvert and prefers shorter discussions

- Multiple framed degrees, certifications, and awards plus photos of
  the person with important people, or framed copies of magazine articles: the person *demands* respect

- A name plaque that lists only the person's first and last name: the person is approachable and friendly. If the name plaque has a formal title
  and lists degrees and/or certifications, the person demands respect.

- Files in boxes, no decorations, no artwork, no plants, no personal
  touches: the person is either new to the organization, has been fired
  and has not yet left, or wishes to leave the organization soon. Alternatively, extensive displays of work-related items say the person
  is insecure since they must display the administrative and mental
  trappings of their job.

- An office with messy piles of papers on every surface, leftover foods
  atop the paper piles, carpet stains, desktop stains, burned out lights
  in the desk lamp, a dirty keyboard, and ripped or torn arm cushions on the office chair shout, "I am totally disorganized." Your concern—Will this person's disorganization spill over to your business
  relationship? An alternative view is a messy office is that the office,

not the person, is a mess and the apparent lack of organization may work for her/him. Despite the mess, the person may be able to find necessary paperwork, keep commitments, follow through on tasks, is knowledgeable, is a team player, and is a solid contributor to the organization. I believe this alternative situation represents a definite minority. A mess is generally a mess!

- Outlandish items on display in an office such as wooden merry-go-round horse, suits of armor, large architectural or structural items, kiddie-size or full-size race cars, soccer nets, or basketball hoops create reasons for passers-by to gawk. **Through the display of this type of item, the person is reaching out and desperately seeking increased personal contact. Conservative office décor with a few small unique items sends a positive—not an overbearing or possibly desperate—message.**

- Political, potentially racist, sexist, homophobic, anti-religious, xenophobic, anti-military, or content otherwise disparaging of any group is a definite no-no. **If you see these messages in a top manager's office, this dysfunctional organization wants employees and customers of only a certain type or style and does not want diversity. Its collective thinking is extremely narrow and not open to new ideas. If you see this type of posting in a middle manager's office or in a break room, the employee rest room, or a worker's cubicle, it is no less insidious—because the organization has allowed freedom of expression to override good taste with no regard for the harm done.**

- Professor Luccioni suggests that humorous posters, ironic bumper stickers, whimsical images, and toys show the office holder doesn't take the whole work thing too seriously. In my view for businesses such as legal, finance, management consulting, technology, and medical/dental, humorous postings are an acceptable way to blow off steam, commiserate with colleagues, and laugh at yourself or the workplace. Generally, these blow-off-steam items would not be visible to guests. Technology organizations in Silicon Valley, Boston's Route 128, Austin, New York City, Florida's Space Coast, Northern California, and Pittsburgh would not be the innovative environments they are without having a socially acceptable way to laugh at themselves.

Humor is one thing; sarcasm is another. **Extensive public displays of sarcastic comments, quotes, bumper stickers, cartoons, posters, and slogans are signs the cubicle dweller or office holder isn't a happy camper. Sarcasm Spells only Dissatisfaction and Dysfunction.**

It's the number, not the presence, of postings that tells the story. One to three postings are acceptable; an individual's entire cubicle wall or office bulletin board filled with sarcastic quips confirms the **D** words—dysfunction, disrespect, and dissatisfaction.

You may be lucky enough to find a wall or bulletin board in a secluded location meant for viewing only by employees. Posting of all sorts of humor—articles, spoofs, April Fools' press releases, mock employee newsletters, bumper stickers, anti-motivational posters, humorously-modified corporate give-aways, changed organizational logos or slogans, fake ads—is okay. In fact, institutionalized *blowing off steam* shows the organization may be aware of its shortcomings and strengths. Hopefully, managers monitor for new and discarded items then advise senior management so they may address changing employee concerns.

Walls in the Executive Suite

Apply the same standards of evaluation to the walls in the executive suite as you applied to the reception area.

EVERYONE KNOWS WHO IS BOSS

At one insurance services company I visited, employees worked in a cubicle farm; the executives worked in large, individual offices with plush furnishings. The employees in sales and sales support worked in very brightly lit, small, cramped cubicles, separated only by four-foot high dividers, giving a fishbowl-like feeling. No one enjoyed any sense of privacy since the low dividers did not really provide individual work areas. The department manager worked in a glass-walled office that overlooked the cubicles.

Executives' administrators, as well as executives, received preferential treatment. Their cherry wood veneer workstations, located in a long softly-lit hall-like space on the second floor used mainly for executive offices, illustrated one more "step up" in a multi-tiered employee environment.

At the highest level of corporate management, spacious executive offices overlooked a manmade pond with a large spray fountain in the center.

- Look at color and tone (bright or dark) of painted walls vs. wallpaper

- Seek thank you letters from students, customers, suppliers, or community groups

- Note the artwork (style, size, professional vs. amateur framing)

- Look for motivational posters (remember, any such poster is the number three sign of corporate dysfunction)

On the Walls of Executives' Offices

The walls of individual executive's offices may differ from those in the executive reception area and its hallways. Look at the degree of individuality. Small changes and subtle touches are fine. However, someone with an entire wall of bright abstract-design wallpaper in an executive suite characterized by walls painted with subdued, earth-tone colors presages a potential loose cannon. Difference is fine; the degree of difference reveals a great deal. What do you see on the walls of each of the VP's offices? Do you see what is essentially the same content—plaques, sports autographs, photos with politicians or celebrities, or artwork of a certain style? The copycat nature of this organization exposes an overbearing or know-it-all CEO, timid VPs, frequently withheld information, and poor internal communication.

The display of children's art is unifying, spiritual, bonding, and appropriate. No matter the child's level of talent, a parent wants to feel connected to

---

Expensive-looking cherry-wood desks, file cabinets, credenzas, and small tables and chairs created a relaxing, lush environment. Fancy artwork and soft lighting contrasted with the brightly lit fishbowl environment of non-management employees.

In the past, I had visited with senior executives of computer system and data communication products manufacturers. These mature technology companies have the revenues and gross profit margins to support fancier offices at higher management levels. The disparity between employee/manager accoutrements at this three-year old, $5 million financial/insurance services company was far greater than at any of those of major computer system and data communication product manufacturers—a gross example of inappropriate, over-reaching, financial miscalculation. Within four years, the organization was acquired for a bargain price.

~~*

his/her child or children. Children's art also humanizes the inhabitant of the office, adding obvious contrast to framed art, professional certifications, or degrees, decorative sculpture, an aquarium, atrium, or individual green plants. Once again, it's a matter of degree—an office with nearly every square inch of wall space covered with children's art work is excessive and distinguishes an executive disconnected from the rest of the organization.

Old grandfather clocks are special pieces of furniture. One of these magnificent clocks may arrive in an executive's office as a family heirloom, relegated to the office because it no longer fits the executive's home decor. The executive may even collect grandfather clocks. In an office environment, the presence of a grandfather clock or any clock which demands attention, whether by its size, style, or auditory intrusion, is a gesture of rudeness, whether intentional or not.

Another type of clock is the art clock. Traditionally, an art clock was a wall clock with photographs, drawings, or brightly colored ceramics on the face . . . long associated with kitschy kitchen décor. The grown-up version of this is the sculptural clock. Sculptural clocks may be small representations of buildings, animals, or any number of non-clock forms—which tend to look overdone in an office environment.

The modern, professional version of the sculptural clock is a finely-finished, intricate, fascinating manual or electronic mechanism—often quite large—perhaps a series of highly-polished, exposed, functional, metal or wood gears or moving metal plates. The elegance of these clocks' movements is almost meditative. A tasteful sculptural clock is an appropriate alternative to wall art, but requires a balance. Since many of these pieces are large, their functions as timepieces need to be secondary to their aesthetic function.

On the other hand, many of these clocks cannot be read in the same way as traditional or digital clocks . . . leaving the visitor who cannot easily read the time at a chronological disadvantage. A clock which a visitor cannot read creates distance between the executive, who knows what it means, and the visitor, who does not. **An executive who feels the need for one-upmanship with a complicated clock or, for that matter, any clever art which requires an explanation to make sense is an insecure executive who will, most likely, be more focused on competing with his peers, employees, and business partners than on building and maintaining effective, healthy business relationships.**

Aside from the art clock used as decorative wall sculpture, clocks should be placed in out-of-the-way locations, not in places of prominence. All clocks should operate unobtrusively—no ticking, whirring of gears, or music. Any clock that chimes on the hour, half hour, or quarter hour is a distraction, interrupts attempts at communication, and disrupts thought processes. If you are meeting with an executive and a clock ticks constantly, then it is hard to focus on anything except that time is passing.

If the clock is too evident, the executive becomes a clock watcher. An executive should be able to estimate the time needed for a meeting and not have to constantly check the clock to ensure s/he is on schedule. Computer applications can be set up to notify the executive of upcoming meetings or conference calls in a timely manner . . . far more efficiently because they can communicate that an event is scheduled as well as what that event is.

The style of clock should match the style of the furniture. **A clock with Roman numerals in a modern or contemporary environment does not fit. It signifies an old-fashioned attitude or over-dependence on core American values. This style of numerals may also serve as a decoy.** Taken to an extreme, a clock with numerals that clash with the design in the rest of the office could signal a thief, malingerer, credit taker, back stabber, or even adulterer.

A display of military mementoes sends an interesting message. This executive is obviously proud of his or her accomplishments while serving in the military. The display may include photos of places stationed or visited, of former GIs with whom they served, of military armament, of military ceremonies, or of the president as commander-in-chief during the years served. What makes this interesting is this person has also accomplished a great deal in the working world, reaching the level of executive. For many who served, no matter what their current accomplishments, their military achievements are most dear to them, especially those accomplishments in times of war. No one can rightfully accuse this person of living in the past; they also achieved a great deal in the business world.

This executive's message is one of pride. Take a second look at the display. How much physical space on the wall does it occupy? A display of medals mounted in a small case and a small photo montage of people, places, or parades places these past events in proper perspective. A large display of medals mounted in a two-foot-by-four-foot ornately-framed case with a red velvet lining places far too much importance on this display. A poster size photo, no matter the subject, gives far too much prominence to the subject. The only exception would be a photograph of the executive receiving the Congressional Medal of Honor while in the service. **An oversize display tells you that person is stuck in the past and longs for the experiences in the military.** A visitor may wish to ask the details behind the photo in order to gauge the importance of that experience to the executive. Be sure to ask when and where that executive was stationed; the executive may not have served in the military but wants to falsely impress visitors.

You may notice sports memorabilia. If you are meeting with an executive watch for extensive displays of autographed baseballs, footballs, sports jerseys, photos, or a combination of items. A couple of small items tastefully included among office furnishings is fine. **However, a near-museum of sports memorabilia tells you this person's priorities are wrong. They really care about sports, not business.** One or more large sports mementoes may represent the extension of that person's childhood dream of athleticism or the remembrance of meeting a famous athlete. Once again, size of the display and perspective are key.

Look for awards on the wall or bookcase, credenza, desk, or wall unit. Examine the nature of the awards and the organizations which presented them. Are these awards for fund raising? Do they recognize community service? Do they acknowledge financial contributions to a community organization? Are any awards related to a religious organization? Veterans' groups? A local *guardian ad litem* program? Political organizations or parties? Industry lobbying organizations? Human rights organizations? Politically-motivated think tanks, such as the Heritage Foundation or the Cato Institute? What about local, regional, national, or international inter-religion committees? Do you see thanks for volunteer service to a government advisory board? Thanks from industry advisory boards?

Each of us reacts differently to the kinds of organizations listed above. The point is: **Why would someone display an award or recognition from a group that espouses certain political, tax, industry, business, or religious beliefs or values? It is incorrect, both politically and business-wise. The person lacks sound business judgment. In this person's mind the lines between political or religious activism and the business world are blurred when they should be distinct.**

Remember, this person invited you to their private space, their office. You were exposed to far more about whom they are, far beyond the images in the lobby, kitchen, main conference room, or restroom. What business person would choose to leave such an impression on a visitor? For a publicly-held corporation, overt display of linkages with political or religious organizations should be unthinkable and unacceptable.

Family-run corporations are a different story. This is precisely where there are no similar boundaries or propriety. Why? These owners answer to no one or to a limited, self-selected, self-serving group of family or close friend overseers serving as Board members.

Once again, the appropriateness of displayed awards boils down to a matter of degree. A few awards represent a balanced approach to work, community, religious organizations, travel, the arts, and family. A full wall of awards tells a great deal, namely:

- The business' city is built around an incestuous network; this person is trying desperately to find a way to enter, then remain in the network

- This person is building a local network in case he/she is dismissed from his/her current job

- The person is insecure and needs constant recognition and acknowledgement and will seek it outside the organization

- This person feels it is necessary to display evidence of others' approval to solidify his/her status

- The person is a social butterfly and networker. Do these extensive activities contribute *directly* to the success of the business?

- Taken to its limit, extensive outside activities imply a less-than-happy marriage. One cannot be involved outside of work every night of the week. At that point, it's an evasive maneuver, possibly one to mask an affair.

Do you see humorous, fake certifications such as those of *Good Ol' Boy* or *Kentucky Colonel?* These belong in the person's family room, den, or home office, not at the worksite. **This is a warning sign of a lack of boundaries or lack of common sense.** This person does not understand the difference between items that are appropriate for an office environment and those that are not.

Awards or recognition from subordinates, even humorous ones, show a sense of bonding and are appropriate in an office environment. One manager I heard of received a GOATT award from his employees. Did the award recognize a great achievement? Hardly. The acronym stood for *Get Out All That Trash*. The manager's office was known throughout the department and the company for being messy. After a major cleaning, the manager added the plaque to the clutter on his walls.

Do you see an autographed photo of the executive with a businessperson, athlete, military figure, newsmaker, actor, or political figure? Seldom do you see just one of these reminders of greatness by association. This person wants visitors to know that s/he is indeed someone, in at least one aspect of their life. However, remember that this person is an executive. That in itself is a big accomplishment! Does this person aspire to a bigger or far different vocation or location? Is that person never satisfied with what they have done? Is it a case of *never good enough*?

Do you see the person's degrees framed neatly and located in a prominent place on the office wall? Once again, this is an unnecessary display. Who cares? The person occupies the position due to their combination of education, experience, expertise, leadership, contacts, and people skills. Education represents only one aspect of that person's qualifications. Often, the displayed diploma is from an Ivy-league or well-known school, which represents more one-upmanship. Is the person's résumé also on display? Of course not. Based on how the executive interacts with coworkers and guests, the visitor will get some idea of that person's education, upbringing, and social interactions. The prominent display of degrees belongs in the person's home office or den.

At the executive level, displaying college diplomas is a warning that the executive feels the need to one-up any visitor. In fact, rather than impressing visitors, the display of one or more diplomas may erect subtle barriers between the executive and the visitor.

Are professional certifications mounted on a wall in the executive's office? An executive may display a professional certification if it related to the executive's business. Accreditations such as Certified Public Accountant, Chartered Life Underwriter, or an attorney license for legal practice in the same state or licensed to practice before a state, federal, or Supreme court are valuable credentials. Industry-specific certifications such as LUTCF or most real estate credentials may be displayed if the executive works in that business.

If the licenses or certifications are not relevant for the current position, they are old news. If the executive displays certifications from training courses, then this is a sign of improved sales abilities, not necessarily better industry knowledge. Many equity and fixed income research analysts, who earned the Chartered Financial Analyst (CFA) designation, proudly display the CFA certificate in their office. However, these individuals seldom meet guests in their office; they are more likely to meet in a conference room. This display represents validation of their financial analysis knowledge and professionalism to peers.

Do you see a small whiteboard, whether hidden behind a wall-mounted closed-door cabinet or mounted out in the open on a wall? There is no substitute for a whiteboard to keep track of a discussion for later reference. More importantly, a whiteboard is essential for drawing diagrams to explain complex interrelationships or keep track of many variables in a given situation. Most importantly, a whiteboard signifies that an executive is willing to listen and learn. **In an executive's office, the lack of a whiteboard or an easel with a tablet of paper, no matter how large or small, reveals that the executive is not open to continual learning.**

What about the opposite situation—one where absolutely nothing is displayed on office walls? Unless the executive just moved in yesterday, there are three options:

- One, the executive is professionally and organizationally secure and does not need to make any statements about who s/he is.

- Two, work is everything. That person's life is empty, reflected by the emptiness of the walls.

- Three, the person does not want to reveal anything about her- or himself. That person wants to be identified by only what they say, write, and do. To not want to reveal anything personal or community-related about him- or herself reflects a need for extreme privacy, almost paranoia.

As a single important data point, the lack of anything on the walls provides direction in your search to better understand this executive. If you find evidence of outside activities, family life, sports, travel, or other interests on the desk, credenza, or bookcase, then this person is secure. If you find work- or profession-related artifacts, then this person eats, sleeps, and breathes work. If you find nothing of a personal nature anywhere else in the office, then the diagnosis of *paranoid* fits best.

Desk/Workspace/Étagère/Bookcase

How many and what kinds of photos do you see? Do you see photos of family, famous people, politicians, athletes, or actors? Are photos mainly of men, women, children, or some of each? How close is everyone standing to one another? Do you see a gap between the executive in the picture and others, especially family members? The executive should be close to family members. If you see a gap, this gap metaphorically represents distance from the individual and those persons with whom you would expect the executive to be close.

Do you see pictures from vacations taken in a faraway place? Do you see photos from industry conventions or meetings? Do you see photos from company events, such as a new product rollout or the celebration of a key company milestone? Do you see photos of holiday parties, departmental or divisional events or milestones, retirement luncheons, or dinners?

Look for a balance or blend of photos, rather than a concentration on one or two topics. **If you see photos of only politicians, actors, musicians, and athletes and none of family or friends, then consider this a warning—the underlying attitude is that of a bigshot; it's-ALL-about-me, or I'm a wanna-be.** If the workspace is filled with pictures and nothing else, take note of the subjects, situations, and locations. **Once again, you're looking for balance. An excessive number of photos of a single topic shows singular, not diverse or balanced, thinking.**

Since this person's life revolves around past events, try to get a sense in your discussion of which topics are most important. You will be better able to determine if this person, despite the executive job position, prefers special people, politicians, places, family, contributing to their industry, memorable events, military functions, actors, athletes, or musicians.

Do you see a copy of any of the *Who's Who* books in the office or, to a lesser extent, in the reception area or conference room? The publisher of this self-promoting book contacts persons in a variety of businesses and professions and asks each to complete a profile. The publisher assembles these profiles and prints the volume in a leather-bound case with gold foil stamped letters on the cover and book spine. This is fine. However, the publisher then sells the book to those who submitted their profiles!

Who's Who is self-serving vanity publishing—and frequently filled with puffery or outright lies. **The presence of any *Who's Who* book by a manager, executive, or board member is my number three sign of organizational dysfunction, after the presence of a filthy restroom and motivational posters on the walls.**

At some point in this person's life, s/he may have felt the need to build a presence in the business or professional world. However, this person, in a leadership position, should now have no real need to justify his/her existence. Anyone could find the person's basic background through a Google or Bing search. **Run, do not walk, from serious dealings with this executive. If the person is the CEO, then watch for signs of insecurity or their need to gain an upper hand in situations where such action is not necessary.**

How many golf-related mementos, knick-knacks, photos of the executive in golf-related scenes, items of equipment, matchbook covers with the names and crests of country clubs or exclusive courses, or photos of famous golfers do you see? One or two smaller items are fine. **If you see an office putting green or the executive's office resembles the 19th hole at a country club, then this person's priorities are backward. They care too much about the game.** While the game offers the opportunity to get to know someone reasonably well, golf is, unfortunately, a time-consuming activity.

The executive may have an inability to prioritize or make decisions, since these items rightfully belong at home in the den, home office, or family room. Most importantly, these *prestige* objects send a message that the executive is of an elevated social class. Other executives are likely to belong to that same class. However, this display sends the wrong message to non-executive visitors to the office.

Do you see collectibles in the office? Collectibles can range from pocket watches and wristwatches, to toys and dolls, to pre-Columbian or 16th century Dutch art, to Lionel trains. In an office environment, an artistic collectible can be displayed neatly among other items of office décor. A small display case mounted on the wall or set on a small table places the collection in proper perspective.

If you see an entire wall display of old Lionel trains, Barbie dolls, watches, or fountain pens, then this is another small warning sign. Once again, this executive does not realize the boundary between what belongs at home and what is appropriate for a business office. The display of one or two large kitschy items, such as an old gasoline pump or buggy from horse-and-buggy days makes an interesting conversation starter. However, when teamed with an entire wall or floor of collectibles, what appears as a conversation starter becomes further proof of excess or lack of boundaries. As in the case of other idiosyncrasies you may observe, display-related dysfunction is a matter of degree.

Has the executive displayed memorabilia from his/her college or graduate school alma mater? Do you see a chair, lamp, pillow, coffee mug, business card holder, photo of a prominent building on campus or school mascot, or sports items imprinted with the school name, nickname, mascot, or insignia? In Florida, the University of Florida Gators versus Florida State University Seminoles rivalry is legendary. In the San Francisco Bay Area, competition between the University of California, Berkeley and Stanford University is extremely strong. In polite company, discussions of Pitt vs. Penn State, Ohio vs. Ohio State,

Michigan vs. Michigan State, Army vs. Navy, and Ivy league rivalries, like discussions of sex, politics, and religion, are humorously forbidden.

Executives who strongly promote their school risk alienating visitors from rival schools. Once again, this is a matter of size of the memorabilia, number of items, and degree of display. You will know when the executive is a rabid fan or major contributor, not just a regular alumnus.

Do you see more than one display of the American flag? Do you see any references to 9/11? If the company flies the flag outside its headquarters or manufacturing facilities, that is fine. However, additional displays of our flag, whether in the lobby, reception area, kitchen, cafeteria, or executive office is overkill—a sign of pandering.

If you see multiple American flags on display, then the company uses that imagery to conceal other dysfunction. To badly paraphrase Shakespeare, "Methinks thee doth divert too much." The chief executive may have control issues, desire a high political office whether or not qualified and temperamentally suited, maintain a too-close relationship with politicians, lack belief in strategic planning, aspire to project a macho public persona, and rely too heavily on key advisors.

Did you observe any clever sayings, elaborately framed, in the executive's office, conference area, hallway, or restroom? Humorous quips, such as those from W. C. Fields or Henny Youngman or Robin Williams, if applicable to business or one of the executive's volunteer activities, provides a different, revealing perspective on that person. A couple of appropriate Dilbert © cartoons work well, too. This display of self-effacing humor humanizes the executive. You should get an impression that the person has a sense of humor and is able to laugh at him- or herself.

If the framed clever saying in any way resembles the content of a motivational poster, then consider this a repeat of the number three warning sign of dysfunction. As in the case of the motivational poster, who is the target of this motivational quip—the employee or the executive in whose office you found the statement? **To rephrase, the person who displays a motivational poster needs the motivation far more than the employees the displayer has targeted.**

Look for a framed *tombstone*, or newspaper clipping that the company went public or completed a secondary public stock offering. Financial executives often display this memento of a company's most significant positive financial event. Chief executives do not generally display this announcement. Sometimes, the CEO or chief financial officer (CFO) will display instead a Lucite® encased miniature version of the printed tombstone. This is a different yet highly acceptable way to call attention to this event.

Check the executive's office for Lucite® mementoes of stock offerings from companies on whose Boards of Directors the executive sits or a company where friends or relatives work. Any Lucite® memento for a company other than the CEO's current company is excessive. The CEO should pay attention to his/her current employer. When the CEO signs financial statements in accordance with Sarbanes-Oxley legislation, the CEO attests to his/her direct knowledge and oversight of the company. If the CEO sits on too many boards for other companies, how can s/he accurately and honestly attest to the veracity of the information submitted to the SEC and stockholders on behalf of the employing company?

Do you see any religious symbols displayed on office walls? The cross, crucifix, Star of David, ichthys (fish symbol), Star and Crescent, Om or Aum, Wheel of Dharma, the Khanda, Yin and Yang, the Torii Gate, Ahimsa Hand, or Baha'i Nine-Pointed Star simply do not belong in a business, government, military, or not-for-profit office environment. These are appropriate at home or in religion-affiliated offices.

Summary

Executive offices are a treasure trove of clues which can help the observer identify organizational dysfunction. Our examination of this important area included its location within the enterprise, furnishings in the waiting area and executives' offices, the presence of electronic devices in executives' offices, the kitchen area, and the executive wash room.

First, are the furnishings significantly nicer than those in individuals' workstations or offices? What did you learn from your examination of the lighting, height of ceiling, artwork, executive spa/Jacuzzi®/exercise area (if present), and beverages served to guests? Did you see evidence of pets being allowed in the office? Did you find fresh flowers or a dish of candy?

Next, were the doors to executives' offices typically left open or were they closed? Did the CEO have a separate conference room for her/his exclusive use? Could you identify a separate entrance or exit for the CEO? Did the CEO have space in his/her office for a small table and two or three side chairs? How much storage space did a credenza or two provide? Did the boss hang her/his overcoat/suit coat on the back of the office door or did you find a separate closet? Did the executive's office have a wet bar or coffee bar?

In this day and age, an executive must possess some level of technical sophistication. You should see a computer terminal, personal digital assistant, tablet computer, and/or cellphone.

As you walk by each executive's office, look at the furniture. Is it all the same? Of do you find a wide variety of furniture styles and colors of wood or other materials? Do the CEO's and VP's offices have healthy plants? Is the door to each office made of all wood, wood with glass inserts, or all glass? Alternatively, if a wood door, can you find a small vertical strip of glass next to the door? Does the CEO work in an L-shaped or a parallel lines-shape workspace? Does the executive suite have its own kitchen?

What did you find in the CEO's office? Did you see lots of pictures of family, friends, co-workers, athletes, disabled children or adults, or politicians? Were the CEO's framed degrees or certifications mounted on the wall? How many and how tall were the piles of papers on the executive's desk? Did you find political or religious items or symbols? Did this executive display many or oversize mementos? What was on the walls of the CEO's office—artwork, clocks, military mementos, sports memorabilia, memberships in *good ol' boy* organizations, photos with famous people, a whiteboard? Did you find a volume or two of any *Who's Who* biographical books? Did you see any Lucite® tombstone commemoratives of stock or bond offerings?

To identify potential signs of dysfunction look closely at: the degree of differences between executive offices, kitchens, rest rooms, and related facilities and those of rank-and-file workers.

~*~*~*~

CHAPTER 22

ORGANIZATIONAL DNA, FUN, & MORE

Up until this point, we have been sensing the structures and objects and attitudinal environment surrounding the people in organizations. We learned how to recognize incongruities and to interpret meaning. Occasionally, we noted a few people as we passed through the building . . . most notably, the receptionist, people interacting in the hallways, and others working at their desks.

In truth, we could have extrapolated most of what we have learned thus far even if no one else was in the building at the time—the evidence is that strong. However, a thorough evaluation of any organization's history and culture must include people-related aspects. If you are a prospective employee interviewing for a job, this can be the most critical consideration of all . . . if you want to ensure an organizational fit.

We will evaluate the organizational DNA:

- How the organization works, plays, and communicates

- Workforce demographics and hiring patterns

- Appearance of employees, executives, and potential employees

- Organizational purpose, problem pasts and power, and decision making

- The position and the hiring process

Organizational DNA

Working together, people form organizations. The genesis of a company is important since the personalities, experiences, egos, idiosyncrasies, drives, plans, and needs of early leaders and employees mesh to create a company's *gestalt* or soul. The founders, the founding circumstances, the organization's early values, and the organizational structure determine the organization's ability to succeed, grow, and adapt. It is important that you learn and fully understand an organization's DNA or culture. Why?

The imprint of the earliest policies, procedures, activities, and values of an organization remain long after founder(s) and early employees have retired, embedded within the organization through transference to subsequent members. *The early group selects those who, it feels, will best continue the organization in the direction it has established.*

Bottom line: **Over time, things may change but not very much. The foundations for an organization's DNA continue to strongly influence the organization long after the company's inception.**

How Does the Organization Work?

Most organizations are best represented by an equilateral triangle with one point at the top and the other two points at the base. The CEO sits at the uppermost point. A slightly wider stratum of vice presidents, typically three to eight, occupies the level below the CEO. Larger organizations may insert a layer of executive vice presidents and senior vice presidents between the CEO and vice presidents. Closer to the bottom of the triangle, an even larger number of directors and managers report to the vice presidents. The widest part at the bottom of the triangle represents the many individual contributor workers, those who have no supervisory roles.

Despite the formal hierarchical structure of an organization, organizations use unique approaches to make decisions. Rarely does the CEO make every decision and order subordinates to follow through. It is important that the job seeker, sales rep, or commercial or investment banker understand how decisions are made at a firm.

- Is the style **top-down** where, as we described, the CEO or possibly a few vice presidents make all the substantive decisions and everyone else implements the given orders?

- Is the style **bottom-up**, where the operating managers and employees make recommendations to the executive staff members who approve these recommendations, and then pass them back to the originating group for implementation?

- Is the style **sideways,** characterized by separate department contributions made at the peer operating level and jointly executed? In this case, the executives are notified only when problems arise or additional coordination is required.

The three described styles evoke vastly different day-to-day operations. The military used to epitomize top-down decision making. The Vietnam War changed the military's rigid decision-making structure, giving field commanders far more latitude and decision-making authority and responsibility.

In the 1980s, IBM was so top-down driven that its decision processes made the U.S. military appear downright flexible! All decisions emanated from the level of corporate vice president or above. However, in response to market, internal, and competitive pressures, former IBM CEOs Lou Gerstner and Sam Palmissano wisely restructured the decision-making style from top-down to bottom-up. Although now a much larger organization than 20 years ago, IBM is more responsive to customer needs.

How does the organization deal with failure? What does the company list as the public cause versus the real cause of the failure? Internally, does a post-mortem meeting accurately pinpoint the problems, rather than assign the blame? Can employees and managers learn from their mistakes? Did anyone ask what they would do differently next time? Were the employees and managers involved demoted, fired or laid off, or *shuffled off to Buffalo*? Can team members laugh at what they did? Can they articulate what have they learned? Have they been allowed to discover the pitfalls and put effective policies in place to prevent future failures?

How Does the Organization Play?

What evidence do you see of fun? What are acceptable standards for employees who need to blow off steam? Here are a few ideas which different companies with different management styles might implement:

- Do members of the company plan and successfully complete Halloween pranks? Employees at Silicon Valley's Sun Microsystems, now part of Oracle Corporation, are famous for their creative pranks which usually include an engineering twist. Do employees wear costumes to work on Halloween?

- Does the company hold pot-luck lunches with ethnic food themes where all participating employees must bring a dish to share—no mooching or freeloading?

- Does the company host picnics? This is absolutely *not* the time or place to drink alcoholic beverages, no matter what everyone is told in advance about the acceptance of beer or wine or malt beverage coolers.

- Does someone in the organization craft newsletters that lampoon the official newsletter?

- Do you see clever mock announcements released on April Fools' Day?

- Are birthdays celebrated or acknowledged each month?

- Does the organization have parties to celebrate company anniversaries or the attainment of key milestones, such as shipping the 10,000th model of a product?

Can you find evidence of fun? Is it obvious? How frequently does the company sponsor fun events or activities? Do you see posters that promote get-togethers? Are these activities designed for the employees, their spouses or significant others, their children or grandchildren, or do you see a combination of activity formats? Do you see photos from fun events on the walls in the reception area? Does the company leave a scrapbook of past celebrations in the reception area? Does the company website boast of past fun events? Do you see photos of employees enjoying these activities?

Does the organization list *specific* fun activities? A general reference to fun is no reference at all. **If the document or website that contains a reference to a *family* like *atmosphere* does not mention specific fun activities, be careful.** Similar to other promises the company makes, it will not keep this promise. Simply stated, a family-like atmosphere can be fun—if you're a member of the family!

Fun is fine. However, make sure fun is appropriate to the industry and the timing is correct. A CPA firm does *not* have fun between January 1 and April 15; it is busy auditing client companies and preparing end-of-calendar-year financial statements for companies until March 15, and preparing individual income tax returns until April 15. Cerebral organizations such as market research or management consulting firms are not likely to offer active sports teams or competitive leagues—fun will probably be more cerebral.

A company should never serve liquor as a normal practice in the office or at any of its functions—even *fun* celebrations. Why? Liability, more liability, and maximum liability—which should be of paramount importance to event planners, risk managers, and executives. Serving liquor within the organizational environment intensifies peer pressure for participants to imbibe. Executives set a truly bad example when they drink with subordinates. Additionally, anyone who has the least problem with controlling his/her behavior while under the influence can end a career in a few hours of bad judgment. As with each branch of the U.S. military, there is a good reason for separate clubs for commissioned and non-commissioned officers.

An overlooked item is how the organization celebrates success. A paycheck is not the only way. Do teams go out for long lunches? Do they go to dinner at fancy restaurants? Go drinking at a bar or dancing at a country club? Does the manager award a day or two off as partial compensation for extensive overtime? Does the group travel for a well-deserved long weekend or weeklong break to a faraway resort? If so, may group members bring spouses or significant others?

How Does the Organization Communicate?

It is a difficult challenge to assess the organization's structure and hierarchy during an interview, plant tour, and selected peer interactions that last in total from two to eight hours. Listen to the exchanges between employees, especially between managers and subordinates. Who talks? Who listens? What is the nature of that communication? Is it strictly directive? Do you sense that subordinates are open and managers supportive? Or does it appear that subordinates are communicating as little as possible because they fear management's dissatisfaction and censure? You may get a sense of what is important in the organization if you ask friendly questions of the receptionist while you are waiting to meet with a manager.

Speak with someone in a department other than the one where you would work. Determine common threads. Determine differences. Determine unspoken issues.

Listen to the receptionist's language: "Mr. Smith will see you," vs. "Bill will see you." Is s/he chewing gum? Is the boss yelling at the receptionist or another employee within earshot of the reception area?

Listen carefully to see if the interviewers focus on a particular trait such as loyalty. Watch for someone acting too *buddy-buddy* at the first interview. As in the case of a first date, this is a *get to know you* meeting, not a prelude to walking down the wedding aisle. Too much friendliness, especially where it is inappropriate, speaks of a phony or a schemer, plain and simple. Beware!

Listen *between the words*: Often someone will say something . . . but, while they are doing that, what are they *not* saying? The more carefully they craft their words around an issue, the more you need to be aware of what they are avoiding.

If you interview more than one person, pay attention to both how the interviewers respond to you and to the interactions between the interviewers themselves. One person could be having a bad day. Snippy reactions between the interviewers communicate underlying power/personality issues which could create an uncomfortable working environment. If your interactions with more than one person do not feel right, trust your gut. **If the interviewer speaks to you in couched, overly-cautious, overly-polite, non-specific language, beware! That, too, is a warning sign. In such a dysfunctional environment, a person must operate carefully and with a mask. Watch your back!**

Language issues—what you say and how you say it—are critical for job seekers. Answer the questions. Do not volunteer more than asked unless you can add a one- or two-sentence example directly related to the question. Do not complain about previous work situations, bosses, co-workers, or companies. Do not bemoan your personal misfortunes . . . nor claim to have out-classed your previous employer/position. You may have been an extremely conscientious, hard-working employee who was unappreciated by a corporate troglodyte (cave-dweller)—but you don't say it if your goal is to get a new job.

The language used in press releases and especially in required financial disclosures is revealing. Does the company spokesperson speak in plain words? Where a simple word or concept will suffice, does the spokesperson use thirty- and fifty-cent words? Do press releases and financial information sound as though they were crafted by someone playing *buzzword bingo*? Similarly, can you tell if the Legal Department was having way too much fun in writing or editing the press release? Do you understand what was written? **Use of inauthentic language characterizes a bunch of phonies, a group that hides critical information, a group of executives and board members that wants to emulate a company held in high esteem, or one which wishes to gain a perceived higher social standing in their industry or local business community.**

Study the organization's website. What does the site emphasize—for example, products, services, employees, community involvement, family ownership, family-like work environment, corporate citizenship, environmental stewardship, or free high quality post-sale service? The website is a formalized communication vehicle where the company has the opportunity to tell the *edited* version of its story . . . as opposed to off-the-cuff comments which may end up misinterpreted. Is the edited version accurate and clear? Or is the communication obtuse, poorly-edited, or full of meaningless platitudes that sound good but mean nothing?

Does the organization place a high value on telling the truth? Is it okay to tell a lie? When? To whom? Does the CEO often lie? **Look for inconsistencies.** People tend to lie when they fear what will happen if they tell the truth. What truth is the liar attempting to cover? Why?

When meeting with managers and peers, what behavioral aspects do they consider important? What happens to employees who are caught by regulatory authorities for actions considered a crime? I know of one person who was suspended years ago as an equity research analyst. A valuable asset to the firm (read: a huge money maker), he was not dismissed. Instead, he was reassigned to a sales position.

Look around. Watch for a group of employees talking in a conference area, going for a run, doing exercises in the company fitness center during the day, chatting with the receptionist, or working in the cafeteria while having coffee. Do you see a balance between work and other activities?

Do you hear laughter? Do you hear groans from bad puns? Do you hear shouting or screaming? A screamer, especially if it is the CEO, is not a good sign. I worked for a screamer at a start-up company. He used his screams to bully, badger, disrupt thinking, gain control, harass, and intimidate others. However, within a few minutes, he forgot what he had screamed about and was able to hold a rational conversation. Out of fairness, he was an equal opportunity screamer, since anyone could become the target of his next scream.

The hub and spoke organizational structure, with the CEO as the hub, guaranteed that he controlled the organization's information flow. Since he was moody and volatile, his executive assistant became the most important person in the company. Everyone would check with her on the boss's mood and receptiveness to bad news. If his mood was sufficiently negative, the news was held up until the next day.

Are the hallways silent since most of the individual contributors are attending meetings? Too many meetings show a lack of organizational maturity, lack of leadership, lack of management training, or lack of managerial qualifications. *Someone* has to get the work done!

Do you see informal groups discussing issues? Impromptu meetings may take place in the coffee room, copier room, empty small conference room, one person's cubicle, or the hallway. The location is unimportant. No one takes notes. No one guides the discussion. It is spontaneous; the right staff members are present and the discussion flows. Everyone contributes and helps solve the problem.

Remember, if you are considering joining or working with an organization, the organizational DNA is not likely to change, regardless of its flaws.

Workforce Demographics and Hiring Patterns

Do you see any women executives in the organization? Women at the director level? Women managers? In this era, the lack of women or the presence of very few in positions of authority is inexcusable. Women now graduate from college at a higher rate than men. Women mature more quickly than men (duh!). Women generally have stronger human relations skills than

---

LANGUAGE, LISTENING, AND A SLICK SALES PITCH

Harriet, a friend with a master's degree in social work administration from the University of Michigan, needed additional sources of income. She scheduled a meeting with June, a representative of a multi-level marketing (MLM) organization. June brought along Jill, the organization's local *trainer*.

To minimize travel for all parties with gasoline priced at $4.40 per gallon, Harriet met these two women at my house, which was conveniently located for everyone. From an adjacent room, I could easily eavesdrop on the conversation.

The discussion started out with pleasantries. Harriet moved the discussion from her recovery from breast cancer, to talk about her 20-year old daughter at college, through a discussion of spiritual philosophies, then to her religious background and beliefs, and finally the history of the treatment of Native Americans. During breaks in Harriet's running commentary, Jill cleverly showed an overly-slick, personal-computer-based marketing presentation. Jill mentioned evening training meetings at a local hotel, a telephone conference call following this meeting to discuss open issues or answer questions, a brochure, and a website upgrade to provide better customer service. June wisely asked qualifying questions of Harriet throughout the presentation.

Clearly, Harriet's focus was not on the presentation. She needed to move from her home within the next three days. She would not admit as much but, based on her responses, was unwilling to commit *any* substantive efforts to this MLM organization. She was talking to June and Jill about anything but the opportunity; they, in turn, were reciting a *canned* pitch which had nothing to do with Harriett.

men. So why not hire or promote women into positions of responsibility?

Here are a handful of reasons to explain the lack of women in management, few of which are reasonable:

- Gender, sexual orientation, religious, or regional discrimination (Southerners prefer to work with Southerners; Midwesterners prefer their own; Easterners are definitely more comfortable with fellow Easterners)

- Lack of qualified candidates

- Lack of personal comfort with a particular person; the hiring manager is not comfortable telling a joke to the best-qualified female individual contributor

---

Bottom line: Harriet was lonely and would tell her story to anyone. In a similar sense, the MLM representatives were desperate to find anyone to sell their products and/or services. Based on Harriet's initial responses to qualifying questions, June and Jill should have stopped the discussion after about 15 minutes. An hour and 45 minutes into the Sunday-afternoon discussion, the resolution was uncertain. As I eaves-dropped, I knew this could go on for a long time with no commitment. Both parties were talking at each other, more interested in being heard than in listening. What a waste of time and emotional energy! A professional sales rep would have found a way to quickly terminate the discussion. This interaction also shed light on the MLM business; this marketing organization would sign anyone with a pulse.

Postscript: I was wrong. The meeting ended just two minutes later, at one hour and 47 minutes. After June and Jill left, Harriet said to me, "Good women. I like the no up-front investment aspect of this program. I will definitely do this." One lonely person plus a desperate, untargeted sales effort for one opportunity to sell a collection of relatively expensive undifferentiated consumer products equaled a very high likelihood of failure. I would have happily eaten my words if I were wrong. Indeed, Harriet needed some successes at this point in her life. This *opportunity* did not look to be the right business to start building success.

Update: Harriet finally looked at the catalog of products for sale. She said the items were overpriced. She could not sell these products.

~~*

- Perceived competition, whether real or imaginary, from a woman
- An interviewer's personal issues with his/her mother

Can you identify any women on the Board of Directors? One recent study showed that the presence of at least one female director on the Board was likely to reduce a company's chances of going bankrupt by 20%. Having two or three lowered the chances even further. (*Financial Times;* May 22, 2012, Special Report: Global Brands, page 3) The article noted reasons for this: "Women, it seems, are good at cash flow, they resist the temptation of getting into debt, and pay attention to managing risk."

Bottom line: **If you do not see any women in positions of authority, beware. Despite whatever interviewers say or what is written on the website, the company does not want to hire the best person for the job.** The company is paternalistic in all the wrong ways. It might: be meddlesome or overly involved in personal lives, make excessive travel demands, maintain strong regional personal preferences (Easterners, Southerners, Texans, Westerners, or Midwesterners), micromanage, over-schedule company events for bonding with other employees, support a fraternity-like environment complete with bawdy humor, or rely on a *cover-for-each-other* culture rather than one which proactively addresses customer complaints.

Do you see any minorities working at the firm? This is especially important at firms with an international marketing, finance, or operations presence. Whether we agree or not, the rules for doing business outside the United States are different from those here. Foreign-born employees or first- or second-generation Americans of foreign descent are a growing part of our country and economy. Surely, many are as qualified as the long-entrenched majority white population (portent for the future: non-white U.S. births exceeded white births for the first time in July 2011).

Many minorities strengthen America through their contributions to higher education. A relatively high proportion of Asians attain advanced degrees in the physical or social sciences. Many teach in these fields. Unequivocally, many other minorities are well qualified for professional-level careers. **If you do not see at least one minority at a firm, especially at an organization that does business in engineering or the physical, chemical, biological or computer sciences, then this company clearly does not hire the best-qualified candidates.** This is business reality.

Similarly, do you see any minority managers or director-level executives? If not, beware. **A firm that hires no minorities is a white person's**

firm; the rules are indeed unwritten and different. Do not sign up as the company's or organization's *first* minority employee. You will be unable to lead it to an enlightened state of working with a diverse workforce. It is already too late—the organization is 20-30 years behind where it needs to be to do business in today's world.

Does the organization hire from an eclectic mix of colleges and universities or is hiring limited to those with a regimented or stylized background? Does the company or organization recruit only from certain colleges, such as Ivy League, local colleges and universities, state colleges or universities, or community colleges?

If the company's business does not require a Department of Defense-issued security clearance, does the organization still prefer to hire veterans or retired military? If you learn this is the case and your background does not match, no matter how good your experience and accomplishments, do not waste your time with this firm. Conversely, if the firm does not have a reputation for hiring veterans, don't apply thinking you'll be the first veteran hired. **Similar to the case of an organization which has not hired and retained a woman or a minority, this company is 20-30 years behind the times.** You don't want to be the person to bring this firm into the second or third decade of the 21st century.

Look at the quality of the employees and start at the top. Great begets great. Good begets good. Average begets average. Quality people are not afraid to hire others who may be smarter in certain areas than they are.

How can we define *quality*? Winning profiles for student graduates include: leadership activities, solid academic credentials, varied extracurricular activities, summer employment, part- or full-time employment while in school, a *can do* attitude, polished appearance, evidence of good grooming habits, and an individual who takes advantage of ongoing opportunities for learning and is willing to try new activities or careers. Beware of an organization where every key employee is a graduate of a particular college, university, certificate program, or vocational school.

Returning to the question of quality, how can we define a quality experienced candidate for employment? Such a candidate has:

- Evidence of accomplishments as a student plus real accomplishments; the candidate *did* something beyond what was expected

- Few or no situations where the candidate was a member of a team or a coordinator or an administrator that failed

- Experience planning or implementing a new company-wide process such as ISO 9001-2008 or 14000

- Proven ability to develop and implement a plan to introduce or design a new product—or to plan and manage the change from one major software package to another

- Skill to plan and oversee major computer system upgrades or changes

- Expertise in conducting research, then installing new or refurbished production equipment despite tight budgets and timelines

- Ability to implement a significant 360-degree employee assessment program

If you are applying for a job as an experienced candidate, re-read your résumé and prepare a list of questions to so you can practice communicating the *details* of what you actually accomplished.

Beware if you discover that all key staff members are graduates of a particular sales training, interpersonal training, or religion-affiliated training program. Unless you fit this narrow definition of highly qualified, you won't fit in. If you research the program and then try to emulate the behavior and words of a successful graduate of such a program, you may succeed at getting hired. You *will* slip up and get discovered. Guaranteed.

Why would you even want to fit or think you can fit into an environment where you realistically do not match the long-established pattern and have little chance for success? If you are desperate, don't be. Take a step back. Regroup. Understand your strengths and weaknesses. Redefine and refocus your job search efforts.

Is the organization listed among the "Top Workplaces" in the local geographic area? If this annual listing is the result of a truly independent assessment, then the firm may be a better-than-average, although not necessarily great, workplace. If an employee at any firm can nominate their firm as a top workplace, then inclusion in the listing shows either employee pride or an executive or manager making a self-serving nomination. A survey of employees at finalist firms not confirmed by an independent panel may expose the inbred, cult-like environment. Even then, some firms may be included if they spend large sums on advertising with the periodical or organization that publishes the list. Before giving too much credence to these lists, be sure to read the footnotes that describe the process for inclusion in such a listing and the requirements for finalists or winners.

Again, check the company or organization website. Do you see any Latinos, Asians, African-Americans, Eastern Europeans, women, or women-minorities on its Board of Directors? The same observations and assessments about the qualifications of minorities and women as employees pertain to minorities and women as Board members.

Good on-line sources for additional information on companies include: www.muckety.com, www.glassdoor.com, www.silobreaker.com (in-depth company information), and www.vault.com. Go to www.zoominfo.com for an effective summary of an individual's background.

To check whether someone has the degree(s) claimed, use www.student-clearinghouse.org and be prepared to pay up to $15 per report. I used this clearinghouse and learned that the self-appointed president of a local not-for-profit job search organization received a degree in physical education, not education as his résumé and website claimed. At that point, his credibility went from low to negative zero. Check, too, with customers, suppliers, business partners, bankers, and ex-employees. Website www.linkedin.com is a good place to find ex-employees of a variety of businesses and organizations, as well as college and private school alumni.

Although it is more difficult to discover, check for lawsuits against the company for discrimination or bullying. In the March 22, 2012 edition of the *Financial Times*, "nearly half the British workforce experience unreasonable workplace behavior within any two week period, while 6 percent experience workplace violence, according to a recent study by academics at Cardiff University and the University of Plymouth." Bullying in the U.K. is defined as, "offensive, intimidating, malicious, or insulting behavior, an abuse or misuse of power through means that undermine, humiliate, denigrate, or injure the recipient." Can the U.S. be that different from the U.K.?

Search also for lawsuits claiming less pay for women and minorities doing the same job as a Caucasian male. Be aware of industry-based discrimination. The financial services industry pays women 55 to 62 cents for every $1 made by men, compared to an all-industry average of 77 cents.

Employee Appearance

Details in employee appearance, however subtle, provide clues about overall corporate health. Obviously, if employees look less well groomed, then something is amiss. Examples include:

- Longer, poorly-groomed hair on men

- More male employees wearing goatees, which may symbolize that the person is *hiding* something

- At companies that ban facial hair, longer sideburns

- If permitted, more visible tattoos or piercings on face, neck, arms, ankles, or legs

- For men, shirts not tucked into trousers

- Inappropriate or borderline hair coloring or styles

- **Many employees with real or imitation brand-name purses, watches, scarves, or eyeglasses. Too many look-alikes warn you of** *groupthink.* **The presence of many knock-off accessories tells you the organization has a high percentage of phonies or wanna-bes.**

Overall, pushing the limits on dress, visible markings, and hair indicate a subtle form of employee rebellion, poor hires, or an individual's poor attitude.

Executive Appearance

Business, government, and non-profit executives should conform to the norms for employee dress described in the previous section. In 2012, a relatively high proportion of men wore moustaches, beards, or goatees. The acceptability of facial hair changes . . . as does the fashion of the office. Let us compare today's practices with executive dress and grooming habits from three-plus decades ago.

In 1975, John Molloy, who established the conservative standard for executive attire, wrote that goatees were unacceptable for business professionals. However, in his book, *Dress for Success*, Molloy stated and justified that moustaches were fine. Full beards were okay, depending on the industry and job function. Molloy emphasized that sales reps should not wear beards unless they needed to cover physical deformities.

Malloy is correct on all points. Goatees, as well as *Fu Manchu* moustaches require a certain pickiness to maintain. **Beards and regular moustaches require regular grooming, but the patchiness of a goatee and the angularity of a Fu Manchu require precision trimming to the point of being an artifice—that is—fake. A goatee on a man who chooses to wear one usually emphasizes a pointed chin or narrow eyes, two physical signs that, when teamed with a goatee, imply untrustworthiness.**

When a goatee or Fu Manchu mustache is combined with the contemporary narrow oval eyeglass frame style which further accentuates narrow eyes, the impression is even worse. Why would someone do or wear any-thing that leaves an impression other than trustworthy and amiable? **Beware of individuals in leadership positions wearing the narrow, horizontal oval eyeglasses that make the eyes appear more narrow—and untrustworthy.**

Appearance of Potential Employees

May we temporarily redirect our discussion? Job seekers, remember that the company evaluates you at the same time you appraise the organization. Someone hires you because you are well qualified, available, have a good attitude—and the chemistry between you and your potential manager and peers is good. You fit in. However, to complete a successful job search, you must play the game. Your résumé must show solid or increasing responsi-bilities and accomplishments, necessary skills and knowledge, and the abili-ties sought by the employer. You must look and act the part you seek. And, despite these challenges, you must come off as real.

Apply the suggestions from the previous paragraph to yourself. Look for signs of personal dysfunction—in you! Correct or modify them, as best you can. You, Mr. or Ms. Job Seeker, can subtly undermine your search ef-forts in so many ways—a poorly crafted résumé; a narrative résumé with ty-pographical errors, misspellings, or poor grammar; a lackluster cover letter; improper spelling of the person's or company's name in the cover letter or the wrong name (!) or gender; gimmickry as part of your résumé and cover letter; applying for the wrong job; or not following application directions from the company's or organization's website.

Let us assume all the steps you take before your interview are correct. In fact they are perfect. The prospective employer cannot wait to meet you. You set up a meeting and it goes badly. You wonder what went wrong.

Organizational Purpose, Problem Pasts and Power, and Decision Making

Organizational Purpose

Does the organization's stated purpose match what it is *actually doing*? Ignore the press releases; look for articles or comments on blogs that tell the real story. Hidden primary organizational purposes include: creating or maintaining a positive image within the industry or a leadership image within the community, establishing a reputation as a strong supporter of the arts/causes/colleges/universities, building close relationships with local governments and tax districts, and furthering religion-based principles and values. Hidden people agendas include: gaining a position of strength in the face of strong internal politics, accumulating ego-driven publicity for key individuals through television/radio/blog/FaceBook presence, one-upmanship, and setting up situations where a colleague looks bad in front of peers, clients, suppliers, investors, and/or supervisors.

Of what is the organization proud? How does the organization's stated purpose translate into day-to-day and long-term decision making? How are things really accomplished—small teams, large teams, a small group of go-to guys and gals, or one go-to person? How does the organization celebrate accomplishments—lunches, bonuses, congratulatory letters and plaque-based awards, paid time off, gift certificates, paid travel, or something unique to the firm?

I read of an international management consulting firm where, to gain an understanding of India, its history, culture, and consumer behavior, an eight-person group of the firm's partners traveled to the country. Once in country, the partners divided into small groups. One group ventured into the hinterland where it encountered a wild water buffalo. The buffalo charged at one of the female partners; quick thinking by another partner diverted the water buffalo away from the lady. **Who decided that wandering the wilderness was an appropriate market research activity? Who failed to consider the associated monetary and safety costs?**

I mention this as a warning: Don't put yourself in a dangerous situation if you don't understand the environment. Yes, you need to gain understanding of a culture, a people, its buying habits, and everyday living challenges, but go to the *people*, not to some unknown wilderness location.

Problem Pasts, Organizational Power, and Decision Making

Let's assume you did extensive research on the executive for whom you will work at your new job. Let's also assume your research uncovered problems at the executive's previous firm serious enough to make the news. Does the executive claim to not know what happened in her/his department at that previous employer? Although the executive may not have been involved in the details or in related day-to-day activities, s/he *knew* what was going on.

How blind and deaf can a top level manager be? Inappropriate personnel activities (affairs between executives or between executives and subordinates), increased risk exposure (especially on Wall Street or in The City), pushing the limits of financial deregulation and decreased oversight, mispricing securities, foreign exchange anomalies, increased use of programmed trading, falsified trading capital, coordinated market making (see: crisis in LIBOR – London Interbank Offered Rate), aggressive profit targets, and more than one rogue trader are not one-of-a-kind events.

How ignorant do these executives expect others to be? The organization's CEO and culture ("it's *only* about money") fostered these activities. Apparently, these managers believed the rarified halls of upper management would serve as an effective cloak for clandestine activities—or their elevated positions sanctified *any* activity—after all, *gods* don't have to follow the rules.

Whether executive management participates in or fails to address questionable activities and/or tries to hide these problems from the board of directors, shareholders, customers, creditors, and employees is not the issue. If the organization's power rests in the hands of those with less than clean histories, beware! You may find yourself in an ethical dilemma or even stuck with responsibility for this executive's next malfeasance.

Who has the *real* power? In many small organizations, the sales department has the power. After all, if there are no bucks, there is no business and no need for anyone else. As an organization matures, power should logically disperse. Watch for mature organizations where the sales department continues to drive all major decisions. Ideally, power should be shared—a five- or six-legged stool where a perfectly horizontal seat visually represents a shared-power environment.

If an administrative function such as human resources, the in-house travel department, or the expense report accounting & payment function tends to drive the organization, then the place is pretty hopeless. Why? No leadership, no sense of purpose, lack of customer orientation, no fun, and no camaraderie lead to high employee turnover, frequent reorganization, and loss of customers.

In a manufacturing firm, employee and visitor safety must be behind every major decision. A sound manufacturing environment requires a balance between marketing, sales, finance, productivity, and safety.

Who gets coffee for managers? Who gets coffee for executives? The correct answer to each question is the manager or executive gets his or her own coffee. By going to the coffee room and pouring their own beverages, they get out of the office for a few minutes and may engage in one or more coffee room discussions.

The alternative—the administrator brings coffee—keeps the executive in the office cocoon. **The executive who requires an underling to fetch his/her coffee is separatist or elitist, and attempting to reinforce an artificial hierarchy, regardless of the executive's claims that he or she is too busy to get the coffee.** This is NOT healthy organizational power.

The Position

If you are considering a position with a company, will your new position fit with the corporate culture? Let's say you are recruited for a brand-new corporate administrative position. The company is divided into many small business units where the bottom-line result is key. Although the organization may need a senior-level executive to coordinate functions and help foster cross-functional efficiencies, the long-standing corporate DNA with its emphasis on growth and profitability, indicates the organization is not ready for this new position.

The Hiring Process

What time is your meeting? If possible, schedule the interview so you may observe how many employees work into the lunch hour or after work. There is a huge difference between individual work styles and institutionalized overtime or excessive attention to the clock. **If you observe a significant number of employees skipping lunch, eating lunch at their desks, or working past 6:00 in the evening, then it is a sign that the company is severely understaffed and is therefore cheap, or the culture rewards time spent at the office rather than measurable results.** You will know the difference when you observe the situation. People who must work late are holed up in their offices, working on projects. Most likely, they attended meetings all day and need to complete their paperwork.

How many *interviews* that span how many days does the company require to make its hiring decision? A total of 10 interviews stretched over a 3-month period aptly describes a tortuous interview process. An interview with 7 managers and peers in one afternoon following three hours of testing and a one-on-one psychological assessment with an industrial psychologist is nearly as tortuous.

How many days does the company need to *receive feedback from interviewers*, psychologists, employment professionals, and possibly the receptionist to make a formal hiring decision? A responsible company will speak with references, do a web search, verify school attendance, and check on degrees. Let us assume that you are the first person the company interviews for an open position. Assume the company needs 5 to 7 work days to schedule and meet all candidates. A reasonable decision timeframe is less than two weeks under the most challenging circumstances.

If a company cannot make a decision in that timeframe, then its culture is clearly one of delay, lack of accountability, and lack of urgency

or an ongoing search for perfection, inability to come to agreement on key issues which leads to the formation of factions, and a possibly overly political environment. By the way, the oft-used phrase, "We're betting the company with each hire we make," is utter nonsense. Within the first two

---

CLOTHES MAKE THE MAN—OR THE WOMAN

Jeanne, a friend and acupuncture physician (AP), applied to work in a local acupuncture clinic. The clinic's owner, also an AP, had a strong positive professional reputation and a thriving practice. He also understood, respected, and could use her training in a particular modality of Oriental acupuncture medicine. His son managed the office; his wife helped with administrative duties.

Limited by tight schedules, Jeanne and the doctor scheduled a meeting for a Sunday afternoon at his clinic. It was the only mutually agreeable time. The meeting came off as scheduled. In a follow-up discussion, Jeanne told me it did not go well. She described the physician and son as dressed somewhat formally. The father wore a polo shirt and khaki-colored slacks. The son wore dark slacks and a long-sleeve button-down shirt. She told me they looked like they might have driven to the clinic following church services.

I asked Jeanne what she had worn to the meeting. She replied that, since the meeting was on a Sunday afternoon, she wore blue jeans and a t-shirt. I did not say a word. The contrasting styles told me she would *never* work with that well-respected professional, despite her solid academic credentials and professional experience. I did not want to hurt her feelings; thankfully, she did not ask my opinion.

I need to share with you one key thought. This was *not* a casual Sunday afternoon introductory get-together—this was a real job interview. Her appearance immediately told the AP and his son that she was not serious about the position and she did not look the part of a professional, although she was. Based on how she dressed for this interview, she killed any chance of employment in the first five seconds they met.

You can always overdress for an interview, even for a meeting scheduled for a casual Friday. You will never go wrong making a good first impression if you are well dressed and well groomed. As they say, "You only get one chance to make a good first impression." True. Absolutely true.

~~*

weeks, the hiring manager and the new employee's peers will know if a new person is going to work out.

How does the organization welcome or celebrate a new employee, if at all? After a prospective employee meets with human resources personnel, hiring managers, peers, and sometimes administrators and support personnel and everyone agrees that person is a good fit, the company may make an offer. If the prospective employee accepts and becomes an employee, what is the process for bringing that employee on board?

To complete the hiring process, a company should have in place a formal employee orientation program. This program should:

- Review company policies and procedures

- Review health, life, disability and travel insurance and, if applicable, waiting periods

- Specify organization-observed holidays plus vacation and sick leave policies

- Reinforce or publicly proclaim key values or aspects of the organization's culture

- Allow for completion of necessary insurance, payroll, and retirement paperwork, with a human resources representatives present to answer questions

- Enable new hires to meet new employees from other departments and start to build a sense of camaraderie

If the company does not have a formal orientation program in place, then this a minor sign of organizational dysfunction. How else will new employees learn basic company beliefs and practices and quickly assimilate?

Summary

In this potpourri-like chapter, we introduced a number of topics necessary for evaluation. First, the organizational DNA. The company's DNA is inextricably linked to the behaviors, attitudes, and goals of the founder(s). One important component of the organizational DNA is decision-making style. It can be top-down, bottom up, or sideways. Be sure to gain an understanding of this important aspect of a firm's day-to-day and long-range operation. Does it appear that managers and senior-level individual contributors suffer from attending too many meetings, many of which are unnecessary?

Second, look at fun. What does the organization do, if anything, to have fun? Unless you're a member of the family, be cautious of places that claim a *family-like atmosphere.*

Third, do you see women and minorities in senior management positions or as members of the company's board of directors? Very simply, the lack of women or minorities tells you the business does not want to hire the best person for the job.

Fourth, grooming and appearance count.

The people aspect is important. Did the local or national business news media report that one executive was involved in a compromising situation? What did the executive say about their involvement? Unexplained or poorly explained executive involvement spells s-e-r-i-o-u-s d-y-s-f-u-n-c-t-i-o-n; what else is that person hiding?

When you are interviewing, listen carefully to what is asked . . . and to the responses to your questions. If everything is couched in neutral or bland language, then the firm is hiding something important. Everyday language should be the norm, not the exception.

Where does the power in the organization rest? Often, it is with sales, since a company needs a sales flow in order to grow.

Does the firm offer a formal employee orientation? When hiring a new employee, how long does the screening process take? Once all the necessary input is collected, how long does it take to make a hiring decision?

Two weeks should be plenty of time.

~*~*~*~

CHAPTER 23

WRAP-UP

We evaluated the exterior, interior, and people-related factors for signs of organizational dysfunction. We discussed safety issues, aesthetics, and signs of deception . . . and the importance of recognizing your *gut response*.

One gut response which has been formalized into a prescriptive practice is *feng shui*. *Feng shui* (pronounced "feng shway"), an ancient Chinese theory about the flow of energy, can be applied to both building interiors and exteriors. Although some people may discount *feng shui* as superstition, many of its principles are actually quite logical. Application of *feng shui* techniques, regardless of whether you believe it has energy-enhancing powers, can improve aesthetics, and increase people's feelings of harmony, balance, and comfort.

Key Feng Shui Concepts and Corporate Dysfunction

Feng shui concepts apply to corporations. A rectangle is the best shape for a corporate building. Square-shaped buildings are also good. Irregularly shaped buildings, such as those L-shaped and U-shaped, are unlucky. Buildings should sit firmly on the ground, without an open parking space underneath. When the building appears to be on stilts, it is not solidly grounded.

The main entrance, accessible by stairs, should be clearly defined and visible. Front lobby imagery is important—high ceilings, a sense of spaciousness, and bright lighting are optimal. If the front doors are made of glass, the elevators should not face the doors.

Feng shui practices apply to the corporate logo. Avoid:

- Logos with too many angular lines or those that resemble arrows or straight lines pointing at your company name

- Abstract designs

- Designs that are excessively *Yin* (masculine) or *Yang* (feminine).

Incorporate the *Five Element* theory (water, fire, wood, earth, metal) into the design of your corporate logo, choosing an element for your logo based on your business or industry. Specifically:

- Property, mining, and real estate companies should stress the *earth* element.

- Electronics companies should highlight the *metal* element.

- Food products and publishing companies should use the *wood* element.

- Banks and financial institutions are best suited to the *water* element.

- The *fire* element is appropriate for restaurants.

Color combinations play an important role in feng shui. Good combinations include:

- Black lettering on a white background

- Silver lettering (water) on a deep purple background (metal)

- Gold lettering (wealth) on red background (good luck)

- Blue with green (together representing the water element).

Feng shui concepts add power when applied to retail store locations. Ideally, a retail store should face a wide road, away from a space where it is sandwiched between larger and higher buildings, and not opposite a "T" intersection, at the end of a long street, or at the end of a *cul de sac*. The store should not have a retail outlet neighbor lacking an obvious main entrance. The front entrance of the store, exterior and interior, should be well lit. The larger the front door, the better for business. If you want to look at it logically, these *feng shui* requirements enhance a store's visibility and accessibility.

Overall, the executive offices and meeting room provide the strongest indicators of a company's, firm's, or organization's health. One of the most important considerations in *feng shui* is the location of the office of the CEO or Managing Director. In theory, if the head of a family or company enjoys good feng shui then, by association, the rest of the family or company will benefit. **The CEO's office is ideally located deep inside the building. Within the office, the power spot is the innermost corner diagonal to the entrance door.** From an applied feng shui standpoint, an office environment is enhanced through the addition of plants, a waterfall, and a photo of mountains or ocean behind the CEO's chair. The CEO's office layout should take into account the following rules. The executive should never sit:

- With his/her back to the door or window

- Directly beneath an exposed overhead beam

- With a pillar corner or edge toward him/her (place a plant to block these interferences)

LOCATION, LOCATION, LOCATION

In my neighborhood, three houses are notable in that a street which intersects the street they are on "runs" straight toward their front doors. According to *feng shui* **principles, this location is considered inauspicious. Logically, such a location could be considered risky since an inattentive driver might fail to negotiate the required turn and end up parked in someone's living room. It happens.**

One house is at the top of a "T" juncture, the other two are at the outside corners of "L" turns. Over the past twenty years, the owner of the house at the head of the "T" juncture, a real estate agent, has repeatedly lost jobs. His two story faces south with a nice lawn, one tree, and minimal shrubbery. For years, I have felt that it aesthetically needed a couple of large red pots planted with flowers on either side of the door. It does. *Feng shui* says a south facing house needs red at the front door to enhance the flow of energy into the house. If I owned that house, those red pots would have been there within a day.

The other two houses face north. For each of them, if a car failed to make the corner, it would end up parked on the front porch. Both houses have been plagued with misfortune—the first owner of one of the houses clipped a bicyclist on a suburban street and killed her. He moved, but was never able to sell the house . . . which has been, over the past 10 years, occupied by new residents every few months.

The second house at the outside corner of an "L" has undergone years of renovation inside and out, but even "fixing" it has not worked. Ever since it was built, people who move into that house got divorced, sold the house, and the next couple that moved in repeated the pattern—this has happened four times in twenty years. Even more disturbing—a couple of those who divorced, even though quite young, subsequently died within a few years.

~~*

- Against a wall that has a lavatory on the other side

One additional feng shui practice tells us the front part of the desk should not be blocked or cluttered with files or paperwork.

Don't believe in *feng shui*? A reasonable explanation for these rules is that an executive sitting with his/her back to the door or window or with a pile of files on the front of his/her desk is not going to be as aware of what is going on outside the office—beyond the clutter or behind his/her back The sound of flushing toilets does *not* enhance concentration. Overhanging beams and pillar corners are irregularities that constrict space (make it narrower). Effective management requires the broadest thinking possible.

Feng shui combinations offer positive and negative connotations for the organization.

- A badly managed company with good *feng shui* will attract decent and hard-working staff; decisions will be good and business judgments will have elements of good luck

- For a well-managed company with bad *feng shui*, good staff will eventually leave and the company will suffer losses or will be taken over or will go out of business. If the bad *feng shui* pertains only to certain offices, then the staff working in those offices will get sick and suffer misfortunes.

The three most important aspects of corporate *feng shui* are:

- The business should operate out of a head office building that enjoys good *feng shui*

- The office of the CEO or Managing Director should be located in the most auspicious part of the building

- The corporate logo should be as positive as possible.

Aside from *feng shui*, here are the major factors that will help you spot organizational quirkiness:

Exterior

- If parking and ramp accommodations for the physically disabled are not available and respected by non-disabled persons, the company does not care about following well established societal and, indirectly, industry rules.

- The company may require identification or pre-clearance from the person you are visiting. If the security guard does not ask for identification or call your host to verify your expected arrival, then safety-related policies and procedures are not consistently followed. What other procedures are not consistently followed?

- If you see reserved parking spaces for executives, this is a warning of dysfunction, since it represents different treatment based on *class* of employee.

- If the business has a messy loading dock, scattered trash, or is not well lit, then this reveals deeper problems.

- **If the interior and exterior of a company vehicle is in poor condition and the vehicle registration is out-of-date, the company does not pay attention to operating details, overlooks other legal requirements, and many departments related to operations will not run smoothly.**

Interior

Since the receptionist is the first person you meet, you will quickly form an impression of the business. If the company has placed the wrong person in this position, expect incomplete or incorrect internal functioning. If the furniture is shabby or too fancy, oversized or not proportioned, uncomfortable, or improper in quality or expense for the stage of company's life cycle—or you hear excuses of, "we're redecorating," the company is inward-looking. If décor includes cheap plastic plants, the company is cheap.

If lights in the exit signs are burned out, the company is not concerned for personal safety and, by extension, may not have good coordination among departments.

Minor points:

- Inappropriate magazines on the table in the reception area tell of an unfocused company.

- Monochromatic art that blends perfectly with the colors of paint, wallpaper, and furniture represents narrow, stultified thinking.

The number three sign of organizational dysfunction is the presence of *any* motivational poster. If management thinks a poster will motivate employees, then it is delusional or living in a fantasy world. Moreover, its key decisions are influenced by an internally focused sense of reality. Reality comes from clues outside the organization—from customers, suppliers, bankers, regulators, journalists, analysts, creditors—not inside.

A critical warning sign: Any evidence of adherence to religious or philosophical beliefs within non-religious or philosophically-based organizations. Such notices are inappropriate.

Run from these hiring "opportunities:"

- If "employee of the month" or "employee of the quarter" commendations are out-of-date, the company shows its lack of concern for employees and lack of overall follow through.

- The display of a sports team booster plaque is a critical negative, since it represents a benefit available to a few, select employees, generally the owners. This is evidence of an organization with well-defined classes, hardly a good work environment.

- What is the tone and content of the notices on the employee bulletin board? This is how the company speaks to its team members. The company will speak to the public through a public relations department or advertising agency.

- If the office numbering scheme is illogical, the company is stuck in the past and its strategic and tactical thinking is muddled.

- If fire extinguisher inspections are not up to date or you are unable to easily reach the fire extinguishers, the company does not care about employee safety. Taken a step further, the firm believes it is too good to obey regulations.

- If the building has not been updated to meet the federal requirements for access by disabled persons, the company is stuck in the distant past and does not respect different classes of employees, visitors, and potential customers.

- Can you find posted maps showing the emergency exit routes from any room in the building? In some states, this is a key safety requirement.

- If required by state law, is the operating certificate posted in the elevator?

- In the kitchen, a dirty refrigerator/freezer, unwashed dishes or coffee mugs in the sink, and any "clean up after yourself" signs show a lack of common courtesy or an "I don't care" attitude on the part of employees. This also highlights ineffective management since employees have not complied with the requests on the signs.

- In the cafeteria, any food safety violation is important, since it relates to employee and visitor health. A separate marked dining area for managers identifies a two-class culture. Does the company manage its cafeteria or use a third party? Unless it is in the food service business, it should use a third party and concentrate operational efforts on its main business.

- In the cafeteria, if employees and visitors are expected to bus trays, how many trays with dishes sit on unattended tables? This indicates poor follow through and a poor attitude.

- If the company charges for coffee or other beverages, is the price reasonable? Do the profits go to an "employee welfare and morale fund," to be used for personal emergencies, to a charity, or back into the company's coffers?

- Poor conditions in the rest room, notably lack of hot water, a mess on the floor around the urinals or commodes, poor toilet tissue quality, lack of antibacterial hand soap, an inoperable hand dryer, an empty paper towel dispenser, many paper towels lying on the floor near the wastebasket, and poor or no restroom accommodations for the disabled reveal the company's attitudes toward cost management, safety, health, maintenance, and even more telling, the intra-company respect or lack thereof between its employees and management. **The condition of the rest room are my "number one" and "number two" indicators of corporate or organizational dysfunction.** (Pun intended.)

- The main conference room provides additional clues about company dysfunction. An oversized conference table shows the company believes it is all about the company, not the client. Inconsistencies between types of furnishings, such as an old-fashioned pull-down movie screen in a room with an elaborately carved conference table and advanced electronics tell of the firm's insecurity. Gross disparities between conference room furnishings and the styles and quality of furniture in other parts of the building signal the company is a "wanna be" or a "pretender."

Look in the executive offices: Separate restrooms or exercise rooms with saunas, Jacuzzis, or showers; displays of religious or political organization's certificates; *Good Ol' Boy* or *Kentucky Colonel* certificates; a wet-bar in an executive's office; a back door to/from the CEO's office; many framed degrees and certifications; lack of a whiteboard or easel; or the presence of any *Who's Who* books warn of a company with a strong "class consciousness," misdirected executive focus, an insecure executive, and lack of leadership. **The presence of any *Who's Who* books in any executive's office is my fourth sign of organizational dysfunction.**

Check out the employees' cubicles. Each cubicle should have sufficient space for the employee and be furnished with file drawers, storage shelves, direct lighting, space for computer and monitor, and a large flat workspace. A mismatch between cubicle design and the architectural style of the building, the presence of storage boxes in hallways and aisles, a notable difference in the quality of lighting and furniture between executive offices and employee cubicles, and cramped cubicle farm aisles show a lack of respect for employees and further highlight an elitist class-conscious organization. Be sure to count the number of Dilbert© cartoons –the more the worse!

People

The lack of women or minorities tells you the firm does not hire the best qualified people. Period. An inefficient, prolonged hiring process characterizes a dysfunctional hierarchy; and the physical signs of employee dissatisfaction determine the daily working environment and effectiveness of the organization. **If a company serves liquor at any company-sponsored function, that is a "red flag" and is my fifth major sign of organizational dysfunction.** The company atmosphere (basically, "Is this a good place to work?") is influenced by the organization's communication style (top down, bottom up, or sideways) and what employees do as a group for fun.

Homes

While this extensive analysis focused on business, not-for-profit, governmental, and military organizations, the factors for dysfunction may likewise be applied to homes. Once again, the condition of the bathroom tells you the most. No need to open the medicine cabinet and inspect medications, personal grooming accessories, hair sprays and dyes, and the usual "unmentionables." What do the sink, the commode, and the tub look like? The floor? Are the mirrors clean and polished? Does the room smell clean or is it overwhelmingly perfumed? See the parallel?

Next, similar to how you analyzed businesses, evaluate the condition of the building and grounds, the kitchen, furniture, and wall displays of art and collectibles. If the house has a home office, check it. Focus on the furniture, layout, books and magazines, artwork, and mementos. Search for inconsistencies. **Sadly, dysfunction of the house easily translates to dysfunction of its occupants. Based on the number and type of dysfunctions you find in the home, it is quite possible, nay, highly likely, to identify early signs of poor marital relationships, health problems, animal abuse, financial issues, hoarding, and poor parent-child relationships.**

Final thoughts

I created two theses: "All organizations are dysfunctional." "All companies and firms suck; it's only a matter of degree." My approach is intentionally not a positive one. Using my metrics you will not be able to identify which firms or not-for-profits will continually be "excellent," "good," or "great." Excellence in one year may deteriorate to lousy in another year—same company, same leadership, changed environment, different reactions.

You will not be able to figure out which companies will make or lose money in any quarter or year. You won't get any hot stock tips on which to trade. On the other hand, you may get a good idea of companies where the CEO is planning to leave, where one or more executives are having extra-marital affairs or are spending too much time on volunteer activities, or organizations where a new strategy is unlikely to succeed.

Yet, things change.

What changes are parts of everyday business? Organizational life cycles, competitive environment, safety and environmental regulatory issues, supplier changes, technology changes, changed banking relationships, changes in consumers' tastes, the discovery and implementation of new operational efficiencies, a new CEO, new vice presidents, new board members, shifted strategic initiatives, input from management consultants, changes to executive bonus criteria, different perceptions of the company by Wall Street and the effect on the stock price and executives' and managers' stock options, changed perceptions of not-for-profit organizations by the community, management of growth/maturity/downsizing/restructuring, changes in the qualifications and work ethics of new employees, and gathering and organization of internal knowledge and processes. WHEW! That's a LOT.

What doesn't significantly change?

Employees' real-time attitudes, overt and subtle signs of organizational and managerial dysfunction, managers' acceptance of second- or third-rate work by employees or contractors, internal politics, one-upmanship, office bullies, the use of *spin doctors* to present a positive corporate and executive image wherever possible, and, unfortunately in this day and age, underlying greed and corruption. **Human nature is a constant.**

Please do not set a significantly higher bar for yourself—expecting instant comprehension of what this book covers; it takes time to understand and apply any set of new concepts. It will take time to train a more accurate and aware *new gut reaction or intuition* after you drop your past inaccuracies, lack of awareness, and *old gut* intuition. Any gain you make will be beneficial. **You don't have to be 100% correct; you need only to be able to see things differently.**

Look around. Make mental or take written notes. Trust your gut. Make the decision that is right for you. You now have the tools so you won't be *bulled* over.

Indeed, knowledge is power.

~*~*~*~

ABOUT THE AUTHOR

Originally from Pittsburgh, Pennsylvania, Bruce earned a BA in economics from the University of Pittsburgh and an MBA in marketing and finance at Santa Clara University.

He proudly served as an Air Force supply and logistics officer. His community service includes 13 years on his homeowner association board of directors, selected as president for five one-year terms. Bruce was elected to the board of directors of a California-based non-for-profit organization that provided education and training for homeowner association Board members and legislative advocacy for 3,900 California-based homeowner associations.

Bruce's business experience spans marketing of computer products; market research on computer systems, software, and computer services; manager of research at an international venture capital firm; management consultant focused on strategic issues at technology companies; and Wall Street equity research vice president focused on stocks of manufacturers of computer systems and board-level data communication products.

Bruce taught as an adjunct professor at Tampa Bay area colleges and universities, including Eckerd College, St.Leo University, and the University of Tampa. He taught 7 graduate and 44 undergraduate courses in marketing, finance, economics, management, and business strategy.

He owned a retail store and a health/life insurance brokerage. Bruce currently owns an income tax preparation business and volunteers as a tax preparer at the local family center in his hometown of Safety Harbor, Florida.

HOW TO CONTACT BRUCE

- Please send your email to:

    bruce@wackyorganizations.com

~*~*~*~